In Work, At Home

Global transformations in employment and labour markets have led to more and more people earning a living at home. This book explores the meaning and experience of this type of employment, clarifying what we mean by homeworking and looking at:

- current research methodologies
- quantitative analyses of global trends
- the emotional and psychological processes of self-management
- household relations.

Presenting statistical analyses of labour markets in North America, Europe, Asia and Australia, together with more qualitative analysis of the experience of homeworking, *In Work, At Home* provides a valuable introduction to a range of issues and debates. These include the development of labour markets, employment relations, managerial strategies and the experience of 'self' in contemporary societies. It will appeal to students across many disciplines such as sociology, business studies, social policy and women's studies.

Alan Felstead is Reader in Employment Studies at the Centre for Labour Market Studies, University of Leicester. **Nick Jewson** is Director of the Ethnicity Research Centre and Senior Lecturer in the Department of Sociology, University of Leicester.

In Work, At Home

Towards an understanding of homeworking

Alan Felstead and Nick Jewson

London and New York

First published 2000
by Routledge
11 New Fetter Lane, London EC4P 4EE

Simultaneously published in the USA and Canada
by Routledge
29 West 35th Street, New York, NY 10001

Routledge is an imprint of the Taylor & Francis Group

© 2000 Alan Felstead and Nick Jewson

Typeset in Galliard by M Rules
Printed and bound in Great Britain by St Edmundsbury Press,
Bury St Edmunds, Suffolk

British Library Cataloguing in Publication Data
A catalogue record for this book is available
from the British Library

Library of Congress Cataloging in Publication Data
Felstead, Alan
    In work, at home: towards an understanding of homeworking /
    Alan Felsted and Nick Jewson,
        p.   cm.
    Includes bibliographical references and index.
    1. Self-employed—United States. 2. Self-employed. 3. Home
    labor—United States. 4. Home labor. 5. Home-based
    businesses—United States. 6. Home-based businesses. 7.
    Cottage industries—United States. 8. Cottage industries. I.
    Jewson, Nick, 1946–   . II. Title.
    HD8037.U5F45   1999
    331.25—dc21   99–29375
                                                  CIP

ISBN 0-415-16299-8 (hbk)
ISBN 0-415-16300-5 (pbk)

Contents

Illustrations

Figure

Tables

Acknowledgements

In the course of carrying out research for this book we have collected and compiled evidence from around the world. This venture has entailed us calling on the goodwill of many friends and colleagues in our quest for international research materials and evidence. The following deserve special mention: Ernest Ackyeampong, Nicola Armstrong, Peter Brosnan, Susan Bryant, Linda Devereux and the National Group on Homeworking, Diane Fieldes, Alison Loveridge, Denise McKenna, Renata Phelps, Wendy Richards, Sean Roberts, Gloria Swieczkowski, Manjeet Tara and the Leicester Outwork Campaign, Yasu Tomita and Michelle Wallace. We would also like to thank the numerous individuals and organisations who responded with information to our fax, email and telephone enquiries. Funding for our own empirical research was provided from two sources: the then Employment Department which funded our doorstep survey of home-located workers and subsequent in-depth interviews with homeworkers, and the Faculty of the Social Sciences Research Board at the University of Leicester which provided funds to allow us to carry out long qualitative interviews with a small sample of home-located producers. In each case we are grateful for the funding provided, although the views and opinions expressed in this book are those of the authors alone. Our empirical enquiries were greatly enhanced by the quality and commitment of the research teams we engaged. We therefore express our gratitude to the following individuals: Delawara Alam, Claire Allen, Ergul Ali, Ahmed Andrews, Munwara Begum, Bruce Bennet, Marina Brooks, Keith Brown, Liz Carney, Champa Chudasama, Diane Geer, Roafa Girach, Lindy Jeffrey, Pat Kirby, Victoria Lawrence, Sophie Mangera, Nikki Masters, Naoimh McElroy, Eleanor McFarlane, Sharon Millington, Eren Noor, Hasmita Pabari, Tracy Palmer, Rakha Pandey, Vida Pearson, Diane Stone, Manjeet Tara, Sandeep Tara, Jackie Sanchez-Taylor, Anne Marie Wainwright and Emine Yigitce. Special thanks are due to Manjeet Tara and Jackie Sanchez-Taylor. However, it is to those we surveyed and interviewed during the course of our empirical work to date that we are most indebted – we hope that we have done justice to their responses, the stories they told and the insights they gave us into working at home. Finally, we would like to thank our respective partners – Lorraine and Marilyn – for their help and support, and especially their forbearance during the final stages of writing this book.

AF, NJ

Abbreviations

ACAS	Advisory, Conciliation and Arbitration Service
BHPS	British Household Panel Study
CATU	Clothing and Allied Trades Union
CIR	Commission on Industrial Relations
CPS	Current Population Survey
EC	European Community
EC LFS	European Community Labour Force Survey
ED	Employment Department (now Department for Education and Employment)
EOC	Equal Opportunities Commission
ESRC	Economic and Social Research Council
EU	European Union
FNV	Vrouwenbond van de Fderatie Nederlandse Vakbeweging
GHS	General Household Survey
HWA	Homeworkers' Association
ILO	International Labour Organisation
LFS	Labour Force Survey
LOC	Leicester Outwork Campaign
LS	Longitudinal Study
NES	New Earnings Survey
NGH	National Group on Homeworking
NHS	National Homeworking Survey
ONS	Office for National Statistics
SARs	Samples of Anonymised Records
SEC	Socio-Economic Classification
SEWA	Self-Employed Women's Association
SEWU	Self Employed Women's Union
SWA	Survey of Work Arrangements
UK	United Kingdom
UNITE	Union of Needletrades, Industrial and Textile Employees
US	United States
WIRS	Workplace Industrial Relations Survey

References to law reports

ICR   Industrial Cases Reports
IRLR   Industrial Relations Law Reports

References to courts

CA   Court of Appeal
CD   Chancery Division (High Court)
EAT   Employment Appeals Tribunal
IT   Industrial Tribunal

Chapter 1

Introduction
Setting the agenda

The field of enquiry

This is a book about people who are in work at home. All over the world they are found in a huge range of occupations and industries undertaking a multiplicity of tasks. They include lace makers in rural India, freelance architects in downtown Manhattan and lockstitchers in the back streets of Manchester. Indeed, they are almost as diverse as those who carry out their work in offices and factories. This broad category of employment we have called *home-located production.*

Home-located production should not be confused with *homeworking* which, in our terms, is much more narrowly defined. The aim of this book is to contribute towards an understanding of homeworking by placing it in the context of home-located production in its entirety. The reader will find that we routinely switch between discussing these two concepts – the foreground and background of our analysis.

Formal definitions of these and other key concepts are provided in Chapter 2. However, it may be useful here to offer a description of the kind of tasks undertaken by homeworkers and the sort of jobs they do. Homeworking is conventionally thought of as involving manual jobs carried out in manufacturing industry and routine service occupations. Substantial numbers of garment makers and machinists fall into this category. However, there are many other occupations involved and, as we shall see, there is a danger of reproducing long-standing stereotypes based on unfounded assumptions. A perusal of *HomeNet* – an international newsletter linking homeworkers and campaigning organisations – indicates the diverse character of the jobs that homeworkers do across the world. Table 1.1 provides an alphabetical list derived from this source and our own research. It is by no means exhaustive but does offer an indication of the breadth and scope of homeworking world-wide.

There are practical limitations to the type of work which can be carried out at home but such restrictions are, to some extent, historically and culturally specific. For example, in the late nineteenth century, nail-making and chain-making in Britain were predominately carried out in people's homes. At that time around half of all British nails and chains were produced in domestic premises in and

Table 1.1 The A–Z of homeworking activities across the world

A	academic gown makers; ambulance kit bag producers; apron makers; Aran sweater knitters; aggarbati (incense) rollers; ambar charkha (spinning) workers; akik (a semi-precious stone) polishers and setters.
B	bicycle light producers; budgie cage makers; brussel sprout peelers; boxer short makers; buckle assemblers; burglar alarm assemblers; badge makers; bath plug assemblers; baby dress makers; ballpoint pen assemblers; ball bearing sorters; bingo ticket book sorters; board game packers; book indexers; belt makers; bolt packers; brass valve assemblers; burger flag assemblers; button packers; beermat producers; bidi (cigarette) rollers and packers; bangle makers; block printers; box makers; bat (cricket) makers; bead makers; bag makers; bookbinders; betel nut crackers; box gluers and folders; bamboo weavers; brick makers; bamboo shoot preservers; broom makers; bell assemblers.
C	camera bag makers; carpet sample makers; Christmas cracker assemblers; card and gift tags packers; Christmas decoration makers; children's clothes makers; curtain rail packers; computer lead assemblers; canoeing jacket producers; curtain makers; cushion cover producers; canvas shoe makers; copper tube sorters; cuff and collar assemblers; comb packers; caps makers; chappatis producers; crocheters; cobblers; Churan (medicine) workers; cooks; chain makers; cotton pod shellers; cashew nut roasters; candle makers; Chinese cracker makers; carpenters; clutch assemblers; cable producers; confectionery packers; chicken deboning.
D	dog collar assemblers; dog coat producers; dress makers; duffel coat makers; draught excluder assemblers; dye makers; dung-cake makers; draw threaders.
E	envelope addressers; electrical switch assemblers; embroiderers; elastic sorters; envelope makers; electric board assemblers; engravers.
F	felt-tip pen makers; firemen's trousers producers; first aid kit assemblers; fur coat producers; football scarves and souvenirs assemblers; firework wrappers; Fairisle sweater knitters; file makers; food processors; food packers; fruit preparers.
G	garment stitchers; grain sorters; gum makers; ground-nut pod shellers; glass painters and blowers; gem cutters; garland makers.
H	hamper makers; hat makers; hanger assemblers; horse blanket producers; handbag makers; hospital gown producers; hook and eye packers; hand-loom weavers; hand fan embroiderers; hairpin packers; herb preparers.
I	inputters of data; Intarsia knitters; insurance claim processors; induction loops for hearing aid producers; ironers; idol makers; ironsmiths.
J	jacket makers; jewellery assemblers; jute workers; jewellery makers; jute toy makers; jam makers.
K	knitters – hand and machine; kite makers; knife polishers; knife makers.
L	leather coat and jacket makers; light socket packers; lobster pot makers; leather bag producers; legging makers; lining assemblers; labellers; leaflet collators; lightshade assemblers; launderers; lace makers; lighter assemblers.
M	make-up case assemblers; medical coat producers; mohair sweater knitters; maggot bag assemblers; manuscript checkers; mountaineering chalk bag assemblers; map packers; mattress makers; mirror ring workers; medicine (traditional/herbal) pounders; match box folders; mirror framers; mop head assemblers.
N	nappy packers; nurses' uniform assembly; nail and screw sorters and packers; net makers; needle packers.
O	onion peelers; overall makers; oil tin washers; ornament assemblers; orchid packers.

P	printed circuit boards producers; plant pot fillers; leather and suede workers; party mask producers; pencil sharpener assemblers; plug assemblers; puppet makers; pottery painters; pillowcase makers; pop sock makers; paper workers; plastic bag cleaners; plastic flower makers; papad rollers; potters; peanut packers; prawn shellers and peelers.
Q	quilt makers.
R	rag pickers; rag doll makers; rattle producers; rug makers; rugby short makers; rosette assemblers; rottweilers (toys) makers; remote control switch assemblers; rope makers.
S	screw packers; shellsuits makers; slipper producers; scourer packers; shoeshine kit assemblers; solderers; stud packers; soft toy makers; skirt producers; shirt producers; sweater knitters; sticker packers; straw sorters; sponge sorters; sample book collators; spice pounders; smock embroiderers; shrimp peelers; suspension assemblers; saddle makers; sock pairers.
T	ticket gluers; tie producers; trouser makers; tight producers; tennis racquet assemblers; typists; telesales workers; tea towel producers; toy soldiers packers; toy makers; tin repairers; tie and dye workers; thread workers.
U	underwear (thermal) workers; umbrella repairers.
V	venetian blinds producers; velvet heart assemblers; 'vileda' cloth packers; vegetable preparers; veil producers.
W	wirers; washers; word processors; weavers; wool shearers; wood carvers; wax makers; waste paper sorters; wallet makers.
XYZ	yoke embroiderers; zip fastener assemblers; zari (gold thread) embroiderers.

Sources: examples taken from Britain, India, the Netherlands, Thailand, Indonesia; Portugal and Bangladesh as reported by HomeNet (various) and Felstead and Jewson (1996: Table 6.2).

around Birmingham (Bythell 1978). However, homeworking should not be regarded merely as a relic of history that is gradually fading into insignificance (Mitter 1986a). Contemporary technological innovations are continuing to create new opportunities for earning a living at home (Huws 1994; Huws *et al.* 1996). Typesetting, for example, has only recently become amenable to homeworking. Before the advent of the microprocessor the manipulation of fonts, print sizes, layout and page make-up was technically complex and subject to occupational closure by craft-trained print compositors (Cockburn 1983). Nowadays, however, even the most rudimentary home computer allows users to undertake all of these tasks with relative ease (cf. Felstead 1988).

Not only technological innovation but also changing managerial strategies are opening up new possibilities for homeworking. Modern methods of controlling costs and regulating labour have introduced the 'hollowed out' corporation, outsourcing, subcontracting, just-in-time supply and the enhanced use of all forms of 'non-standard' employment (Felstead and Jewson 1999). These may offer new opportunities to relocate paid work into the home (e.g., Boris and Prügl 1996). In addition, there remain a number of trades which have for long relied on homeworking. Foremost among these are the garment and clothing industries (Phizacklea 1990). Here, only parts of the production process have been revolutionised by technology. Assembly, in particular, remains dependent on human labour – for example, overlocking edges to prevent them from fraying and lockstitching garments together. These activities are still carried out using latter-day variants of the sewing machine invented in the mid-nineteenth century (Rainnie 1984). Thus, a contemporary A–Z of homeworking covers a range of 'old' and 'new' activities.

The variety of work carried out in the home widens much further when the broader concept of home-located production becomes the focus (e.g., Hakim 1987a; Kraut and Grambsch 1987; Nadwodny 1996; Lafferty *et al.* 1997). Journalists, artists, lawyers, architects, accountants, consultants, teachers and a host of other freelance workers who earn a living at home fall into this category. A looser definition, including those who work at home *some* of the time, captures even more of the working population (Presser and Bamberger 1993). Hence, to seek to construct an 'average' picture for such a disparate group – at least as far as the work they do, how they do it and what rewards they get – is highly misleading, as later chapters will show.

Why study working at home?

What attracts sociologists, economists, geographers, psychologists and business analysts to the study of people who earn their living at home? Why are homeworkers of interest to policy-makers and managers? We hope that the answers to these questions will emerge during the course of this book. However, the following comprises a preliminary indication of some of the more intriguing aspects of home-located production that make it an absorbing and engrossing field of research.

- Home-located production and homeworking bring together two great spheres of contemporary social life – home and work – that have become increasingly differentiated during industrialisation.
- World-wide the numbers of homeworkers and home-located producers appears to have sharply increased in recent decades – although the rate of increase has not always matched the heroic expectations of futurologists, management gurus and some academics.
- Mass access to the Internet heralds an immanent and revolutionary leap in the number of jobs that could *potentially* be done at home for all or part of the time.
- The growth of home-located production and homeworking are part of a larger shift in the character of labour markets which has resulted in the proliferation of 'non-standard' employment.
- Working at home has sometimes been portrayed as a utopian solution to the principle ills of modern society, promising to restore work satisfaction and rejuvenate family relations.
- Campaigners and some academic researchers have highlighted the grim realities faced by many of those who work at home, emphasising their poor terms and conditions, their relative disadvantage compared to workplace peers, and the stresses they encounter in reconciling 'two worlds in one'.

- Homeworking is concentrated among some of the most deprived groups in the labour market – such as women and ethnic minorities – but this is not true of home-located production in general.
- Juggling the twin demands of paid employment and domestic life in the same locale calls forth distinctive coping strategies that shape the emotional and psychological dispositions of home-located producers.
- Although the attitudes of home-located producers have much in common with the personality types currently demanded by 'leading edge' managerial ideologies, employers often appear to regard working at home as problematic.
- Working at home poses problems for conventional modes of labour organisation, control and surveillance that are of interest to both trade unions and management.
- The growth of home-located production raises a raft of social policy issues – including such matters as transportation, urban and rural planning, architectural design, electronic infrastructure, commercial property values, health and safety, and employment law.
- Despite the significance of these trends, home-located production and homeworking remain under-researched and conceptually confused.

The origins of this book

This book arises from our own experience of researching people who work at home. Although its scope is very broad, it does not purport to deal with all the issues and themes that scholars in the field have raised. It does not, for example, consider the social and economic history of homeworking, which has been discussed elsewhere (Boris 1994; Boris and Daniels 1989; Pennington and Westover 1989; Bythell 1978). Nor does it highlight the operations of transnational corporations, that lock increasing numbers of homeworkers and home-located producers into global economic networks of dependency (Mitter 1986a; Boris and Prügl 1996; Tate 1996a, 1996b). Instead, this book focuses on the many enduring puzzles and unresolved questions that we have encountered in the course of our work. Our aim here, then, is to address what we regard as some of the most challenging issues entailed in studying people in work at home. We will introduce these themes by briefly recounting the history of our involvement before, in the next section, stating specifically the questions tackled in each chapter.

In 1994 we successfully bid for a government-funded research contract – sponsored by the then Employment Department (ED) – to carry out one of the largest surveys of homeworkers ever conducted in Britain. In this way, we began a hectic year – subsequently extended to 15 months – in which we undertook a wide range of different research activities in a variety of geographical settings. This very stimulating period rapidly caused us to question many aspects of home-located production and homeworking that previously we had taken for granted.

Along the learning curve we managed to complete the project and publish our findings (Felstead and Jewson 1996). In the process we discovered a great deal. However, we reached the end of the project with as many questions as we had begun.

At this point, we felt that conceptual clarification was urgently needed. Some of our early thoughts in this area were published the following year (Felstead and Jewson 1997). In addition, a range of new empirical questions surfaced in our minds, including some which the remit of the ED project had prevented us from exploring. Foremost among these were a number of issues concerning the ways in which home-located producers manage to combine the demands of domestic life with those of paid employment. Accordingly, with the support of a small grant from the Faculty of the Social Sciences Research Board at the University of Leicester, in 1997 we undertook a qualitative study of 23 home-located producers. This was completed in 1998 and the findings are published for the first time in this book. Although only a small study, the rich interview data we obtained shifted our focus yet again to an examination of the meaning and experience of working at home.

An even more undeveloped area of research concerns the management process of home-located production and especially the consequences and implications it has for the organisation of work as a whole. Does home-located production prompt the redesign of jobs both inside and outside the workplace, or are traditional management controls – such as piece rates – applied to the invisible workforce? We have surprisingly little evidence to answer these questions. This has opened up another research agenda which we are currently pursuing with the financial support of a research grant secured under the Economic and Social Research Council's (ESRC) Future of Work Initiative. This project will, in addition, further investigate another facet of home-located production that has increasingly figured in our analysis of those who are in work, at home: that is, the social relations of home and household. These constitute the social and spatial context of home-located production and indeed are its defining feature. Although often acknowledged as having vital significance for the understanding of home-located production relatively few researchers have investigated these relationships in-depth. Many questions and issues, therefore, remain to be thoroughly explored.

This, then, briefly sketches the history of our research in this field to date. In order to explain further how we arrived at the agenda for this book we need to excavate some of the layers of this experience in more depth. There are two reasons for this. First, at various points in subsequent chapters, we will draw upon the results of different facets of our work in developing the argument and analysis. It is necessary, therefore, to explain the methodologies we adopted and our use of terminology. Second, the chapters address problems, issues and questions we encountered in the practical exigencies of doing research and in wrestling with the challenges they posed.

Analysis of official data

Many of our initial and continuing research questions – how many, how often, who, where, what, when and so on – were quantitative in nature. Not surprisingly, therefore, we turned – as have many others – to official data sets, with their large samples and government-backed resources, for the answers.

We began work on the Employment Department (ED) project with an examination of available British official data sets, such as the quarterly Labour Force Survey (LFS), Workplace Industrial Relations Survey (WIRS) and the 1991 Census. It immediately became apparent that none of these contained answers to all of our questions and that each used different definitions. It was, therefore, very difficult to compare results. Despite an apparent wealth of data, there were many traps for the unwary; for example, the same terms were commonly used in various data sets to describe different categories of people who work at home. The first lesson we quickly learned, therefore, was that official statistics require careful and detailed investigation of the assumptions, definitions and techniques of data collection and compilation. The implication is that national and international comparisons are fraught with difficulties.

We decided to focus mainly on the Census because it gives a geographical slant not available elsewhere. The results of the 1991 Census provided us with a national picture and enabled us to select local research sites for further work (Felstead and Jewson 1995). The results were not always what we expected, particularly with respect to rural areas where there were many more people working at home than we anticipated. This once again raised our suspicions about the conceptual and operational basis of the figures. It also heightened our awareness of theoretical and semantic problems in framing apparently simple and readily understood survey questions.

Despite these reservations, the Census alerted us to the possibility that home-working and home-located production may by no means be confined to traditional geographical areas and a limited number of social groups. This, combined with an emphasis in the ED brief on an investigation of so-called 'untypical' geographical areas, made us suspect that home-located production is a more ubiquitous and diverse phenomenon than often imagined. Much of the limited research which has been done in Britain comes from and tends to be carried out by campaign groups (e.g., Yorkshire and Humberside Low Pay Unit 1991; West Yorkshire Homeworking Unit 1992; Huws 1994). Valuable though this work is in many respects, it has the unfortunate effect of confirming stereotypes of home-workers. This is because much of it has been conducted in the localities where campaigning groups are best organised and funded – which happen to be industrial cities with long-standing clothing and garment industries. Official data, however, led us to wonder whether this image has obscured a more complex and varied pattern. Exploration of this issue became one of the objectives of our further work using other methods.

Doorstep survey

We decided to initiate a large scale doorstep survey in four geographical localities in Britain, urban and rural, focusing on nine local areas. The latter corresponded to electoral wards or (in Scotland) postal sectors that figured in the Census. The survey entailed calling on approximately every other household in all residential streets. Our researchers knocked on 15,623 doors in all. In order to make the questions short and concise, it was decided simply to ask whoever answered the door: 'Have you, or anyone else in your household, done any paid work at home during the last twelve months?' Those who responded positively were asked how many people were involved and what type of work they had been doing. Individuals in manufacturing and lower-status service sector jobs were asked whether they would be willing to participate in an in-depth interview.

Quite a few colleagues doubted whether this strategy would yield useful results. Nevertheless, with a great deal of trepidation, we embarked upon this not inconsiderable task. Fortunately, the doorstep survey was a success. Its aim was to obtain a quantitative measure of the numbers of people who work at home. We were able to generate figures for each electoral ward/postal district which were congruent and plausible in the light of other official estimates. There were, however, problems. These included households where there was no reply, difficulties in operationalising responses and negative returns from respondents who we had every reason to believe were earning a living at home.

The doorstep survey was also used to generate a sample of homeworkers for in-depth interview (discussed on pp. 9–10). Again, we were pleased with the outcome. In some areas most of our in-depth interviews came from doorstepping, although in others we had to resort to 'topping up' from other sources. Our success owed much to the very high quality of the research teams employed in different parts of the country. These were selected in the light of local circumstances, ethnic and gender differences, and the anticipated anxieties of potential respondents. Their skills in establishing rapport and making contact with respondents, who were often cautious and uncertain, were essential to the outcome of the project. All this experience made us focus on the problems of searching for subjects. Indeed, there was a period when we were almost obsessed with ways of making contact with potential respondents, some of which proved to be much more effective than others.

A further aim of the doorstep survey was to generate estimates of numbers of homeworkers in a range of different types of localities, including areas renowned for homeworking and others which appeared to have little history. This proved to be extremely revealing. In one location, in particular, we were told by local economic analysts that we would find nothing. However, on the ground we discovered a rich and complex pattern of homeworking and home-located production, albeit one different in detail from so-called 'typical' areas. This led us to believe that earning a living at home is more widespread than is commonly realised and extends into a surprising range of activities. We began to suspect that much previous research had only seen the more visible part of the iceberg.

In-depth interviews

The doorstep survey generated a sample for in-depth interview. These were conducted with a total of 338 respondents across the local areas, making ours the largest study of homeworkers conducted in Britain. The interviews provided detailed information about a wide range of aspects of their employment, work tasks, health and safety, pay, fringe benefits, qualifications and household characteristics.

Our experience has shown that, contrary to much advice, large scale and intensive door-knocking can generate a significant sample of homeworkers willing to be interviewed. However, in some areas suspicion of doorstep canvassers was so great that we were forced to resort to additional methods. This made us aware of the special difficulties and sensitivities involved in interviewing homeworkers. We became wary of projects that, in searching for subjects, do not adopt special procedures that take account of these issues (cf. Hakim 1987a).

The in-depth interviews represented a turning point in our understanding. They enabled us to listen to the voices of homeworkers explaining, in their own words, their experiences and feelings, the circumstances they encounter and the challenges of their everyday lives. This prompted a further set of research questions which have become increasingly prominent in our thinking.

Many of those interviewed were faced with economic hardship and high levels of stress. The terms and conditions of homeworkers are among some of the worst encountered in the labour market and these were fully reflected in the accounts of our respondents. However, our findings contrasted with those of some other researchers in at least two respects. First, we identified a small group of homeworkers whose earnings were relatively high. Second, our estimates of *average* hourly pay were consistently higher than some other studies, although we also detected some individuals who received abysmally low wages. In part, of course, our higher average reflected the presence in our sample of the better paid. Even allowing for this, however, we became increasingly intrigued by the problems of describing and identifying the *precise* character of the labour market disadvantage endured by homeworkers. Much of the debate surrounds competing estimates of the average hourly rate. Less attention is devoted to questions such as: is an average figure a reliable or meaningful barometer of low pay? How are average hourly rates calculated when most homeworkers are paid by the piece?

Whilst our interviews left us in no doubt that a large majority of homeworkers are badly paid and receive virtually no fringe benefits, we were repeatedly impressed by the resilient and resourceful way in which they responded to their difficult circumstances. We formed the view that homeworkers typically generate active and creative coping strategies. We suspected that, in emphasising their deprivation, some authors have obscured the capacity of homeworkers for struggle and resistance. A major research issue thus became seeking to understand the choices and constraints faced by those who work at home.

Closely related to issues of autonomy and struggle are those surrounding relationships between homeworkers and employers. The stories and anecdotes of our respondents frequently referred to the dynamics and nuances of this relationship. It became apparent that employers and their agents adopt a range of strategies for managing homeworkers that are distinctive and sometimes in contrast to those which they adopt with respect to workplace employees. To our surprise, we also discovered that there was little published work on this theme, despite the fact that it was one constantly discussed by respondents. Our current research for the ESRC takes this as one of its central themes.

Our interviews also highlighted the pressures experienced by homeworkers in their attempts to reconcile paid employment and domestic life within one space. This is a theme commented upon by many researchers. However, it rarely forms the focus of detailed investigation in its own right. Moreover, as we listened to the experiences of our respondents, we became increasingly aware of the diversity of their household circumstances and their responses to them. We were increasingly struck by the heterogeneity of what might, at first sight, appear to be an homogeneous form of economic activity. With some notable exceptions, however, the social science literature on homeworking provided us with few clues to an understanding of the complex interaction of home and work.

Qualitative interviews

Many of the questions which emerged from the in-depth interviews were beyond the scope of the ED project. However, with the support of a small grant from the Faculty of the Social Sciences Research Board at the University of Leicester, we were able to carry out a series of long qualitative interviews with a small sample of home-located producers. Our 23 respondents – including eight homeworkers – were recruited by 'snowballing' techniques. This study, adopting an investigative methodology, had two aims. First, to illuminate the processes by which those who work at home generate strategies of resistance and control. Second, to situate these in the context of their household relationships and domestic regimes. We hoped to map ways in which the dynamics of household relations – including the creation of personal identities and inequalities of power – interacted with those of the labour market. The range of types of home-located producers included in the sample enabled us to take a wider perspective on these issues than we had been able to do in our earlier work.

Once again, the discipline of listening to those who *live* home-located production proved immensely rewarding and interesting. An immediate outcome was a strengthening of our suspicion that home-located production involves distinctive processes of struggle. On delving into the transcripts we unearthed a series of psychological dispositions and social practices through which home-located producers struggle to control *themselves* – and thus gain a greater purchase on their relationships with employers, clients and other household members. These 'technologies of the self' became an increasing focus of interest to us.

The qualitative interviews also explored the pressures, tensions and sources of support inherent in the household relations of home-located producers. We collected quite a substantial volume of information about the specifics of household regimes – but it proved to be much more difficult to establish the underlying rules, values and beliefs that guide decision-making. We came to the view that this is, in part, because the latter are deeply embedded in more or less taken-for-granted assumptions and practices. We designate these as 'household understandings'. Home-located production is particularly interesting because it problematises household understandings by potentially putting established domestic regimes in jeopardy. This theme has emerged from our recently completed work and has increasingly become a focus of our attention, and forms one of the central themes in our current ESRC research.

Plan of the book

In this section, we will move from an exposition of the development of our research to outlining the agenda of this book. The chapters emerge from the 'suspicions' and 'hunches' that have driven us over the last few years.

Chapter 2 – 'Conceptualising the field' – confronts head-on the thorny question of definitions. The distinctive feature of home-located production is its spatial location; quite simply, it refers to all market-based ways of making a living at home. However, this covers an extremely heterogeneous group occupying different positions in the labour market. It is, therefore, essential to identify different *types* of home-located producer. We develop a typology based on an analysis of their social relations of production, and thereby generate our own definition of homeworkers. The chapter goes on to outline some of the concepts that are used later in the book to analyse the household context of home-located production – in particular, the notion of 'household understanding'. As far as we are aware, our approach and our definitions offer a distinctive perspective. The terminology spelt out in this chapter is used throughout the book. One of the problems of developing a unique set of terms is that of referring to the results of the work of others who have adopted different conceptualisations. Wherever possible in drawing on other research findings we have 'translated' the categories of others into our own terms. For example, the well-known study of Allen and Wolkowitz (1987) uses the term 'homeworkers' to describe the group that we call home-located wage labourers. On the occasions when it has not been possible to translate the terms of other researchers into our own, we have put them in inverted commas. However, where we have quoted our interview respondents, we have not changed their words nor attempted to translate them into our terms.

Chapter 3 – 'Searching for subjects' – examines the range of ways in which researchers throughout the world have attempted to select and recruit samples of home-located producers. Here, we explore the means adopted by social scientists to investigate what is generally accepted to be one of the most 'invisible' segments of the labour market. The chapter documents the implications of relying upon particular techniques in generating a research sample.

Chapter 4 – 'Taking a count' – tackles one of the most fundamental but complex quantitative issues: how many home-located producers are there? The chapter reviews estimates from around the world, covering official, academic and other sources. Our argument is that no single study offers the definitive answer, but that the contribution of each may be appreciated in the light of the conceptual analysis found in Chapter 2. We also highlight the formidable array of technical problems that confront a comparative analysis of different counts within and between countries.

Chapter 5 – 'Revealing diversity' – focuses upon the social characteristics of those who work at home. It presents a wide range of international research findings and evaluates the extent to which popular stereotypes of home-located producers are confirmed by the evidence. It concludes that different kinds of people are involved in different types of home-located production. Confusion reigns when one piece of the jigsaw is taken to represent the overall picture. Moreover, a review of research findings strongly suggests that each category of home-located producers includes a substantial minority with unexpected backgrounds.

Chapter 6 – 'Documenting the grim realities' – presents and interprets research findings from across the world on the working conditions of home-located producers in general and homeworkers in particular. Not only do many have poor pay and conditions but they also suffer disadvantages *relative* to their workplace-located peers. The spatial location of, and managerial strategies towards, homeworkers makes collective organisation and government regulation difficult. However, the chapter provides examples of innovative campaigning strategies that have managed to make a difference.

Chapter 7 – 'Struggling for control' – is the first of several that focus attention on the meaning and experience of working at home. It evaluates competing arguments about the freedoms and constraints encountered by home-located producers. Some researchers have portrayed them as tightly controlled, others regard them as relatively autonomous. Our argument is that those who work at home are subject to a range of limitations and restrictions derived from their relationships with employers and with other household members. Nevertheless, we also argue that they are characterised by high levels of self-motivation, self-discipline and self-organisation. These attributes – which, ironically, employers increasingly seek from their workplace-located employees – entail personal dispositions and capabilities that we describe as 'technologies of the self'.

Chapter 8 – 'Managing the self' – explores specific features of 'technologies of the self' characteristic of home-located producers, all of which involve management of time and space within the home. These are grouped around two themes: the management of spatial and temporal boundaries *between* the home and the outside world, and the management of spatial and temporal boundaries *within* the household. By these means, home-located producers seek to reconcile the disparate demands of paid employment and domestic life. The analysis presented in this chapter is derived from the findings of the qualitative interviews, described above, and is supported by extensive quotations from our respondents.

Chapter 9 – 'Combining home and work' – argues that underlying the specific characteristics of particular 'technologies of the self' can be found more general strategies. Furthermore, it is suggested that the opportunity to pursue one or other of these is, in part, determined by the nature of household relationships. The concluding part of the chapter presents a typology of connections between, on the one hand, strategies for combining home and work and, on the other, forms of household understanding. This analysis represents an initial – and speculative – attempt to forge an understanding of an issue that is central to home-located production but which is surprisingly under-researched and under-theorised. We doubt this will be the last word on the subject but we hope that it will stimulate debate and promote further research.

Chapter 10 – 'Mapping the broader perspective' – presents an overview of the themes of the book and locates its central arguments and findings within the context of broader contemporary social science.

Conclusion

The inspiration for this book comes from reflection on our research experiences and an attempt to chart future directions. This is not, therefore, a conventional textbook – although it does offer a comprehensive and wide-ranging perspective on the character of home-located production and homeworking. It is not a straightforward review of the literature – although it does assemble and interpret a large volume of research materials from across the world. Nor is it a research monograph – although the text includes original quantitative and qualitative research findings. What this book does offer is an exploration of a series of crucial but contested research issues. In each chapter we not only pose questions but also dare to provide answers – sometimes controversial, always open to further debate. Taken together, the chapters address a range of different intellectual tasks, including conceptual clarification, evaluation of research techniques, analysis of quantitative measurements, interpretation of qualitative materials and hypothesis formulation. Throughout, however, we urge the reader to bear in mind the subtitle – _Towards an understanding of homeworking_. Our analyses and arguments are provisional. They will be justified if they inspire others to do better.

Chapter 2

Conceptualising the field

'When *I* use a word,' Humpty Dumpty said in a rather scornful tone, 'it means just what I choose it to mean – neither more nor less.'
(Lewis Carroll, *Through the Looking Glass*, original emphasis)

Introduction

There is no single, internationally recognised, definition of 'homeworking'. Even within a single country definitions can differ widely. While many studies have gone to considerable lengths to specify who is – and who is not – included, few have offered theoretical justifications for their choices (among the exceptions are Allen and Wolkowitz 1987; Walker 1987; Dholakia 1989). Empiricism has, therefore, obscured theoretical clarity. Our aim in this chapter is to go some way to correct this deficiency.

The spatial location of home-located production is its defining feature – the single attribute that all types of home-located production have in common. We conceive this space as a 'field' within a series of overlapping social relationships (cf. Bourdieu 1990b). The totality of relationships within this field – including the interactions, tensions and contradictions between them – is our focus. To be in work at home is to experience two worlds of meaning and organisation within one locale. Our analysis, therefore, focuses on the distinctive conjunction of social relations of production and reproduction this entails.

This book seeks to follow through the implications of this starting point and to bring together insights into various aspects of the total organisation of home-located production that are commonly presented in isolation from one another. In this chapter, we will begin by conceptualising the social relations of home-located production and then proceed to contextualise these within the life of the house-hold. The implications of the juxtaposition of these two sets of relationships within the lived experience of the home will gradually unfold throughout the following chapters of the book.

Social relations of home-located production

We shall begin to develop our conceptual framework by examining the social relations of production of those who work at home. These refer to the relationships
between various economic agents in the production process, whereby one party
mobilises the labour of another. It is immediately apparent that the production
relations of people working at home vary enormously. However, although these
differences are sometimes acknowledged in empirical studies they are rarely incor-
porated into theoretical frameworks or conceptual models. This, in turn, is
reflected in slippage in the use of terminology. As a result confusion frequently
arises about exactly which category or group of people working at home is under
discussion. A basic but not uncommon error, for example, is to assume that the
social characteristics and employment conditions of homeworkers, as we have
described them in Chapter 1, are typical of home-located producers as a whole.
This misunderstanding has led to claims that in Britain there are 1.2 million
homeworkers engaged in basic manufacturing and service jobs – when in fact this
is the figure which approximates to *all* those working *at and from* home in whatever capacity.

For these reasons, we have developed a typology of the social relations of
home-located production which generates a series of categories – and associated
terms – that we adopt throughout this book (see Figure 2.1). At the most general
level, we use the term *home-located production* to designate economic activity by
members of households who produce within their place of residence commodities
for exchange in the market. Those who engage in such work we call *home-located
producers*. We include within the scope of our definition all of those involved in
such work, whether on a part-time, full-time or occasional basis. This includes
those who work at home for only *some* of the time. Home-located producers may,
furthermore, have other workplace jobs which they pursue at the same time as
working at home. They may regard home-located production as a secondary or
supplementary source of income.

The term 'home-located production' embraces a very wide variety of different
types of activities, people and social relations. It is therefore imperative to disaggregate this complex and diverse group in terms of the contrasting social relations
of production of the members. The first step is to distinguish between those who
employ others – and who therefore have control over the labour power of others –
and those who do not. The former group we call *home-located employers*. It
includes, for example, hotel owners or publicans who live 'on site' and who
employ bar staff or cleaners. It follows, however, that it does not include live-in
proprietors who run guest houses without any hired help.

Those home-located producers who do not employ others we denote as *home-
located workers*. This corresponds to a category we used in our earlier work
(Felstead and Jewson 1996). They are themselves a heterogeneous group. Some
exercise a considerable degree of control over their market and work situations;
others do not. Further analytical distinctions are needed, therefore.

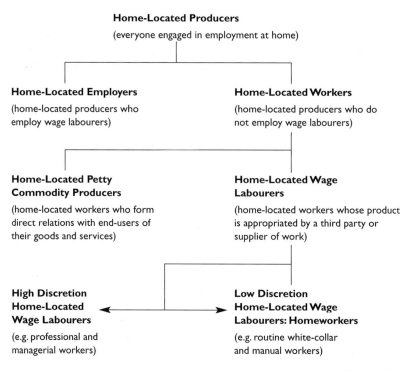

Home-Located Producers

(everyone engaged in employment at home)

Home-Located Employers

(home-located producers who
employ wage labourers)

Home-Located Workers

(home-located producers who do
not employ wage labourers)

**Home-Located Petty
Commodity Producers**

(home-located workers who form
direct relations with end-users of
their goods and services)

**Home-Located Wage
Labourers**

(home-located workers whose product
is appropriated by a third party or
supplier of work)

**High Discretion
Home-Located
Wage Labourers**

(e.g. professional and
managerial workers)

**Low Discretion
Home-Located Wage
Labourers: Homeworkers**

(e.g. routine white-collar
and manual workers)

Figure 2.1 **A typology of positions within the social relations of home-located
production**

It is important to differentiate between *home-located petty commodity producers*
and *home-located wage labourers*. Home-located petty commodity producers do
not employ others but do form *direct* relationships with the end-users of their
goods and services. They include, for example, mechanics, accountants, childminders, hairdressers and craft workers who sell their services and wares directly
to the public. Although they do not have significant control over the labour
power of others, they are in a position to receive the full benefits of the sale of the
goods and services they produce. Their life chances and social relations of
production are in contrast to those who deliver their product to a third party, or
a supplier of work, in exchange for wages. We will call this group *home-located
wage labourers*. Examples include mechanics or accountants who are employed at
home by a firm or business. Home-located wage labourers are, therefore, econ-
omically dependent on a third party or parties – mediating between themselves
and end-users.

It necessarily follows that home-located wage labourers are always in some
kind of managerial relationship with an employer or supplier of work. Their relations of production imply some form of supervision, monitoring or control of
their output. This may take different forms, depending upon circumstances.

However, it is of great importance to recognise that the social and geographical distance between home-located wage labourers and management problematises such relationships for both parties. It generates a series of issues and uncertainties that are characteristic of home-located wage labour as compared with workplace-located wage labour.

Problems for both employers and workers arise from the absence of continuous supervisory contact. Employers may fear that work will not be completed by the required deadline, that quality standards are not being met or that materials are being stolen. Workers also face uncertainties as a result of their intermittent contact with suppliers of work. They may feel that they are not given guidance about problems they encounter, that work loads are unpredictable or that wages will not be forthcoming when pay day comes around. In the office or factory it is typical for the time, space and pace of work to be externally regulated. This is partly due to the presence of supervisors and managers but is also inherent in the general social organisation and physical layout of the workplace. Those who work at home are not subject to the same kind or level of external constraints on their working day and their work location. They must generate and maintain for themselves the temporal rhythms and spatial boundaries of their employment. Thus, a part of the managerial function is delegated to home-located wage labourers and internalised within the daily routines they construct for themselves. There are elements of self-management inherent in home-located wage labour. These themes are developed further in Chapters 7 and 8.

Among home-located wage labourers there are wide differences in opportunities and life circumstances – including command over the allocation of jobs and distribution of rewards. It is necessary, therefore, to identify criteria for differentiating between those with more and those with less power within the labour market. Various approaches might be adopted in distinguishing labour market segments among home-located wage labourers. They might, for example, be grouped according to occupation, industry, technology or skill. We suggest, however, that a useful distinction can be drawn between those with relatively *high discretion* and those with relatively *low discretion* jobs. In this context, discretion refers to the extent to which qualities of judgement, problem-solving, decision-making and originality are key attributes of the labour process. Low discretion work is predictable, routine, standardised and rule-dominated; high discretion work is variable, complex, creative and choice-dominated (cf. Jaques 1956, 1967). Discretion should be conceptualised as a continuum rather than a dichotomy. Elements of discretion and repetition are inherent in all jobs but a sliding scale can be envisaged (Fox 1974).

Discretion can, in practice, be roughly translated into a division of occupational types: in descending order, professional, managerial, craft, clerical and routine manual. However, these only represent a proximate mapping of the discretion levels involved. Thus, for example, in general home-located solicitors probably do enjoy much higher levels of discretion than home-located secretaries – but, in practice, junior legal staff might be given routine work to do at home while the personal assistant to the senior partner in the firm might do highly sensitive and responsible tasks at home.

We hypothesise that the degree of discretion in the work task itself is of crucial relevance to the experience of home-located wage labour. Task discretion should not be confused with the need for self-direction referred to above. All forms of home-located production require self-discipline and self-motivation. However, the levels of discretion inherent in the job task do shape the strategies of control open to management in seeking to regulate wage labourers as well as the strategies adopted by wage labourers in coping with the demands of their situation. The problems of supervisory and managerial relationships are characteristic of both low and high discretion home-located jobs. However, the options open to both parties in the employment relationship vary with the degree of task discretion exercised by workers. Thus, the concept of discretion may provide a more sensitive criterion for distinguishing between the social relations of home-located wage labourers – and hence their command over resources, rewards and authority – than occupational titles or the manual/non-manual divide.

It is now possible to identify the social relations of production characteristic of the group who are the principle focus of this book. Low discretion home-located wage labourers we designate by the term *homeworkers*. They may be engaged in routine clerical activities (e.g., data entry or transcribing), low-discretion manual tasks (e.g., packing boxes or stuffing envelopes) and routine service activities (e.g., on-site security or catering). There are some manual jobs done at home that entail high levels of discretion, reflected in higher wage rates and better terms and conditions. In the terms of our definition, we would not designate these as homeworkers. However, there are difficult practical problems in operationalising these distinctions (cf. recent debates surrounding the new Socio-Economic Classifications (SECs) introduced by the Office for National Statistics – see O'Reilly and Rose 1998; Blackburn 1998; Prandy 1998; Rose 1998).

Focusing on the issue of discretion enables us to highlight within our conceptual model the issue of relativities between home-located and workplace-located wage labourers who belong to the same occupation or, indeed, work for the same firm. Home-located workers are often said to be given job tasks that involve lower levels of discretion than their peers in the office or factory. This, in turn, may damage their future career prospects and shape their trajectories in the labour market. Home-located wage labourers may thus experience deprivation of high discretion tasks *relative* to comparable others. This may affect those in basically high discretion jobs as much as those at the other end of the continuum.

The allocation of low discretion tasks to home-located wage labourers may be due to several factors. They may not be present when the interesting jobs are being handed out in the office. Their relative invisibility at home may not give them the opportunity to show off what they can do and to claim the credit, leading seniors to underestimate their capacities. However, there may be a more systematic and deliberate reason. Employers may seek to minimise the risks and problems inherent in the managerial relationship by only allowing the simplest and most routine tasks out of the office into the home.

The capacity of any individual to access high and low discretion forms of home-located wage labour in part reflects the quality and amenities of their place of residence. Thus, for example, a telephone is essential for a clerical worker who is required to use a modem, possession of a car may be of vital importance to a garment maker who is required to collect work from a factory, and a personally owned computer may be an enormous advantage to a professional working at home. In these circumstances, the quality of the environment generated within the household in fulfilling the tasks of social *re*production can have a direct relevance to the market power of the home-located wage labourer. It should also be noted that different kinds of home-located production require contrasting work spaces and facilities. Moreover, they may impinge upon domestic life in a variety of different ways depending on the degree of noise, pollution and hazards involved. Thus, the market power of home-located wage labourers is intimately connected with the social relations of their households.

Before turning to an examination of the social relations of households, however, there is a further point which it is appropriate to make at this juncture. The concepts we have used in order to distinguish between contrasting social relations of production among groups of people who work at home also enable us to mount a theoretically based critique of the concept of 'telework'. 'Telework' has been variously defined and operationalised – some of the most interesting and eminent research work being that of Huws and her colleagues (Huws 1993, 1996b; Huws *et al.* 1990, 1996). However, whatever approach is adopted, it is impossible to escape a technological basis for identifying the criteria which define 'teleworkers' – typically involvement with some form of information technology or other remote communications devices in the work process. Criteria such as these do not focus on the social relations of production. In terms of the classificatory system developed here, they may include home-located employers, home-located petty commodity producers, high discretion home-located wage labourers, and home-workers. The concept of 'telework' thus confuses rather than clarifies our understanding of home-located production. It is not derived from an analysis of *social* relations but rather from an implied or explicit technological determinism. In this book, we shall avoid using the terms 'telework' and 'teleworker' in our own analysis. We shall only use them when referring to what others have written or said.

Social relations of the household

The distinctive feature of home-located production is that it takes place in a locale – the home – which is also the primary site of social *re*production in capitalist societies. The social relations of reproduction impinge upon those of production in ways that require specific analysis. Just as the different *types* of home-located production need to be considered, so too do the differing household *contexts* within which this work is carried out.

Our detailed conceptualisation of the ways in which home and work are combined by home-located producers is developed in Chapter 9. In that chapter we spell out a series of analytical distinctions concerning the characteristic features of different types of households and the ways in which home-located producers reconcile conflicting demands. These arguments emerge from the themes developed throughout the book. We have avoided presenting them in full here because we do not want to overload the early part of the text with terms and concepts that are not put to use until later on. However, readers may wish to read Chapter 9 in conjunction with this chapter. They are the two most theoretical parts of the book. In this section, we shall confine ourselves to some 'ground clearing' exercises that set the stage for the more elaborate analysis that is to follow.

A preliminary, but crucial, conceptual distinction concerns the extent to which work is spatially located within the place of residence. It is vital to distinguish between people who: work *at home* (e.g., someone who packs Christmas cards in their spare room); work *from home* (e.g., a jobbing plumber); and work *in the same grounds and buildings as home* (e.g., a smallholder or concierge). Although this division may at first sight seem straightforward, it routinely leads to confusion and is one of the issues that accounts for much of the non-comparability of data sets. People who work from home or in the same grounds and buildings as home are less likely to experience the full impact of the conjunction of the social relations of production and reproduction in their lives. Their work activities tend to take them away from the spatial location of much housework and childcare. In contrast, those who work *at* home are far more likely to experience the cross-cutting pressures of two worlds of meaning, organisation and value. They typically have to negotiate some kind of reconciliation or settlement between the public and private spheres within the home itself. In this book, we shall use the terms home-located production and homeworking to refer exclusively to those who work *at* home.

There is an important aspect of these definitions that deserves further clarification. As we made clear earlier in this chapter, we include in our definition of home-located producers those who work at home *some* of the time as well as those who work at home *all* of the time. Hence, a management consultant who works at home for half of the week and who visits clients from home in the remainder of her working week would fall within the scope of this book. However, a management consultant who worked entirely from home would not be included in our analysis. This should be borne in mind with respect to the sample of respondents who participated in our qualitative interviews.

The spatial location of home-located production necessarily places gender issues right at the heart of the analysis. Although all employment relations may be said to entail issues concerning male and female identities, home-located production is gendered in ways that are distinctive (see, for example, Allen and Wolkowitz 1987; Boris and Daniels 1989; Boris 1996; Huws *et al.* 1996; Christensen 1988). Household and family relationships incorporate deeply ingrained notions of masculinity and femininity. These are the context of the activities, roles and responsibilities of home-located production. To a significant degree gender is constructed through taking responsibility for and completing specific domestic tasks that are identified with masculinity and femininity (Berk 1985; West and Zimmerman 1987; Coltrane 1989; Warde and Hetherington 1993). Hence, the introduction of relations of production into the home has different consequences for male and female home-located producers – as well as for other household members.

There are, however, two further points to make. First, homeworking in particular, and to a lesser extent home-located production more generally, is sometimes discussed as if it were solely the preserve of women. This fails to acknowledge that more home-located producers are male than female. Even among homeworkers, as we have narrowly defined them, a sizeable minority are male. However, very little is known about the ways in which men who work at home reconcile the demands of employment and household. Too often discussions of homeworking women have taken precedence over an analysis of gender divisions among homeworkers.

The second and more fundamental point is that, while gender divisions are of critical importance, it is also essential to capture the diversity of types of households within which gender relations are embedded (Benjamin and Sullivan 1996; Gregson and Lowe 1993; M. Anderson *et al.* 1994). The household context of home-located production cannot be fully encompassed within a dualistic analysis of masculinity and femininity. It is necessary, therefore, to identify different forms or types of household relations.

We suggest that the social relations of households revolve around a series of allocation processes, negotiated on the basis of explicit and implicit rules. Two such processes are central to the ordering and lived experience of household life; the domestic division of labour, and the management and control of household finances (M. Anderson *et al.* 1994; Warde and Hetherington 1993; Morris 1987, 1990, 1993; Pahl 1983, 1989; Vogler 1989; Vogler and Pahl 1993, 1994). Households differ on both these dimensions. Each comprises a range of constraints and opportunities with contrasting potentialities and possibilities.

Members of households may be more or less equal with respect to the distribution of domestic labour and the management of financial resources. We may, therefore, identify a continuum between relatively egalitarian and relatively hierarchical households. Egalitarian households commonly seek views of all members and involve them in reaching a consensus. This often entails processes and techniques of negotiation and compromise. In hierarchical households decisions are made by some members and received by others.

Whether egalitarian or hierarchical, households also differ in the extent to which members carry out tasks and exercise powers jointly or separately. We may, therefore, identify a continuum between relatively joint households and relatively segregated households. In segregated households members have discrete tasks and spheres of authority which are their sole responsibility and which are different in kind to those of other household members. There is a clear separation between the spheres of competence and activity of each individual. In joint households, tasks are shared, decisions are made together and domestic life is conducted in collaboration with other members.

Households incorporate values and assumptions within which members devise and maintain boundaries in time and space between their activities and relationships. The domestic division of labour and systems of financial management reflect and reinforce spatial and temporal divisions, both within the home and between the home and the outside world. Those who engage in home-located production must manage the introduction of work processes and relations into this context.

Control over resources and the division of domestic labour – and the associated organisation of household time and space – may be the subject of calculated and deliberate decisions. More usually, however, they are derived from practices, beliefs and values that are habitual or taken-for-granted. We describe these as *household understandings*. These are based upon deeply held assumptions about what are perceived to be fundamental features of human behaviour, commonly regarded as 'second nature', normal, appropriate and decent. In a similar vein, Silverstone *et al.* (1994) identified what they called the 'moral economy' of the household. This refers to 'the capacity of households to define a distinct social, cultural and economic regime for themselves, different from that dominant in the public world' (Haddon and Silverstone 1993). Household understandings, thus, have much in common with Bourdieu's concepts of 'practical logic' and 'habitus' (Bourdieu 1990a, 1990b).

Home-located production frequently problematises household understandings because it introduces principles and practices derived from the workplace into the home (cf. Bulos and Chaker 1993, 1995). Overt statements of the principles of household understandings are relatively rare and are usually confined to exceptional moments of conflict, celebration or 'rites of passage'. More commonly, they are not formally stated – as in a contract – but are expressed symbolically, implicitly and intuitively (Christensen 1988). It should not be assumed that household understandings necessarily specify a tightly knit and inflexible set of behaviours. Indeed some may, as a characteristic feature, call for processes of individual negotiation and idiosyncratic decision-making between the parties. Nor should it be assumed that household understandings preclude ongoing and endemic disagreement. There may well be a lack of congruence between the assumptions of different parties to the understanding. Such differences in perception may not be antithetical to their operation – indeed they may even be central to their success. Disputes, disturbances and disagreements, however, are occasions on which the principles of household understandings may be expressed directly or explicitly articulated.

Household understandings are constructed around personal ties of sexual partnership, marriage and parenting. They are made and negotiated in the context of strong emotions that typically constitute a major element of personal identity and biographical meaning. The renegotiation or redefinition of these ties in the context of home-located production may, therefore, be problematic.

In Chapter 9 we distinguish four ideal types of household understandings. Each represents a complex set of constraints and opportunities that face members who undertake home-located production. These, we suggest, shape the strategies adopted by those who seek to combine home and work. The implication is that we need to examine the dynamics of the household *as a whole* in order to understand the actions of home-located producers.

Conclusion

We have outlined a number of conceptual distinctions with respect to the social relations of production and those of households. Together, the totality of these relationships constitute the field of this book. In this chapter we have differentiated several types of production relations among home-located producers. We have also introduced the concept of 'household understanding' in an attempt to capture the features of social life in the home. In Chapter 9, we spell out four different ideal types of household understanding and explore the implications of each for attempts to combine home and work.

The thesis of this book is that the various ways in which the two worlds of home and work impinge upon one another create a complex mosaic of social relations that characterise a range of different types of home-located production. Thus, people with the same occupation, but living in different types of household, may well generate contrasting solutions to similar challenges – manifested in the organisation of space and time in the home. Similarly, it follows that households with similar sets of values and practices – household understandings – may generate a variety of different work regimes with respect to different types of home-located production. The logic of our conceptual framework, therefore, is that home-located production is intrinsically diverse and multi-faceted.

Chapter 3

Searching for subjects

> Unlike most other employment, homework does not form a distinct and organised section of the industrial world, but an unknown country without chart or beaten tracks, in which the boundaries and landmarks are continually shifting, so that the investigator has practically to grope his [*sic*] way through it.
>
> (Irwin 1902: 8–9)

Introduction

The above statement has certainly stood the test of time; it is just as true now as when first uttered a century ago. One of the main reasons why homeworking is still an 'unknown country' is the practical difficulty researchers find in identifying subjects for study. Indeed, in the course of researching this book we have been forced to draw on a range of different kinds of research studies simply because paid work in the home is often hidden from view. There are many reasons for this invisibility, including *inter alia* unclear legal status, fear and disapproval of employers and other family members, rapid turnover, and a general reluctance by disadvantaged groups to reveal themselves to official gaze. Thus, identifying who does work at home, in what capacity, is not easy to do. One of the consequences of this difficulty has been the tendency for social scientists to adopt a particular technique in generating a research sample and then to generalise their conclusions to homeworkers – or even home-located producers – as a whole. It is, therefore, appropriate that early on we provide the reader with an overview of the different methodologies adopted by researchers in searching for subjects.

We by no means claim to be the first to review the methodological problems entailed in carrying out our research in this area (e.g., Allen and Wolkowitz 1987; Phizacklea and Wolkowitz 1995). Furthermore, methodological compromises have often been forced on researchers by a lack of resources and time rather than a lack of analytical awareness. In this chapter, however, we have sought to assemble a comprehensive review of research methods, commenting upon their efficacy by drawing on examples from around the world and teasing out the implications of different approaches for an understanding of home-located production.

Most researchers focus on home-located producers rather than on employers and suppliers of work. The balance of this chapter reflects these preoccupations. The text itself contains minimal references to specific studies since annotated details of their methods and foci are given in a series of tables which accompany the text. The chapter concludes by arguing that the nature of home-located production makes it empirically as well as conceptually problematic to study. The research methods adopted are likely to shape our perceptions of working at home. Each study offers new insights into what still remains largely uncharted territory, throwing light on some questions at the same time as leaving some unresolved. We will begin by looking at official data sources and then move on to consider doorstep surveys, direct appeals, chasing known points of contact, documentary evidence and surveys of employers.

Official data sources

Probably one of the most cost-effective ways of searching for subjects is to carry out secondary analysis of official data sets. These obviously have to be ones which enable the researcher to identify those who work at home. Population censuses, labour force surveys and household surveys come under this heading.

Governments in all modern industrial societies require accurate information on national populations, their characteristics and how they are changing. Population censuses are one technique routinely used to provide regular information on a wide range of topics. Typically, completion of census forms by all households is regular and compulsory. The most common interval between censuses tends to be ten years, although some countries such as Australia and New Zealand have one every five years.

For those studying home-located production, censuses are of interest since most of them carry a 'travel-to-work' question. This usually, though not always (see, for example, Census of Population Office (Singapore) 1994), allows respondents to declare that they or members of their household 'work mainly at home'. On this basis, research on the extent, growth and characteristics of those who work at home has been carried out in many countries. These include the US, Canada, Australia, New Zealand, India, Hong Kong, Finland and the UK (see Table 3.1).

However, census data do have their drawbacks. Reliance on travel-to-work questions results in imprecision as to where the work is actually conducted (Hakim 1998). It could be in the environs of the home (i.e., in the grounds or buildings surrounding the home) or in parts of the home otherwise used for domestic purposes (see Chapter 2, pp. 20). Another problem is that forms are often filled in by one household member on behalf of others, thereby generating inaccuracies. For example, all the activities of household members may not be known to the person filling in the form. They may be deliberately concealed from view, not regarded as 'real work' or simply not visible to the form-filler. Furthermore, the work may not be acknowledged by home-located producers and/or form-fillers for fear of enquiry by housing authorities, benefit agencies or tax officials.

Table 3.1 Searching for subjects using official sources of data about people working at home

Research method and examples	Techniques for identifying subjects	Type of production relations
Analysing official data sets		
Kraut and Grambsch (1987), Silver (1989), Nadwodny (1996), Walker (1987), Loveridge et al. (1996), Dholakia (1989), Wong (1983), Lui (1994), Salmi (1996), Pugh (1984) and Felstead and Jewson (1995)	Analyses of the 'travel-to-work' Census question in countries such as the US, Canada, Australia and the UK.	Home-located production, examples of disaggregation.
Horvath (1986), Deming (1994), Presser and Bamberger (1993), Akyeampong and Siroonian (1993), Akyeampong (1997), McLennan (1989, 1996), Madden (1992), Eurostat (various), Felstead (1996) and Lafferty et al. (1997)	Analyses of Labour Force Survey data in countries such as the US, Canada, Australia, the UK and across the European Union.	Home-located production, with some examples of disaggregation.
Abrera-Mangahas (1993), Laurie and Taylor (1995) and Foster et al. (1995)	Analyses of household surveys in countries such as the Philippines and the UK.	Home-located production, with some examples of disaggregation.
Analysing official records		
Hakim and Dennis (1982)	Analysis of official British Wages Inspectorate data on the pay and earnings of workers in the clothing and toy manufacturing industries. Data on 500 homeworkers and 500 inworkers who were working for 74 firms based in Lambeth, Wandsworth and Southwark in the winter of 1978–1979.	Homeworking.
Mitter (1986b)	Analysis of discrepancies in the official employment and output figures for the British clothing industry.	Homeworking.

Research method and examples	Techniques for identifying subjects	Type of production relations
Rubery et al. (1986b)	Updates Mitter's (1986b) analysis of the official employment and output discrepancies for the British clothing industry.	Homeworking.
Suzuki (1993) and Kamio (1995)	Registration of homeworkers with local authorities by employers. Registration required under the Japanese Industrial Homework Act 1970.	Homeworking.
'Piggybacking' official surveys		
Hakim (1987a)	Uses 1981 Labour Force Survey in UK as a sift survey for the National Homeworking Survey of England and Wales. The NHS was carried out later that year. A total of 1,287 'home-based' workers were interviewed.	Home-located production, with disaggregation to, inter alia, manufacturing homeworking.
Marshall (1992)	Uses the Argentine Household Survey to identify those working in the clothing and footwear industries in Buenos Aires. Out of 112 households with at least one member working in either one of these industries, 68 interviews were completed including 34 homeworkers (p. 54).	Homeworking.
ILO (1995)	Respondents selected from lists held by officials in four areas in Vietnam. Industries with high proportions of women workers were targeted. In total, information on 565 home-located workers was collected, 90 per cent of whom were women.	Home-located working.
Salmi (1996)	Respondents to a survey on living conditions in Finland in 1986 were asked about their place of work. Those who worked at least half of their time at home were asked to fill in a questionnaire. 195 home-located producers were surveyed in this way.	Home-located production.

Aside from these collection difficulties, the data once gathered may not allow for detailed analysis. Census data often consist of *counts* of individuals with particular characteristics. Each individual is commonly not represented as a single *case*. This is to protect the anonymity of individuals, since censuses typically present data on small areas and hence there is a danger that particular respondents could be identified if all of their characteristics were known. For the social scientist, however, presentation of the data as counts limits the analyses possible. It may not be feasible, for example, to generate a count of homeworkers – as we have defined them in Chapter 2 – or to cross-tabulate variables. Furthermore, it may not be possible to undertake statistical analysis based on the characteristics of each case, such as testing the hypothesis *ceteris paribus* that women are more likely than men to do particular types of home-located production.

In some countries these problems have been addressed. One solution is to give researchers access to census extracts which contain individual-level records for a small proportion of the population but for large geographical areas, thereby protecting the anonymity of respondents (Marsh 1993). Among such data sets are Census Microdata (US) and Samples of Anonymised Records (UK). Most notably they have been used by researchers to isolate the factors strongly associated with working at home by holding all other factors constant – see, for example, the work of Kraut (1988) for the US and Loveridge *et al.* (1996) for New Zealand. In terms of searching for subjects these provide a potentially rich source of information as well as a high degree of quantitative accuracy. However, they remain a largely untouched source, although Hakim's (1998: chapter 7) work represents a recent exception based on the UK SARs.

Labour force surveys are another source of official data. They typically entail periodic interviews with relatively large samples selected from within national labour markets. The advantages they have over census materials are their frequency and the inclusion of more direct questions about the spatial location of work. However, they do not always carry relevant questions in every trawl. In the US, for example, the Current Population Survey (CPS) is carried out monthly but questions on respondents' places of work have only been included every six years. In Australia, the monthly Labour Force Survey (LFS) asks questions about place of work every three years. Data are more readily available in the UK where respondents to the quarterly LFS are asked every six months about their place of work (see Table 3.1).

Figures compiled from labour force surveys do not suffer from some of the drawbacks typical of census data. They are collected and coded on an individual case basis and made available for analysis in that fashion. They are therefore amenable to tabular analysis of the researcher's own choosing as well as non-tabular procedures such as multivariate analysis. However, such surveys are subject to a degree of sampling error, which restricts the reliability of their conclusions. This becomes particularly problematic when disaggregating groups since small cell counts carry large sampling errors and may, therefore, be unrepresentative. Other problems include respondents who may be reluctant or unwilling to declare that they work at home, despite guarantees of confidentiality. Participation in these surveys remains entirely voluntary, unlike most censuses, and hence there will inevitably be some who simply refuse to take part.

Another source of official data are household surveys, which sometimes provide researchers interested in home-located production with valuable information (see Table 3.1). However, in practice, both the inclusion of relevant questions and appearance of the survey itself may be irregular. For example, a household survey in the Philippines included, on a one-off basis, questions on place of work but, as far as we are aware, this has not been repeated (Abrera-Mangahas 1993). The drawbacks of this type of data collection are similar to those of labour force surveys; that is, the non-disclosure of certain work activities and their voluntary nature.

Another way of seeking information on working at home is to analyse official records which may gather relevant information. This type of research has been carried out in countries such as Japan and the UK (see Table 3.1). Employers may be required to register details of the people they employ who work at home with the local authority. Government agencies may focus on particular industries to ensure compliance with the law. Another approach is to suggest that discrepancies in official output and employment data indirectly indicate patterns of home-located production not otherwise detectable. Mitter (1986b), for example, argues that anomalies between official British data on productivity, investment and employment can be taken as evidence that significant amounts of economic activity have shifted into unrecorded homework (see Rubery et al. 1992).

Official data sets can also act as means of identifying respondents eligible for further research. In other words, they can act as sifts for surveys of particular groups of home-located producers. One can find examples of this sort of 'piggybacking' in the UK, Argentina, Vietnam and Finland (see Table 3.1). However, if there are anxieties on the part of those working at home in responding to official government surveys in the first place, this is likely to be aggravated even further by a second survey – this time focused on activities some may regard as, at best, semi-illegal. None the less, 'piggybacking' does relatively easily pinpoint individuals who work at home, thereby facilitating the collection of specific information on the work they do and the circumstances under which they do it.

Given the problems of official data, researchers have pursued other ways of searching for subjects. Three are of particular importance; that is, door-knocking, direct appeals and chasing known points of contact. The main problem all of them face is the difficulty of generating a large or representative sample. We will consider in turn how each of them measures up to this challenge.

Doorstep surveys

One way of generating a sample of people to interview is to carry out a doorstep poll. Studies of this type have been carried out in several places in the UK as well as in South Africa (see Table 3.2). However, a major problem faced by such a technique is that only a relatively small proportion of a country's labour force

Table 3.2 Searching for subjects by carrying out doorstep surveys of people working at home

Examples	Techniques for identifying subjects	Type of production relations
Hope *et al.* (1976)	Systematic house-to-house survey carried out in a North London neighbourhood where homeworking was thought to be prevalent. 216 households canvassed at times when husbands were least likely to be at home. 11 interviews generated in this way.	Homeworking.
Cragg and Dawson (1981)	Door-to-door approaches using professional market researchers in areas in three English cities thought to have an above average incidence of homeworking. £8 financial incentive offered. Out of 900 contacts, seven possible interviews were gained, only one of whom was interviewed. Elsewhere 22 contacts were generated, of which 12 were interviewed.	Homeworking.
Allen and Wolkowitz (1987)	Knocked on every door within specified areas in Bradford. 4,190 households surveyed, from which 90 interviews were secured.	Home-located wage labour.
SEWU (1995)	House-to-house survey carried out in and around Cape Town and Durban in areas thought most likely to contain home-located producers. 601 households surveyed, 69 per cent of which had at least one person working at home.	Home-located production, with some disaggregation.
Felstead and Jewson (1996)	Doorstep survey calling on every other household in four contrasting areas in Britain, including 'typical' and 'untypical' areas. 15,623 doors were knocked on. £10 paid per interview. 'Snowballing' and placing adverts also used. Total of 338 in-depth interviews carried out.	Homeworking.

works at home. For example, the largest doorstep survey of which we are aware knocked on 15,623 doors in four locations in Britain (see Chapter 1, pp. 8–9), yet over half either refused to answer the door or were out. Of those who were contacted, 3.4 per cent worked at home in some capacity – in our terms, home-located workers – and a further 7.3 per cent declined to answer either way (Felstead and Jewson 1996: 21). In other words, even if one assumes that *all* the refusals were working at home, nearly 16,000 household contacts were made in order to identify at most around 800 people within the scope of the survey. Thus, doorstepping draws many 'blanks', making the costs of mounting such a survey relatively high. In order to maximise the number of positive responses, doorstep surveys often focus on cities, neighbourhoods and even particular streets thought to have an especially high incidence of the type of home-located production. This information may come from local knowledge, the presence of factories known to use such workers nearby, observations of regular loading and unloading of materials, and/or data from the census. Surveys of this type range from those which focus on just a few streets to more systematic 'house-to-house' surveys of much larger areas, such as electoral wards. Several strategies are commonly deployed to reduce suspicion on the doorstep and enhance participation. These include: financial compensation to respondents for lost earnings; an array of identity badges and information leaflets to distance the researchers from official agencies; and the use of doorstep interviewers with characteristics in common with people living in the area.

Doorstep surveys have several advantages. They can be locally focused, ensuring that a close rapport between potential interviewees and interviewers is established. They also enable the interviewer to weed out those excluded from the remit of the research at the point of contact, such as home-located producers who do not fall into the required category. However, many of their disadvantages relate to the cost of carrying out research of this type. Locating a sample is likely to be time-consuming, expensive and labour intensive even under the best of circumstances. Researchers, therefore, often have recourse to complementary techniques, such as 'snowballing' from those already interviewed (see pp. 35–37). In addition, most doorstep surveys can only hope to cover tightly bounded geographical areas. Cost has other implications. The spectre which haunts the doorstep survey is that of not finding a sample at all. As already highlighted, in order to maximise the chances of recruiting cooperative respondents, the temptation is to concentrate efforts on 'typical' areas. This runs the risk that survey findings become a self-fulfilling prophecy; that is, they reproduce hunches, assumptions and prejudices with which researchers entered the field. The few studies that have been conducted in 'untypical' areas suggest that home-located production may be more prevalent, and characteristic of different social groups, than commonly realised (Felstead and Jewson 1996). The representativeness of doorstep surveys is, therefore, in question. However, the literature does not always acknowledge this drawback and sometimes misleadingly implies that local results are typical of the national picture.

Direct appeals

Another way of generating a sample for survey research is to make direct appeals to members of the public who work at home, requesting them to come forward. The main channels that have been used to make such appeals have been popular magazines, radio and TV broadcasts and adverts in the press. Appeals to magazine readers, for example, have generally taken one of two forms. Sometimes a questionnaire is printed in an edition of the magazine itself and those who work at home are asked to complete and return it by post. Alternatively, regular subscribers are mailed a special questionnaire. Radio and TV appeals have been less prominent. Access to these media often depend on perceived 'newsworthiness'. Advertising in print media has taken several forms which have been used singly or in combination. One tactic is to place adverts for respondents in the press. Another tactic is to generate news stories for the national, local and/or specialist press, thereby generating a wave of publicity for the survey. While yet another is to put adverts in places such as supermarkets, shops, community and advice centres, health centres, doctors' surgeries and launderettes.

In comparison with doorstepping, the most obvious benefit of these approaches is that they avoid making unnecessary contacts with those outside the scope of the investigation. Appeals are also typically made to a much larger group of individuals than is possible by commissioning doorstep surveys. For example, Christensen (1988: 4) launched her appeal in *Family Circle*, a magazine read at the time by around 19 million women living in the US (see Table 3.3). Some 14,000 women responded, approximately half of whom worked exclusively at home. On a smaller scale Phizacklea and Wolkowitz (1995) gathered over 400 responses to a questionnaire included in one of the best-selling women's magazines in Britain.

Direct appeals also have disadvantages. First, the channel through which the appeal is made can have a major bearing on who responds. Magazines and newspapers have distinctive audiences, potentially skewing the sample. The same is true of radio shows and TV programmes. Second, respondents are 'self-selecting' and 'self-initiating'; that is to say, they must actively take steps to put their names forward to researchers. In these circumstances, some types of people are more likely to respond than others. The criticism of public appeals has, therefore, been that they attract the most dissatisfied rather than a broad cross-section of opinion and circumstance. However, it might be argued that respondents coming forward are likely to be drawn from *both* ends of the spectrum. Certainly, they are likely to be among the most vocal and articulate members of the audience. There may also be other mediating factors such as household relations, material circumstances, time availability and so on. Third, although it is possible to make some estimate of the extent to which the audience of the appeal is representative (for example, via analysis of readership figures), it is extremely difficult, if not impossible, to calculate how many *eligible* respondents see, hear or listen to the appeal but fail to respond. Fourth, appeals have rarely been made in ethnic minority languages, hence respondents have typically been skewed towards native language speakers

Table 3.3 Searching for subjects by launching direct appeals to people working at home

Research method and examples	Techniques for identifying subjects	Type of production relations
Appealing to magazine readers		
Christensen (1988)	Survey of Family Circle readers in the US in January 1985. 14,000 women responded, of whom 7,000 worked exclusively at home.	Home-located production.
Olson (1989)	Survey sent out to a random sample of 5,000 subscribers to two computing trade magazines in the US. Carried out in the mid-1980s. It generated 807 replies.	Home-located production.
Phizacklea and Wolkowitz (1995)	Survey of Britain's best-selling women's monthly magazine, Prima. Carried out in September 1990, generated 401 usable responses from women.	Home-located production.
Making radio appeals		
Brown (1974)	Radio appeal made on a popular British radio programme (Jimmy Young Show on Radio Two). A total of 107 letters were received, 50 manufacturing homeworkers were contacted to provide more information on their jobs.	Homeworking.
Richards (1994)	Radio appeal made on an Irish radio programme (Gay Bryne Show on RTE Radio 1). This was supplemented by an article in the Evening News. 46 letters were received as a result of the appeal, 19 of whom were sent a questionnaire.	Homeworking.
Using adverts in the press and elsewhere		
Cragg and Dawson (1981)	Placed local press advertisements in newspapers or wide distribution free sheets, along with adverts in shop windows in four English cities. This generated 96 contacts, of which 32 were interviewed.	Homeworking.
Huws (1984)	Issued Press Release in collaboration with the research sponsors – the UK's Equal Opportunities Commission. Wave of publicity generated. Feature articles in computer magazines, national and local press, and in women's magazines. 119 contacts made, 78 completed questionnaires for analysis.	Homeworking.
Bisset and Huws (1984)	Homeworkers were mostly sought through media appeals. Press releases were sent to local and national newspapers, press and television in Britain. A total of 52 interviews were completed.	Homeworking
Cummings (1986)	Followed up 'job wanted' adverts in the Sydney press, placed advertisements for interviewees in the Sydney Morning Herald and asked employment agencies for contacts. Only the first of these yielded any interviews – 21 in all.	Home-located working.
O'Donnell (1987)	Elaborate advertising strategy including translation of questionnaire into 12 different languages, widely circulating copies to a variety of different groups, taking out adverts in the ethnic and regional press, publicising the research on TV and radio, distributing the questionnaire to registered workers and organisations of freelancers across Australia. 224 completed questionnaires were returned.	Home-located working disaggregated by occupational group.

Research method and examples	Techniques for identifying subjects	Type of production relations
Probert and Wajman (1988a)	Two groups sought – programmers and word processors. Programmers sought via contact with computer user groups, advertisements in the computer section of the *Australian*, software contacts and word-of-mouth. This generated 26 interviews. Word processors were contacted by scanning the local suburban newspapers and noticeboards in shopping centres which carried adverts from those seeking work at home, advertising for interviewees in community-based centres, and word-of-mouth. 13 interviews generated.	Home-located working disaggregated by group.
Dawson and Turner (1989)	Interviews generated by a range of techniques, including approaching the clerks' union, asking employers, placing adverts in local newspapers and on university noticeboards, launching a poster campaign, writing articles for local newspapers, computer magazines and local employment guides, and appealing on radio programmes. This generated 20 interviews.	Home-located working.
Schoeffel *et al.* (1991)	Placed advertisements in most of the major daily newspapers in New Zealand, computer magazines, special interest publications and on computer bulletin boards. Generated 37 responses, from which 31 questionnaires were eventually completed.	Home-located working.
Yorkshire and Humberside Low Pay Unit (1991)	Contacted community and advice centres, health centres and doctors' surgeries, local hairdressers and other places women might go. A basic leaflet and poster were produced carrying a local phone number from where free advice could be sought. Fact Packs and newsletters were widely distributed and translated into Urdu. 56 interviews were completed.	Homeworking.
Haddon (1992)	Interviewees contacted via 'teleworking' magazines, enquiries to firms and other organisations, and via a network of personal contacts.	Home-located production.
Haddon and Silverstone (1993)	'Teleworking' households were recruited by the following: 'teleworking' support organisations; personal contacts; requests to employing organisations; and a national newspaper article based on the research. 21 households interviewed, all but one in the South East of England.	Home-located production.
Phizacklea and Wolkowitz (1995)	English language adverts for respondents placed in local daily newspaper and in wide circulation 'free' newspaper in Coventry. Advert translated into four South Asian languages and placed in a multilingual 'free' newspaper. This generated a sample of 30 white, English-speaking homeworkers, but only two Asian homeworkers.	Homeworking.
Harris (1997)	Glasgow-based project. An article publicising the study in a free newspaper, a local daily evening newspaper and the *Scotsman*, a Scottish national daily newspaper. In addition, leaflets, noticeboard pleas and 'snowball' techniques were deployed. A total of 36 questionnaires were completed, but only nine respondents reported having had any homeworking experience.	Homeworking.

(although there have been some notable exceptions in Britain and Australia). Finally, responses have to be thoroughly sifted. Appeals often generate responses from people *seeking* rather than *doing* work at home. Some misinterpret what is required and others may simply be outside the concept under investigation.

Chasing known points of contact

Chasing known points of contact typically involves an investigative methodology in which leads are followed up and a network of respondents is developed. Among the most widely used techniques are: 'snowballing'; observing and visiting home-located producers; contacting employers, campaign organisations, and workers' and other associations. The benefits include focusing on those who are likely to be eligible for inclusion in the research, establishing rapport by means of personal contact and the opportunity to obtain personal recommendations when making further introductions. Another advantage is that the researcher may gain information about relationships *between* respondents. This could be invaluable, for example, in establishing the way in which 'word-of-mouth' recruitment operates.

'Snowballing' is the most widely used technique of this type. Examples can be found *inter alia* in Britain, the US, Hong Kong, Mexico, Turkey and Iran (see Table 3.4). The technique is a relatively simple, pragmatic and cost-effective way of generating a sample. Contacts are made through a mutual acquaintance, who might be a neighbour, friend, colleague, teacher, social worker or trade-unionist. These introductions are then used to generate another round of contacts on the basis of 'a friend of a friend'. In this way a research network can multiply quickly, although typically the number of leads diminishes once a circle of friends, neighbours or relatives has been thoroughly explored.

Those who have used this technique readily acknowledge there is no guarantee that respondents are statistically representative of large populations, since there is no sampling frame from which to draw. The technique is perhaps best deployed to examine the circumstances of specific groups – such as homeworkers in the East End of London or carpet weavers in rural Turkish villages. 'Snowballing' by its very nature is likely to uncover a relatively homogeneous group of individuals simply by virtue of the fact that each newcomer is introduced into the research by one of those already included. To counter this tendency, several 'snowballs' are often set up with a view to accessing different networks of contacts as well as minimising the risk of reaching a 'dead end' too quickly. These are set off in different parts of the area under focus and/or with different acquaintances. Nevertheless, the research material produced tends to be relatively local and small scale in nature.

Another way of creating points of contact with known home-located producers is to carry out participant or non-participant observation. Participant observation typically entails taking employment as a home-located wage labourer, or setting up in business as a petty commodity producer or in some other capacity. It is hoped that contacts will be established with others undertaking similar roles. In the case

Table 3.4 Searching for subjects by chasing known points of contact with people working at home

Research method and examples	Techniques for identifying subjects	Type of production relations
'Snowballing' from established contacts		
Shah (1975)	Initial contact with homeworkers made through mutual acquaintance and interviews then conducted on the basis of 'a friend of a friend'. Five starting points dotted around the East End of London generated 56 interviews.	Homeworking.
Hope et al. (1976)	Contacts made through playgroups, neighbours and friends known to the women who carried out the research. Ten interviews in North London secured in this way.	Homeworking.
Bagihole (1986)	Focused on the clothing industry in Nottinghamshire. Procedure yielded interviews with 24 women clothing homeworkers which started with an acquaintance.	Homeworking.
Benería and Roldán (1987)	Interviews carried out in 15 neighbourhoods in Mexico City. Contacts made in each via a variety of initial contacts, including local health workers, school teachers and personal acquaintances. 140 women homeworkers were interviewed.	Homeworking.
Berik (1987)	Analysis of carpet weaving in ten villages in Turkey. Civil servants, merchants, friends and first-generation migrants helped set up village contacts and from there the 'snowball' of weaver interviews began. A total of 133 weavers were interviewed, 94 of whom worked at home.	Home-located working.
Beach (1989)	The 'snowball' began with two names suggested by a community acquaintance. Each interviewee was then asked to name two more people they knew who worked at home. From these, 15 families were identified, with a total of 57 men, women and children participating in the research. All white, rural, middle-class families living in the US.	Home-located production.
Bulos and Chaker (1993)	Interviews with six home-located workers selected by a variety of means. These included 'snowballing' from friends, family, neighbours and colleagues. Contacts were also gained from a Tenants' Association and a local trade union official.	Home-located working.
Mitter et al. (1993)	Interviews with 17 Bangladeshi clothing homeworkers carried out in the London borough of Tower Hamlets. Access facilitated by Bangladeshi youth worker on local estate and the involvement of a help agency.	Homeworking.
Lui (1994)	Interviews with 50 middle-aged women homeworkers in Hong Kong secured by 'snowballing' from four social workers known to the researcher. Interviews with 16 employers and agents yielded from contacts elicited from homeworker interviews.	Homeworking.

Research method and examples	Techniques for identifying subjects	Type of production relations
Wolkowitz (1996)	'Snowballing' from parents of a particular North London school. 32 home-located workers were interviewed.	Home-located working.
Ghavamshahidi (1996)	Informants were introduced to the researcher via male relatives in two carpet weaving areas in Iran. Contact was first made with merchants, then middlemen and then to home-located carpet weavers. From there, the 'snowball' continued to others in the neighbourhood. A total of 37 carpet weavers were interviewed.	Home-located working.
Carney and Brent (1997)	Used 'snowballing' plus advertisements in newspapers and radio (in English and Asian languages), a poster campaign and a survey of Health Visitors in the Sheffield area. All but a few of the 18 interviews were generated as a result of 'snowballing'.	Homeworking.
Generating contacts from observation		
Hsiung (1996)	Spent three months in satellite factories in Taiwan. All the factories produced wooden jewellery boxes. Researcher worked without pay for two weeks in six factories and visited about thirty others. Unspecified number of interviews with homeworkers completed as a result.	Homeworking.
Miraftab (1996)	Researcher lived and worked with a homeworking family in Guadalajara, Mexico. Gained contact with others living and working in the neighbourhood. 12 interviews with homeworkers and their families produced as a result, plus sketches and maps drawn of their living and working space.	Homeworking.
Generating contacts from employers		
Olson and Primps (1984)	Examination in the US of 14 pilot 'work-at-home' schemes and six high-technology companies where working at home was informally permitted. Interviews with participants were carried out.	Home-located wage labour.
Leidner (1988)	Analysis of four known 'work-at-home' programmes, all in the financial sector. These included two separate departments in the Continental Illinois National Bank of Chicago, the First National Bank of Chicago and Wisconsin Physicians Service Insurance Corporation.	Home-located wage labour.
Costello (1988)	Interviews with managers and clerical homeworkers presently or formerly employed by the Wisconsin Physicians Service Insurance Corporation.	Homeworking.
Gerson (1993)	Survey of secretarial, typing and word processing service providers as listed in Yellow Pages in 24 US cities. 222 agreed to cooperate. From these, 106 homeworkers and 260 office-based workers were identified. 87 per cent response rate to questionnaire. Results based on final sample of 297 women.	Homeworking.

Research method and examples	Techniques for identifying subjects	Type of production relations
Huws et al. (1990)	Research carried out in 14 'teleworking' companies. Managers and 'teleworkers' interviewed in each – 14 managers and 119 'teleworkers'.	Home-located wage labour.
Brosnan and Thornthwaite (1997)	Interviews with 14 homeworkers working for the same company. Company participated in Queensland, Australia survey of employers' use of 'non-standard' work. Company identified itself as an employer of homeworkers and amenable to a follow-up study.	Homeworking.
Huws et al. (1996)	Survey of home-located translators in Europe working for a British-based translating company. Distributed 500 questionnaires, 188 responses received.	High discretion home-located wage labour.
Rangel de Paiva Abreu and Sorj (1996)	Survey of 100 female seamstresses who worked at home in Rio de Janeiro, Brazil. Respondents identified from address lists supplied by three garment firms as well as 'snowballed' from co-workers interviewed.	Homeworking.

Using campaign contacts

Research method and examples	Techniques for identifying subjects	Type of production relations
Crine (1979)	Postal survey of readers of Home News, the Low Pay Unit's monthly newspaper for homeworkers. 46 responses received.	Homeworking.
West Yorkshire Homeworking Unit (1992)	Interviewed homeworkers with whom the organisation was currently in contact. From this, 50 interviews were produced.	Homeworking.
Huws (1994)	Survey of 175 homeworkers known to local campaigns in ten cities in England. £10 honorarium paid to interviewees.	Homeworking.
Phizacklea and Wolkowitz (1995)	It took four months for a newly appointed, Punjabi-speaking local authority officer to find 17 Asian homeworkers willing to be interviewed. All of these contacts were made by 'snowballing' within the local community.	Homeworking.

Generating contacts from workers' and other organisations

Research method and examples	Techniques for identifying subjects	Type of production relations
Ahrentzen (1990)	Sample from the National Alliance of Homebased Businesswomen, the Cottage Industry File from Dun's Marketing Services, professional organisations and corporations known to have 'teleworking' programmes. Also personal contacts. 104 home-located producers interviewed in five US cities.	Home-located production.
Granger et al. (1996)	Postal survey of members of the Society of Freelance Editors and Proof-readers in Britain. A response rate of almost 50 per cent was obtained from a single mailing – 371 completed questionnaires were returned.	High discretion home-located wage labour.

of non-participant observations, the researcher is likely to visit producers in their homes and observe them in action. Studies of this kind have been carried out in Taiwan and Mexico. The advantages of these methods include the benefits of first-hand experience and acquisition of detailed insights. This is likely to add to our understanding of such elusive issues as wage setting, management techniques, household organisation, and so on. One of the difficulties is that home-located producers tend to be geographically scattered and socially isolated from one another. Entry into employment, for example, by no means guarantees contacts with others in a similar situation. As a result, such studies tend to be relatively small scale. However, what is lost in breadth may be gained in depth.

Employers, too, can provide an avenue for identifying and surveying those working at home. Though rarely used, this offers an interesting approach. Here, the strategy is to construct the sampling frame by asking firms to supply the names and addresses. Two different tactics may be deployed. The first involves focusing on case-study employers, known to make use of home-located wage labour. Examples include studies of high technology professionals, insurance workers and bankers in the US, seamstresses in Brazil, and translators across Europe. The second entails a two-step approach. Initially, large numbers of employers are surveyed in order to discover which firms make use of home-located wage labour. Names and addresses of respondents are then drawn up with the cooperation of relevant employers (see Table 3.4).

There are several benefits of making contacts through firms and businesses. The employer's 'seal of approval' may help to allay fears of potential respondents – indeed, it is noticeable that response rates to surveys of this kind are often quite high. When focusing on a particular industrial sector, there may be an added bonus that a thorough picture of employment policies and practices is obtained. Working with employers may also permit researchers to identify comparator groups of workplace-located employees within the same firms. Against this have to be set various drawbacks. Most notable is the reliance on employer cooperation. Not only are researchers dependent on employers' willingness to *participate* in the survey, they are also reliant on them for providing a *complete* list of workers. This means that the research can be seriously skewed towards 'best practice' employers and 'best case' workers rather than producing a truly representative picture. The case-study approach has an additional disadvantage in that it often leads researchers to concentrate on industries and firms that are famous – or indeed infamous – for employing home-located wage labourers. A large scale survey of all the firms in an industrial sector or locality may spread the net wider and generate unanticipated results.

So far in this section we have discussed recruiting respondents via informal networks. Chasing known contacts may also involve establishing or developing links with formal organisations which, in one capacity or another, are involved in home-located production. Prominent among these are organisations such as local groups, national bodies, trade unions, voluntary organisations and local authority units. Many of these conduct research in their own right. In addition, in the course of their welfare and other campaigning work they come into contact with home-located producers. With appropriate permissions, this may provide social scientists with a source of respondents.

British examples of research directly conducted by such groups include a survey carried out by the Low Pay Unit, an independent body whose main objective is to document and eradicate low pay in Britain. In April 1979 a questionnaire was included in its bi-monthly newsletter for homeworkers – 46 replies were received. More recently, campaign organisations such as the National Group on Homeworking (NGH) have done much the same by administering question-naires to homeworkers with whom they are in touch. Elsewhere, local authority officers have provided researchers with a route into the lives and experiences of those who work at home.

The major advantage of chasing contacts via campaigning organisations is that respondents may place greater trust in researchers, enabling them to pursue ques-tions that might otherwise be considered threatening. However, the use of campaign contacts encounters specific drawbacks of its own. The very fact that homeworkers are in contact with a support organisation makes it more likely that they have a problem or grievance with their employer. The particularly dissatisfied or abused are more likely to be picked up as a result of such a method. Furthermore, homeworkers belonging to such organisations may have been drawn into membership via participation in other support networks, such as political, community or women's groups. More isolated or intimidated homeworkers are less likely to take part. One should, therefore, interpret research based on this technique with caution.

Other formal organisations that may provide researchers with a means of chasing known contacts include trade unions, networks of 'teleworkers', pro-fessional bodies, trade and business associations. In practice, however, these sources have been relatively rarely tapped. They hold out the promise of speed-ily providing a targeted sampling frame, rather than wasting resources on those whose work is not carried out at home. However, this has to be balanced against a number of drawbacks. First, the rules for membership of these organisations may, in fact, have more to do with employment status than place of work. Membership of freelance associations, for example, is not necessarily indicative of working at home. In certain jobs – such as freelance proof-reading – this is likely; in others it is not. Second, it is often not clear whether members of these organisations are representative. Third, the scope for surveys of this kind is limited by the absence of relevant organisations among many types of home-located producers.

One of the major benefits of chasing known points of contact is that it allows researchers to establish trust and credibility with respondents who may be reluc-tant or suspicious. Moreover, it offers the prospect of obtaining at least some empirical data. However, as with doorstepping, it runs the risk of simply con-firming what researchers already know, thus not generating new bodies of evidence.

Documentary evidence

While not the exclusive preserve of the historian, documentary evidence has been used to greatest effect by researchers from this discipline. There are several notable examples in Britain and the US (see Table 3.5). The use of historical documents illuminates contemporary developments and gives a voice to women and men who were once engaged in home-located production. Historical research thereby gives a new dimension to the search for subjects. However, the difficulties encountered are considerable. In the first place, surviving records kept by merchants and man-ufacturers are relatively rare since many businesses were small and ephemeral and, in any case, most ceased trading a long time ago. Even if documentation once existed, only a small proportion is likely to survive today. The historical records of the experiences and attitudes of homeworkers themselves are rarer still. For these insights, one frequently has to rely on 'second-hand' information gleaned from autobiographies, a few private letters, official enquiries, newspaper articles, legal cases and interviews with surviving relatives. Moreover, many of the surviving doc-uments comprise comments on home-located production by those not directly involved in the work – such as philanthropists, clerics, government officials and novelists. Much of this material provides qualitative rather than quantitative data.

Our focus in this book is primarily on contemporary patterns of home-located production. We do not intend, therefore, to dwell further on the complex series of historical debates which go beyond our remit. However, we could not fail to notice the paucity of *contemporary* research that utilises documentary sources. This is particularly surprising given the volume of, and the detail contained within, present-day written materials.

Campaigning organisations, referred to above, have amassed large quantities of documents of various kinds. Writers such as Rowbotham (1993) and Tate (1994a, 1994b) provide an indication of the value of such sources. Local organisations – such as the Leicester Outwork Campaign and the West Yorkshire Homeworking Unit – have extensive case notes relating to their advice, welfare and support func-tions. Many also issue periodic newsletters, magazines and information packs. These provide a ready source of detailed information about the lived experience and working conditions of homeworkers. In addition, these organisations also have generated extensive volumes of minutes, agendas, reports, memos and letters that provide fascinating insights themselves. There are also national and interna-tional organisations which lobby on behalf of homeworkers. They, too, represent a mine of documentary information.

Court cases – such as industrial tribunals – provide especially interesting informa-tion and insights. Legal discourse involves collecting and presenting 'the facts of the case', hence revealing to researchers a great deal about the background of individ-ual subjects. Moreover, the process of legal argument and advocacy revolves around the construction of interpretations and meanings attached to evidence. These cases provide an extremely fruitful avenue of research – but one which has largely been ignored. Much more attention has been paid to government documents. The

Table 3.5 **Searching for subjects by analysing documentary evidence**

Examples	Techniques for identifying subjects	Type of production relations
Bythell (1978)	Examination of the role and extent of 'outwork' in several nineteenth-century industries in Britain, including textiles, clothing, and boot and shoe. Relies on information provided by magistrates, Poor Law officials, Parliamentary enquiries, journalists and autobiographies.	Homeworking.
Pennington and Westover (1989)	Disparate sources of information from contemporary novels, oral evidence from daughters and granddaughters of homeworkers, local newspapers, national and local enquiries, and trade union records. Focuses on homeworking in Britain since the beginning of the Industrial Revolution.	Homeworking.
Boris (1994)	Library search of numerous sources, including official records, legal case law, workers' associations, women's organisations, private collections and consumer groups with the aim of tracing the history of homeworking in the US.	Homeworking.

procedures of government sometimes prompt enquiries into home-located pro-duction which result in the collection and publication of views, opinions, depositions, minutes, evidence and reports. Examples include the work of the Employment Committee of the British House of Commons and, in the US, the Department of Labor.

Documentary sources are not only produced by formal organisations and insti-tutions. The testimony of home-located producers themselves is of special interest. However, many of those who work at home are among the most deprived and hard pressed members of the labour market. These groups are not likely to pro-duce extensive written accounts of their daily lives. Nevertheless, diaries, autobiographies and letters are not entirely absent. Moreover, researchers may themselves ask homeworkers, and others, to keep a documentary record of their daily activities reflecting on their working experiences and household relationships.

It should be remembered that documentary sources do not have to take the form of text. Photographs and other images can be very illuminating. Home-located producers themselves may play an active role in producing such images. In the last few years, a whole new realm of documentary evidence has opened up. The Internet provides quick and easy access to many different types of text as well as channels of communication with subjects. The latter, however, are currently heavily skewed towards certain occupational groups who are 'wired up'. Contacts with subjects via the Internet have the merit of potentially becoming *continuous* and *interactive* – transcending the rigidities of the more one-way forms of com-munication often entailed in, for example, postal surveys.

It is unlikely that busy people will take time to cooperate with such ventures unless they feel a sense of involvement and commitment to the research. This, in turn, may depend on establishing a close *collaborative* working relationship between subjects and researchers, based on mutual trust and respect. Such a relationship may raise fundamental questions about research design and authorship. Moreover, it may bring respondents together, for example, in writing groups or Internet bulletin boards. This may influence their perceptions of and attitudes towards home-located production itself.

Surveys of employers

Research on employers – the demand-side of home-located production – is relatively rare. Indeed, this is largely reflected in the balance of this book. Nevertheless, the study of employers is vital. Chapter 2 makes it plain that the social relations of production are the starting point for any thorough analysis. This necessarily entails examination of both parties and their interaction.

Various channels have been explored to make contact with employers. These include regulatory bodies, official surveys, telephone polls, postal questionnaires, subcontracting chains and key informants (see Table 3.6). Ironically, most of the data collected in this fashion has not focused on employers themselves but has, instead, sought to gather information about the numbers of homeworkers they employ. Far less research has been conducted on strategies used by management to regulate and control a remote workforce. However, this managerial relationship has long been recognised as problematic. Indeed, Marglin (1974) suggests that in the late nineteenth century a major incentive behind the development of the factory system and the decline of outwork was the desire to secure greater control over labour.

A problem encountered in employer surveys concerns interpretation of the data gathered. As discussed in Chapter 2, there is considerable confusion about the definition of homeworking. Terms such as 'freelancing', 'agency working' and 'outworking' are used in surveys of this type without making adequate distinctions (e.g., Callus *et al.* 1991: 33–34). There is, therefore, no way of telling how questionnaires are completed. A further complication is that some firms use agents or subcontractors who employ homeworkers. This may or may not be reflected in survey returns. The issue of subcontracting thus raises a fundamental issue: that is, who is the boss? (cf. Felstead 1993). The elaboration of subcontracting chains frequently links multinational companies and high street retailers with small back street sweatshops in the developed and undeveloped world. These often entail intermediaries and other agents. It has to be recognised that the relationship between homeworker and employer is multi-layered and multi-faceted. Tracing subcontracting chains is therefore a matter of the greatest theoretical and empirical interest, but has so far received scant attention (Tate 1996a; Mitter 1986a).

Table 3.6 Searching for subjects by conducting surveys of employers

Research method and examples	Techniques for identifying subjects	Type of production relations
Carrying out surveys via regulatory bodies		
CIR (1973)	Survey of plants in the Pin, Hook and Eye and Snap Fastener Wages Council sector in Britain. Eight of the nine eligible plants employed a total of 760 homeworkers between them; most by one plant. 30 homeworkers were interviewed.	Homeworking.
ACAS (1978a)	Survey of plants in the Button Manufacturing Wages Council sector in Britain. 79 plants surveyed. About 380 homeworkers were employed by the industry at the time of the survey. Most employed by just six plants, the rest being fairly evenly distributed over a further 27 plants. 46 firms claimed not to use homeworkers at all. Employers provided lists of homeworkers, 57 (i.e., 15 per cent) of whom were interviewed.	Homeworking.
ACAS (1978b)	Survey of plants in the Toy Manufacturing Wages Council sector in Britain. Postal survey to 421 plants. Of the 153 respondents, 87 (53 per cent) indicated that they used homeworkers, 68 of whom reported that they did so regularly. During the survey week, a total of 2,679 were being used. 151 interviews with homeworkers from 17 firms were carried out, supplemented by a further 27 interviewees identified from local authority lists.	Homeworking.
Carrying out surveys via official surveys		
Hakim (1985)	'Piggybacks' on the 1980 Workplace Industrial Relations Survey (WIRS). This consisted of interviews conducted in a broadly representative sample of 2,040 establishments employing more than 24 employees in Britain. 160 employers made some use of 'outworkers'.	Homeworking.
Carrying out telephone surveys		
Huws (1993)	Telephone survey of 1,003 employers in Britain carried out by professional market research company. 113 were employing some people who spent at least half of their working time based at home.	Home-located wage labour.
Carrying out postal surveys		
Lui (1994)	Survey of the employment practices of industrial establishments in the Tsuen Wan district of Hong Kong. 29 employers identified as using 'outworkers'.	Homeworking.

Research method and examples	Techniques for identifying subjects	Type of production relations
G. Anderson et al. (1994)	New Zealand survey of over 2,000 workplaces eliciting 638 usable responses. Several questions on arrangements for working at home were asked among many others on employment practices.	Home-located wage labour.
Standen (1997)	Survey of 202 of the largest organisations in Western Australia, each with more than 200 employees. Four-page postal survey mailed to Human Resource Manager in each organisation which specifically focused on working at home. 97 replies received.	Home-located wage labour.
Tracing subcontracting chains		
Tate (1996a)	Through the European Homeworking Group (set up in 1994), at least five homeworkers in four European countries (Greece, Italy, Portugal and the UK) were interviewed using a common questionnaire along with another five key informants. From this, those involved in the subcontracting chains were identified. In Greece, Italy and mainland Portugal this focused on the leather footwear industry, in Madeira the focus was on embroidery, and in the UK various sectors were examined but the main focus was on the clothing industry.	Homeworking.
Using key informants		
Hendry (1994)	Uses key informants in local government and industry to build up a sample frame. Firms then contacted by telephone to request interviews. 24 interviews with clothing manufacturers and subcontractors in Britain.	Homeworking.

Conclusion

This chapter has been about searching for subjects. We have reviewed and evaluated a range of diverse techniques, with examples drawn from around the world. These include: using official sources of data; carrying out doorstep surveys; launching direct appeals, chasing known points of contact; analysing documentary evidence; and conducting surveys of employers. Details of research studies incorporating these approaches have been provided in Tables 3.1 through to Table 3.6. More general themes and issues have been discussed in the text. We have seen that identifying a cooperative group of respondents is a difficult practical problem faced by all researchers in this field. Different approaches focus on different subjects. Hence, ways of searching for subjects should be tailored to the specific questions under examination. No single strategy is likely to be able to provide all the answers. For example, national estimates of home-located production are readily available from official data sources such as population censuses and labour force surveys, but provide little insight into the experience and meaning of working at home. Other ways of identifying subjects, such as direct appeals, shed little light on the numbers involved but may give a better indication of the working conditions endured. Furthermore, evidence drawn from one approach may serve to confirm or modify the results of another. Some of the most successful pieces of research have been based on a combination of different techniques each revealing a part of the overall picture (e.g., Phizacklea and Wolkowitz 1995; Haddon and Silverstone 1993). However, we should bear in mind that triangulation – the cross-referencing of contrasting methods – may compound rather than eliminate important sources of bias. As we have noted in our review, a number of quite different ways of searching for subjects suffer from a common problem. For example, both doorstepping and chasing known points of contact can confirm the assumptions and prejudices with which the researcher began. It may be of relevance here to note that some categories of home-located producers are studied more frequently than others. Thus, although a reading of official data sets suggests that in Britain there are at least as many home-located petty commodity producers as homeworkers, there are far more studies of the latter than the former.

Searching for subjects is a perpetual challenge. It is very difficult to corroborate the validity and reliability of the detection process; i.e., to establish just how much of the homeworking workforce remains hidden from view. It is, therefore, essential that researchers are frank and open about the approaches they have adopted so that at least the provenance of their findings are clear to all.

Chapter 4

Taking a count

> How many people do homework, what kind of work they do and whether it is increasing are the first questions people ask about homeworking . . . Comparatively little is known about these aspects of homeworking in quantitative terms, and this makes it all the more necessary to examine how existing estimates of the extent of homeworking have been calculated.
>
> (Allen and Wolkowitz 1987: 30)

Introduction

The objective of this chapter is deceptively simple – to count numbers of both home-located producers and homeworkers. It will provide details of national estimates from countries around the world. While not claiming to be globally comprehensive, this is – as far as we are aware – the first time such an undertaking has been attempted in depth (ILO 1994: 6–8).

A major outcome of such an undertaking is the discovery of a wide range of contrasting, and apparently conflicting, estimates *within* most countries for which data are available. This inevitably begs the question: which count is correct? Rather than seeking a figure for the true extent of the phenomenon, this chapter argues that the range of estimates serves to shed light on different types of home-located production (as outlined in Chapter 2). A second objective of this chapter, therefore, is to plot differing national estimates against our theoretical framework. Regrettably, such an exercise quickly reveals the wide variation in definitions and terminology used within and between societies and by different groups of researchers. There is no agreed nomenclature or conceptualisation. Hence, counts often diverge for technical and theoretical reasons, which must be made explicit when comparing figures. The variety of estimates available reflects the contrasting conceptual and methodological approaches adopted by researchers.

This review concentrates on estimates from three great regions of the world: North America, Australasia and Europe. These are societies that provide us with the most reliable and detailed counts of people working at home. However, it is, of course, the case that home-located production of various kinds flourishes in developing societies (Mitter 1986a; Boris and Prügl 1996). Little is known about home-located production in Africa, for example, although it is known to be extensive in Egypt, Kenya, Morocco and Tunisia (Direction des Statistiques Sociales 1991). Although the anecdotal and observational evidence is extensive, these countries typically do not produce reliable labour market statistics on which researchers can draw. In addition, there are major theoretical and conceptual difficulties in measuring the extent of home-located production in the Third World. As we have defined it, home-located production comprises a unique conjunction of the social relations of capitalist production and those of the household. In short, home-located production cannot come into being prior to the emergence of the separation of home and work. It is fundamentally different from what is commonly referred to as the system of 'household production' which preceded it in many European and other societies (Bythell 1978; Thompson 1967; Berg 1987). In many contemporary Third World societies forms of production analogous to these earlier pre-capitalist modes are still much in evidence. In these societies there is, therefore, a considerable difficulty in identifying those households which are engaged in home-located production itself. These dilemmas are too complex and numerous for us to attempt to resolve here. Instead we have confined ourselves to an examination of the counts for a number of Third World countries, commenting on the theoretical and technical issues they raise.

National estimates of home-located production are derived from two main sources: official estimates based on government collected statistics and non-government sources. For many labour market issues, official data sets are the first port of call for researchers, policy-makers and interested parties. While home-located production is no exception to this rule, the absence of questions on place of work often limits the number of relevant sources. Indeed, according to the International Labour Organisation (ILO) (1994: 6) 'very few' countries have the *technical* capacity to measure the extent of working at home within their national boundaries. Moreover, it is our contention that fewer still have the capacity to disaggregate home-located production into its constituent parts. We attempt to reveal both technical and theoretical differences between existing official estimates. Non-government sources range from grass-roots 'guestimates' by interested bodies through to academic social science work. Many of these are more specific in focus and, in some cases, have a more refined theoretical basis. They are, however, usually based on smaller samples, and often relate to specific industries.

United States

The US is relatively well served with official data sets, although resulting estimates of the numbers of people currently working at home vary widely (see Table 4.1). At one extreme, analyses based on the 1980 Census of Population suggest that only 1.3 million people, or 1.6 per cent of the non-farm labour force, regarded home as their main place of work. This compares with 3.6 per cent in 1960 and 2 per cent in 1970 (Kraut and Grambsch 1987: 412; Kraut 1988). At the other extreme, a set of supplementary questions added to the May 1985 monthly Current Population Survey (CPS) of 60,000 households suggested that as many as 17.3 million people did some work at home. Of these, 8.4 million worked for at least eight hours per week and almost 1.9 million worked entirely at home (Horvath 1986). A set of differently worded questions, added to the CPS six years later, yielded a total figure of almost 20 million or 18.3 per cent of those at work (Deming 1994). Other estimates fall somewhere in between (e.g., Silver 1989).

These variations can be explained in several ways. First, they are the result of differences in criteria for inclusion in the count, especially those based on numbers of hours worked at home per week. This cut-off point varies significantly within and between data sets. Higher estimates reflect lower thresholds (Horvath 1986; Silver 1989).

A second source of variation concerns whether 'working at home' is taken to include work done *at* home, *from* home or *in the same grounds and buildings as one's home*. For example, the US Census and the CPS appear – as far as can be discerned from published sources (see Table 4.1) – to adopt quite different criteria. The CPS seems to focus on a narrow definition comprising only those who work at home. In contrast, Census-based estimates are derived from travel-to-work questions (see Chapter 2, pp. 20) and hence are likely to include all those who work at, from or in the same grounds and buildings as home. To add to the confusion, estimates based on the *same* data source can sometimes vary in the way they analyse spatial issues. For example, Kraut and Grambsch (1987) estimate that in 1980 there were 1.3 million people working at home in the US, while Silver (1989: 110) gives a figure almost three-quarters as much again (2.2 million, or 2.3 per cent of those employed). Both are based on the 1980 Census. The former attempts to exclude those working in the same grounds and buildings as their own home by removing the farm labour force from the count whereas the latter makes no such attempt. The more recent figure of 3.4 million (or 3 per cent of the employed) who were recorded as working at home by the 1990 Census also includes farm labour (US Department of Commerce 1998b: 1).

A third source of variation in official US estimates concerns whether *unpaid* work is included. The unpaid bookkeeper in a family business conducted from home would be classified as working at home in some surveys and not in others. The Census and 1991 CPS estimates apply only to respondents who were in paid work in the data collection period. However, the 1985 CPS estimates included respondents who took some work home from the office for which they were not specifically paid.

Variation in the US official estimates can, therefore, be explained less by differences in the theoretical concepts deployed than by the narrowness or width of the technical focus. So, for example, estimates based on whether *any* work is done at home widens the focus, while those based on whether work is done *mainly* at home narrows it. US estimates make little attempt to exclude particular groups on account of their position within the social relations of production. In general, they capture home-located production – the broadest concept in our schema. The only

Table 4.1 Taking a count in North America

Estimator	Counts	Data source
United States		
Horvath (1986)	More than 17 million people regularly did some of their scheduled work at home. Almost half worked at home for less than eight hours a week, nearly 8.4 million worked at home for eight hours or more in the reference week, and almost 1.9 million worked entirely at home.	Current Population Survey, May 1985 (supplementary survey)
Kraut and Grambsch (1987)	In 1960, 3.6 per cent of the non-farm labour force 'worked at home as their principal place of work in the reference week' (p. 411). In 1970 the figure was 2 per cent and in 1980 it was 1.6 per cent (or 1.3 million).	Census of Population, 1960, 1970 and 1980
Silver (1989)	Data from the 1960, 1970 and 1980 Censuses indicate that working at home fell, both absolutely and relatively, over the two decades – from 4.7 million (7.2 per cent) in 1960 to 2.2 million (2.3 per cent) in 1980.	Census of Population, 1960, 1970 and 1980
Deming (1994)	Almost 20 million non-farm persons were engaged in some work (paid or unpaid) at home as part of their primary job, representing 18.3 per cent of those at work. However, only 37.2 per cent of these were paid specifically for the work done at home.	Current Population Survey, May 1991 (supplementary survey)
US Department of Commerce (1998a)	The 1990 figures reveal a dramatic increase in the number of people who worked at home, up 56 per cent from 1980, to 3.4 million people (or 3.4 per cent of the employed population).	Census of Population, 1990

Estimator	Counts	Data source
Canada		
Akyeampong and Siroonian (1993)	About 6 per cent of the Canadian workforce 'performed some or all of their regularly scheduled hours of work at home' (p. 9). For the majority it was a requirement of the job.	Labour Force Survey, November 1991 (supplementary Survey on Work Arrangements)
Nadwodny (1996)	Around 1.1 million Canadians worked at home in 1991. The proportion of people working at home in non-agricultural paid occupations doubled over the previous decade, rising to 6 per cent in 1991 from 3 per cent in 1981.	Census of Population, 1991
Akyeampong (1997)	Around 1 million Canadian employees regularly did 'some or all of their paid hours of work at home' (p. 48).	Labour Force Survey, November 1995 (supplementary Survey on Work Arrangements)
Statistics Canada (1998)	Excluding those who worked on a farm, a total of 819,000 people, or 6 per cent of the employed labour force, usually worked at home in 1996. However, comparability of these data with previous Censuses has been compromised by the inclusion of an additional response category; 'No fixed workplace address', in the 1996 Census. This more rigorously excludes those who work from home in the published count.	Census of Population, 1996

notable exclusion is that of the farming community, many of whom would, in any case, be excluded from the theoretical typology outlined in Chapter 2 because they work in nearby fields and buildings rather than at home.

A further issue likely to affect the size of any estimate concerns whether or not all work activity is included. Failure to collect data on people who 'moonlight' at home in a second job, or who occasionally work at home, can potentially be significant. One estimate is that the numbers of Americans who were 'moonlighting' grew from 4 million in 1970 to 5.7 million in 1985 and multiple jobholding among women grew especially rapidly (Stinson 1986).

Canada

In contrast to the US, Canada has only recently begun to collect official data on people working at home (see Table 4.1). In 1991 the Canadian government carried out a survey of the weekly, daily and hourly routines of the workforce. This covered the incidence of shift work, flexitime, on-call work, 'moonlighting' and, of particular interest for current purposes, working at home. The Survey of Work Arrangements (SWA), as it was known, gathered data on each of these issues. It was carried out as a supplement to the November 1991 Labour Force Survey (LFS). However, only paid workers (those working for a wage or a salary) were interviewed. The self-employed were excluded on the highly debatable grounds that 'they have wider control over their work schedules than do paid workers' (Akyeampong and Siroonian 1993: 8). The exclusion of the self-employed has the effect of underplaying the prevalence of some types of work arrangement, such as 'moonlighting' and home-located production. On the other hand, workers who performed any of their regularly scheduled hours of work at home were included in the count. This inclusiveness is in line with the CPS approach adopted south of the border. On this basis, 5.8 per cent of Canadian workers in 1991 were recorded as working at home (Siroonian 1993: 50). This figure is corroborated by analysis of the 1991 Census which suggests that 6.2 per cent of the employed labour force (excluding agriculture) worked at home. Comparison with the 1981 Census suggests that numbers had doubled over ten years (Nadwodny 1996: 17). More recent data suggests that this trend has continued well into the 1990s, with the proportion working at home rising by half as much again between 1991 and 1995 (Akyeampong 1997: 48). Although the results of the 1996 Census have recently become available (Statistics Canada 1998), the published counts are not comparable with previous Census counts since they make a more determined effort to exclude those working from home.

The growth of homeworking in Canada is associated with broader processes of restructuring, such as the fragmentation of production and the substitution of homeworkers for factory-located employees. In the Canadian clothing industry, for example, the number of officially recorded workers has fallen by half over the 1987–1992 period. The clothing union – the Union of Needletrades, Industrial and Textile Employees (UNITE) – estimates that 77 per cent of current production in

Ontario is being carried out in workplaces with fewer than 20 workers, and that there are at least 2,000–3,000 homeworkers in Toronto alone (quoted in Tate 1994a: 75).

In some respects Canadian estimates are based on narrower criteria than those of the US, in others they adopt a wider focus. By including individuals who do some or all of their work at home, they are relatively broad in scope. However, by excluding the self-employed, the SWA count is more restricted than most US estimates. In our terms (see Chapter 2, pp. 16) the effect of this exclusion is that many home-located employers and home-located petty commodity producers are likely to be under-counted. Moreover, many homeworkers – as we have defined them – are legally categorised as self-employed or perceive themselves to be so (Felstead and Jewson 1996). For these reasons, the Canadian SWA figures may underestimate the extent of home-located waged labour.

Australia

As in Canada, the shift from factory production to homeworking is regarded as a significant development in Australia. Union estimates are that homeworkers in clothing, for example, outnumber factory workers by about fourteen to one. This gives a national figure of 329,000 homeworkers in the clothing industry, with 144,000 in Victoria and 120,000 in New South Wales alone (Textile, Clothing and Footwear Union of Australia 1995: 5). Official estimates of the extent of people working at home in Australia stem from two sources – the Census and a special supplement to the monthly Labour Force Survey (LFS) of households (see Table 4.2). These estimates are available on a regular basis – every five years in the case of the Census and every three in the case of the LFS. Yet despite their presumed reliability, they come up with widely differing estimates. For example, the 1981 Census suggests that 5.6 per cent of employed males and 9.5 per cent of employed females worked at home, whereas the 1989 LFS equivalent figures are 1.8 per cent and 6 per cent respectively (Walker 1987; McLennan 1989).

The differences between the Census estimates and those based on the LFS may be attributable to the relative inclusiveness of the two measures. However, the pattern is not a simple one. With respect to work location the Census probably has a wider rubric than the LFS but with respect to eligible employment the LFS adopts a broader remit. Census estimates rely on answers to questions about the daily journey to work and are hence likely to include in the count many farmers who work in fields and buildings adjacent to their homes. Counts based on the LFS explicitly exclude the farming community. This difference is highly significant since almost half of those working at home according to the Census are in agriculture. Indeed, by removing them from the count, the LFS and Census estimates become broadly comparable.

However, in other respects LFS estimates are more inclusive. The LFS collects information on respondents' second jobs, whereas the Census limits itself to main jobs only. Moreover, the LFS estimates include people who work some of the time

Table 4.2 **Taking a count in Australasia**

Estimator	Counts	Data source
Australia		
Walker (1987)	Overall, 451,000 people worked at home on the day of the Census (7.2 per cent of the employed population).	Census of Population, 1981
McLennan (1989)	Over 1.75 million workers (22.8 per cent) worked some hours at home, of these 266,600 (3.5 per cent) worked more hours at home than they did elsewhere.	Labour Force Survey, April 1989 (triennial supplement)
Madden (1992)	Over 2 million workers (26.4 per cent) worked some hours at home, of these 307,900 (4 per cent) worked more hours at home than they did elsewhere.	Labour Force Survey, March 1992 (triennial supplement)
McLennan (1996)	About 2.1 million workers (25.8 per cent) worked some hours at home, of these some 343,300 (4.1 per cent) worked more hours at home than they did elsewhere.	Labour Force Survey, September 1995 (triennial supplement)
New Zealand		
Loveridge et al. (1996)	In 1986, 47,682 people – accounting for 3.8 per cent of the total workforce – worked at home. By 1991 their absolute numbers had fallen to 45,948 but they held their own as a percentage of the workforce.	Census of Population, 1986 and 1991

at home as part or as an extension of their job. This would include, for example, teachers who prepare lessons at home. Nevertheless, in practice, there is a strong tendency for analyses and estimates derived from the Census and LFS to focus on those who 'usually' or 'mainly' work at home rather than those who do so on a partial basis.

New Zealand

While Australia has two official data sets from which to draw, New Zealand has just one – the Census of Population carried out every five years which incorporates a question on travel to work (see Table 4.2). Many of the difficulties of using the Census as a source of information are readily acknowledged by those who rely on it (Loveridge *et al.* 1996). These include problems we have already come across elsewhere, such as differentiating between those who work *at*, *from* and *nearby* home. This is of particular relevance to the treatment of the agricultural labour force. In terms of our theoretical perspective, a further difficulty with the New Zealand Census is that the data only provide a very general picture. The way information is recorded makes it difficult to focus on the various types of home-located producers we identify, such as home-located wage labourers and home-located petty commodity producers.

Loveridge *et al.* (1996: 19) suggest that in New Zealand between 1986 and 1991 home-located production, as we have defined it, changed in both expected and unexpected ways. Against a background of a rapid increase in unemployment and part-time work during the second half of the 1980s, it was predicted that it would increase. However, while home-located production excluding agriculture rose from 3.1 per cent in 1976 to 3.8 per cent in 1986, no further increase was recorded in the 1991 Census. Indeed, the absolute numbers actually fell from 47,682 in 1986 to 45,948 five years later. It was only because the non-farm workforce shrunk by 7 per cent that the proportion remained stable. This is in contrast to the Australian situation, where available figures from the LFS suggest steady growth in recent years from 3.5 per cent in 1989 to 4.1 per cent in 1995 (McLennan 1996).

Looked at from our typology, it is clear that the Australian and New Zealand estimates measure the extent of home-located production in its entirety. Virtually no attempt is made to break down this category into its constituent parts, apart from the exclusion of farmers from some of the estimates. The resulting estimates, therefore, vary according to the technical scope of the counts rather than their conceptual focus.

European Union

The compilation of comparable statistics on labour market issues at the level of the European Union (EU) has been a priority since the Community was first established. Although labour market statistics existed in all member states, the sources used, the definitions adopted, the methods of data collection deployed and so on, differed to such a degree that comparison at the Community level was virtually impossible. In order to combat these problems the Statistical Office of the European Communities (Eurostat) has regularly organised the European Community Labour Force Survey (EC LFS).

The first EC LFS was carried out among the six original member states of the Community in 1960. From 1968 to 1971 it was carried out annually and from 1973 to 1981 it became biannual, although the basic features remained unaltered. The survey moved back onto an annual basis in 1983, where it has remained until today. However, the period 1983–1991 saw the introduction of a revised set of concepts aimed at improving comparability between member states and, as far as possible, with other countries. The survey was once again updated in 1992. This decision was influenced by a number of developments in the labour market thought to affect the information requirements of the 1990s. Among these was the recognition that structures of employment were altering to such an extent that certain patterns of work previously regarded as 'unusual' were becoming commonplace. The EC LFS was, therefore, revised with effect from 1992 to collect data on persons 'working at home' for the first time (Eurostat 1992: 7, 54). This means that – in contrast to other piecemeal attempts to measure the extent of home-located production in Europe (e.g.,

Table 4.3 **Taking a count in Europe**

Country	Percentage of employed workforce aged 15 or more working at or from home*				
	1992	*1993*	*1994*	*1995*	*1996*
Euro12	4.9	4.2	4.6	4.6†	4.6†
Belgium	11.6	11.3	11.1	10.8	10.1
Denmark	11.0	10.3	11.8	11.0	11.0
France	0.8	2.6	5.5	5.4	5.0
Germany	5.2	5.1	5.1	4.1	5.0
Greece	1.7	2.3	1.8	1.6	1.4
Ireland	20.6	19.5	18.6	18.2	7.1
Italy	5.5	5.1	4.5	4.6	4.6
Luxembourg	5.5	6.9	6.3	6.9	6.1
Netherlands	5.6	6.4	6.8	6.8	6.8
Portugal	4.4	3.9	4.0	3.7	3.5
Spain	0.8	0.7	0.6	0.6	0.6
United Kingdom	7.6	2.7	2.7	2.6	2.6

Source: Eurostat (1993: 136–137; 1994: 136–137; 1995: 146–147; 1996: 146–147; 1997: 146–147).
Notes
* These figures refer to persons who spend half or more of their working hours at or from home.
† This figure refers to the Euro15.

Meulders *et al.* 1994: chapter 6) – we now have, in theory at least, a common EU-wide data set from which to draw.

The published data reveal some interesting patterns over time within member states as well as contrasts between them. The count of those working at home in the EU as a whole has remained remarkably stable at around 5 per cent of the working population, but this figure masks many contrasts between countries. In 1995, for example, the incidence ranged from a mere 0.6 per cent in Spain to 18.2 per cent in Ireland (see Table 4.3). Furthermore, some member states appear to be experiencing dramatic upsurges, while others are experiencing marked declines. In France, for example, working at home tripled between 1992 and 1993, and then doubled again the following year. Thus, according to these figures, in just two years the number of French men and women working at home rose sevenfold. Elsewhere, the data tell a different story. In Ireland, the proportion of the workforce working at home fell by well over half between 1995 and 1996, while in the UK it fell by two-thirds during the period 1992–1993. Such dramatic swings within a 12-month period strongly suggest that there are major problems associated with collection and compilation of these counts. Moreover, as we shall show below, the UK official data sets do not confirm these surprising results.

It is the stated intention of the EC LFS to provide a 'harmonized and synchronized' labour force survey of households of persons living in each member state. With this in mind, Eurostat adopts a clear and precise definition, to be applied across the Community, of who is to be counted as 'working at home' and who is not. However, there are a number of technical aspects of the operational-isation of this concept that distinguish it from other counts we have encountered elsewhere. It includes both the self-employed and employed. However, if the place of work comprises a separate unit (for example, a doctor's surgery or a public house) adjacent to the person's home but with a separate entrance, then work is *not* considered to be done 'at home'. The same goes for farmers when working in fields or buildings adjacent to their homes. Employees are only included in the count if they have a formal employment contract which includes the monitoring of work completed by timesheets, additional payments for heating and lighting incurred while working at home, and the provision of any tools and equipment required. Also qualifying for inclusion are travelling sales representatives who work *from* home but who do most of their work at other locations. However, unlike US estimates based on the CPS, the EU figure does not include those who take work home because of personal interest or pressure of time. Eurostat respondents are asked to estimate the time spent working at home. Counts distinguish two categories: those who 'usually' work at home (i.e., half or more of the days worked during the four weeks prior to interview) and 'sometimes' work at home (i.e., on at least one occasion during the four weeks prior to interview) (Eurostat 1992: 47).

It might be thought that, although the Eurostat conceptualisation appears idiosyncratic, at least it is precise and provides a basis for international comparison. However, in spite of their apparent precision, closer inspection of aspects of the technical construction of the data casts doubt on their reliability. First, the published tables refer erroneously to persons who 'usually work *from* home' (our emphasis), whereas in actual fact it is designed to capture those who work *at* and *from* home. This may, in part, explain a second anomaly. As hinted at earlier, the EC LFS suggests that working at or from home declined precipitously in the UK. However, this may be more to do with misclassification than anything else. It would appear that respondents working from home in 1992 were – correctly according to EC LFS protocols – entered as 'usually working from home' in the published tables but were *not* included in the years which followed. While we are not in a position to probe into the reliability of the EC LFS estimates for other countries in the same way, the UK example should serve to caution against pre-suming that Eurostat has achieved its goal of comparability, at least as far as the working at home data are concerned.

The EC LFS has been extended to include the new member states of Finland, Sweden and Austria. However, all but the most recent data from this source refer to the 12 member states only. As a result, the series for these new member states is short. At the time of writing, the 1996 figures were 8.6 per cent in Finland, 11.2 per cent in Austria and 6.6 per cent in Sweden. The Finnish data are particularly interesting since they suggest a tripling of the numbers who identified their workplace as their home in the decade since the 1985 Census (Salmi 1996: 148). However, the comparability of these figures is questionable. Very little information is provided about the provenance of the Census figure. For example, we are not told how people identify their workplace as their home, details of their work location, and other criteria utilised in determining their inclusion in the count.

The history of Eurostat, therefore, is one of increasing clarity in the definition of terms and an attempted harmonisation of measures across the continent. However, it appears likely that serious difficulties remain with regard to putting these principles into practice.

Britain

In contrast to many countries, with the exception of the US and possibly Australia, Britain stands out as far as official data are concerned. While labour market researchers elsewhere in the world are limited to a few, often dated, official sources, British researchers now have recent, national and up-to-date data sets at their disposal. These paint an increasingly complex and rich picture (see Table 4.4).

After an absence of 50 years, a Census question enabling the identification of those who work at home was reintroduced in 1971. A count of 1.5 million people, or 6 per cent of the labour force, was obtained (Hakim 1980: 1105). In our terms this figure corresponds to home-located producers. Some researchers expressed dissatisfaction (e.g., Pugh 1984) with this count on the grounds that it was based on a broad definition, including many groups that have little in common. Pugh therefore argued that some form of disaggregation was urgently required. She based her estimates on a narrower definition, originally developed in the Homeworkers (Protection) Bill 1978, which attempted to give home-workers – as we would define them – the same employment rights as other workers. Her aim was to provide a 'realistic' picture of homeworking in Britain, to set against the 'inaccurate figures' and 'misleading information' which result from the adoption of a broad definition (ibid.: 1). To achieve this aim, Pugh used the Longitudinal Study (LS) which is based on a sample of all individuals born on four dates in 1971, comprising approximately 1 per cent of the population of England and Wales. This data set allows greater manipulation than is possible using the Census counts alone.

Pugh (1984) identified a broad figure – equivalent to our home-located producers – of 819,020 people working at home, 4.0 per cent of those employed in England and Wales. By making a number of fine-grain distinctions, she broke down this category into a series of smaller groups. She eventually arrived at a figure of 87,400, or 0.5 per cent of the employed workforce, engaged in what we (and she) describe as homework. Sadly, Pugh does not appear to have continued with this pioneering and most promising line of investigation. Nor, as far as we are aware, have other researchers. Instead, in the 1980s a different research agenda emerged.

The British government initiated a programme of research in Autumn 1979 with the aim of providing more information on the extent, characteristics and experiences of people working at home. This culminated in a specially designed national survey of what were called 'home-based workers' carried out in Autumn

Table 4.4 Taking a count in Britain

Estimator	Counts	Data source
Pugh (1984)	According to the narrow definition contained in the Homeworkers (Protection) Bill 1978, 87,400 persons were homeworking in 1971 (0.5 per cent of the employed population). This corresponds very closely to our definition of homeworking presented in Chapter 2.	Longitudinal Study (1 per cent sample survey of the 1971 Census)
Hakim (1987a)	Hakim estimated that in England and Wales 658,250 people worked at or from home. Of these, 229,800 worked at home (excluding childminders).	National Homeworking Survey, 1981 (sift survey of 1981 LFS)
Laurie and Taylor (1995)	Of all those in employment in the sample, 6.7 per cent worked at or from home, 3.9 per cent worked at home and 2.8 per cent worked from home.	Wave One of British Household Panel Study, 1991
Foster et al. (1995)	Some 5 per cent of working respondents fulfilled 'a number of criteria: (i) either they worked in their home or same grounds and buildings as their home; (ii) or their usual pattern of working involved some days working from home and some days away from home so long as they had worked at home on at least one day and had not worked away from home on more than nine days in the two weeks prior to interview; (iii) and the informants' job does not require them to live at their work premises or in accommodation provided by their employer' (p. 55).	General Household Survey, 1993/1994
Felstead and Jewson (1995)	It is estimated that in 1991 1,162,810 people worked at home in Britain, constituting 5.0 per cent of the working population.	Census of Population, 1991
Felstead (1996)	Estimated that over 250,000 people had main job as homeworker in terms of the definition presented in Chapter 2. To this one can add another 55,000 people whose second job was that of a homeworker.	Labour Force Survey, Spring 1994
Employment Gazette, now Labour Market Trends (various)	Persons working at home in their main job varied from 622,000 to 698,000 with the percentage figure ranging from 2.5 per cent to 2.9 per cent of those employed.	Labour Force Survey Spring and Autumn quarters

1981, the results of which were eventually published six years later (Hakim 1987a). This became known as the National Homeworking Survey (NHS). The 1981 Labour Force Survey (LFS) was used as a sift and sampling frame for follow-up interviews. For reasons of cost, the NHS was limited to England and Wales, although it was claimed to be broadly representative of Britain.

The breadth of the NHS allows comparisons to be made between a wide variety of types of home-located producer. Its sweep included a range of spatial locations of work and patterns of employment. However, the survey excluded almost one-third of what were described as 'home-based workers' who happened to be in construction, road haulage or a family business – on the grounds that 'much is already known about these types of home-based jobs' (Hakim 1987a: 7). Resulting estimates for 1981 produced figures of 658,250 'home-based workers' and 229,800 people who worked at home (childminders excluded). To this could be added an estimated 284,000 'home-based workers' in construction, road haulage or a family business and a further 750,000 people who had live-in jobs (Hakim 1987b: figure 1). It should be noted at this point that Hakim's notion of 'home-based workers' does not correspond to any of the categories of home-located producers we outline in Chapter 2 since it includes both those who work *at* and *from* home. It has been argued that this conflation in part accounts for the relatively optimistic – some would say rosy – picture that emerged from the NHS (Allen and Wolkowitz 1987). Hakim goes on to subdivide this broad category into manufacturing and non-manufacturing sectors. She also distinguishes those who work at and from home (Hakim 1987b: 94). To confuse matters further, however, she calls the former group 'homeworkers', although in our theoretical framework we designate these as 'home-located producers'.

The NHS was a conceptual and empirical watershed that proved to be very influential. For a generation, it was the most widely quoted piece of empirical research among both academics and policy-makers. Nevertheless, over the years it attracted a barrage of methodological criticisms. These included the dangers of reliance on official data gathering, failure directly to gather information on ethnic minorities and use of over-complex research instruments (e.g., Phizacklea and Wolkowitz 1995; Felstead and Jewson 1996, 1997). Even today, it continues to have a major impact on research in Britain and elsewhere. For example, a recent analysis of the British Household Panel Study (BHPS) – a national household panel survey of individuals about their employment, income and attitudes – mirrors the NHS approach by adopting the same definition of a broad category of 'home-based workers' and then subdividing the population into specific segments (Laurie and Taylor 1995: figure 1). The most significant difference is that the BHPS questionnaire precludes the possibility of employees recording that they worked mainly *from* home, but allowed the self-employed to do so. Consequently, those reported as working from home are all self-employed and the total numbers of those working from home may, therefore, be underestimated. The BHPS data suggest that in 1991 6.7 per cent of all those in current employment were in 'home-based' jobs, with 3.9 per cent working at home and the remaining 2.8 per cent working from home (Laurie and Taylor 1995: 8).

Other official British data sets also contain useful information. In 1993/1994, for example, the General Household Survey (GHS) included questions intended to collect data on working at home for the first time since the annual survey began in 1971. Informants were asked to identify where they worked in their main job. They were given four options: somewhere separate from home; in different places using home as a base; at home or in the same grounds or buildings as their home; or a combination of home and somewhere else. Those falling into the third category were described as 'homeworkers' – yet another use of the term which is widely at odds with our definition. It is also different from Hakim's use of the term, described above. The resulting GHS category was, in principle, large and wide ranging – yet only 5 per cent of the sample of 18,492 respondents qualified for inclusion. This is even more surprising given the fact that the survey was designed to pick up those who regularly did *some*, but not all, of their work at home. When this approach was adopted in the US, large counts were produced (see earlier discussion).

Alongside one-off attempts at measurement, in Britain regular counts are provided by the Census of Population and the Labour Force Survey (LFS). The Census counts only capture a broad measure, but they do permit comparisons over time. They show a sharp rise in numbers from 777,170 in 1981 to 1,162,810 in 1991, an increase of two-thirds (Felstead and Jewson 1995: 96). However, it should be remembered that Census figures are based on responses to a question about mode of daily travel to work rather than a direct question about place of work. As a result, counts from this source are likely to conflate those who work at and nearby home. In this regard – though not others – Census definitions are similar to those of the GHS but differ from those of the NHS and those outlined in Chapter 2 of this book.

The LFS incorporates yet another definition, but one which is more in tune with our own way of thinking. From 1992 a work location question was introduced to the Spring and Autumn quarters of the LFS. This enables home-located production *as we define it* to be monitored on a half-yearly basis. According to these figures, the number of home-located producers has risen from 656,000 (or 2.7 per cent of the employed population) in Spring 1992 to 698,000 (or 2.9 per cent) in Autumn 1995 (*Employment Gazette*, December 1992: 617; *Labour Market Trends*, June 1996: LFS32). However, in 1997 LFS-based data were published incorporating a second definition running alongside the first. Published LFS counts, therefore, simultaneously incorporate two definitions, one of which is similar to our concept of home-located production and another which is much broader. The latter includes those who work at and those who work in the same grounds and buildings as their home. There is an obvious potential for confusion here, with the broad definition figures suggesting that one in twenty women and one in thirty men work 'at home' (*Labour Market Trends*, August 1997: LFS43).

One of the benefits of the LFS compared to the Census is that data are more readily available for further analysis. It is possible, therefore, to operationalise crudely our definition of homeworkers on LFS data. Such an exercise suggests a sharp increase in recent years. In the NHS study, Hakim used the LFS to derive a one-off estimate of 100,000 homeworkers *as we define them* (Hakim 1987a: 41). Thirteen years later, the Spring 1994 LFS suggested that their numbers had risen to 300,000 (Felstead 1996: 230). This was notwithstanding the decline of manufacturing industry in this period – an important source of homeworking jobs.

Britain is distinctive not only in having an extensive collection of official estimates but also many other non-government sources which provide alternative counts. Indeed, it has been argued that reliance on official data sources can be misleading. Huws (1996a: 5–6) makes this point by comparing the official figures for the inner London borough of Tower Hamlets with local estimates. According to the 1991 Census, there were only 1,210 people working at home in the borough (Felstead and Jewson 1995: 98). Yet, 'economic development officers in Tower Hamlets suggest that 8,000 homeworkers or more would not be an unreasonable figure for the numbers working at home in the clothing industry during the busy season' (Mitter *et al.* 1993: 4). This discrepancy is remarkable when one considers that the larger unofficial figure refers to *one industry* and a conception akin to our *narrow* definition of homeworking, while the smaller official figure refers to *all industries* in the locality and a much *broader* measure. One of the explanations may be the fears and anxieties generated particularly among the deprived and disadvantaged by official surveys and investigations. For example, it is striking that according to the 1991 Census one in 23 employed residents in Harrogate were working at home, compared to just one in 133 in Tower Hamlets. From this Huws concludes that

> middle-class people who do not go out to work – who may include such diverse groups as farmers, novelists, management consultants, architects, shopkeepers, hoteliers, publicans and those living from unearned income – are much more likely to record themselves as home-based than working-class people.
>
> (Huws 1996a: 6)

There are, however, dangers in accepting this critique in full. Whatever the deficiencies of official data sources it is at least possible to investigate their methodology and reasoning. In some cases, unofficial figures offer little more than guesstimates which are very difficult to verify (e.g., Birmingham City Council 1993; Dundee Inner City Neighbourhood Action Centre 1984; Elwin 1994). We turn, therefore, to more rigorous non-government counts provided by academic researchers.

A door-knocking survey of 4,190 households in Bradford and the surrounding area reported that 2.6 per cent of those answering the door were doing home-located wage labour (Allen and Wolkowitz 1987: 45). More recently, we have carried out a similar door-knocking exercise of our own within selected wards/postal sectors in four different locations in Britain (see Chapter 1, pp. 8–9). A total of 15,623 doors were knocked within four areas. Where our interviewers obtained an answer, some 3.4 per cent reported at least one member of their household had done paid work at home during the last 12 months (see Felstead and Jewson 1996: 7–8). Survey researchers were also encouraged to record systematically any hearsay evidence. Such evidence strongly suggests that some of those involved in home-located working were reticent about declaring their work activities on the doorstep. Our doorstep survey results may, therefore, be treated as bare minimum estimates of the extent of home-located work in each of the four areas.

Another technique for evaluating the veracity of official counts is to develop an *indirect* measure of the extent of homework in particular industries. Rather than relying on individual respondents, who may be unwilling or unable to declare they work at home, this approach draws on officially collected output and employment industry data which are assumed to be more reliable. This approach was first adopted by Mitter (1986b) and has since been updated and revised by Rubery *et al*. (1992) for the British clothing industry.

For much of the 1970s and early 1980s, productivity in clothing continued to rise while investment was static or, if anything, began to decline. Mitter (1986b) argues that this apparent paradox can be explained by a shift in patterns of employment, comprising a decline in the number of officially recorded employees in the industry accompanied by a rise in the number of 'invisible' workers – particularly those working at home. Labour productivity is defined in terms of the relationship between gross output and the number of employees known to be working in the industry. Labour productivity will, therefore, tend to show an upward trend, even in the absence of technical change or work intensification, if some employment shifts from the official to the 'hidden' economy. Mitter (1986b) focuses on one sector of the clothing industry, commonly known as the fashion trade, to estimate the extent of the shift. On the assumption that real productivity levels in the industry remained stable at 1978 levels, she calculates that implied employment was 13,100 higher than the level actually recorded for 1983. Furthermore, assuming that workers in the informal sector are more likely to be part-time or irregular than their formal sector counterparts, the number employed in the fashion trade may by 1983 have increased by 17,030 over the 1978 base figures (ibid.: 70–71). On this basis, it is suggested that official estimates for the size of the manufacturing homeworking labour force may grossly underestimate its true extent (ibid.: 74). However, there is no way of telling what proportion of these informal workers carried out work in their own homes. Evidence on the existence of clothing 'sweatshops' suggest that at least some worked informally on employers' premises and as such could not be regarded as homeworkers (Phizacklea 1990).

Rubery *et al*. (1992: 93–95) have subsequently replicated Mitter's (1986b) estimates, but with two important modifications. First, their estimates are based on more up-to-date output and employment figures. Second, and more significantly, they adopt the more conservative assumption that the jump in productivity in

1979–1981 might well reflect the shakeout of low productivity firms. Hence, they make the assumption that productivity remained constant from 1981 rather than 1978. However, even based on these less heroic assumptions they still conclude that 'the use of homework in clothing is higher than estimated in national surveys and has increased at least in the first half of the 1980s' (Rubery *et al.* 1992: 94).

Philippines

In setting out to provide a national estimate of the number of people working at home in the Philippines researchers have confronted many of the issues identified above, as well as some new ones specific to a developing nation (Abrera-Mangahas 1993). Statistics on home-located production are noticeably sparse in many countries of the world, but this is especially the case in developing nations (Korns 1993). Moreover, in many cases home and work have not been wholly differentiated. What constitutes 'work' in small scale family production and subsistence agriculture is difficult to define precisely since it is the household rather than the individual which is the focal point.

The National Survey of Homeworkers in the Philippines was based on interviews with a representative national sample of 1,200 households conducted in 1989 (see Table 4.5). It sought to establish a comprehensive picture of the working population by asking respondents three questions. First, 'do you have a job or a means of livelihood?' Those answering affirmatively were considered to be in the working population. This is more or less standard practice across the world. The survey's novelty came in the next two questions. Those denying that they had a job or means of livelihood were asked what their main activity was during the week before interview. They were offered a list from which to choose, which included helping in the family business, looking for work, studying, taking care of the children and doing the household chores. Those choosing the option 'helping in the family business' were included in the working population, regardless of whether they were paid or not. Third, those who selected other responses were directly asked whether or not they helped in the family business. An affirmative response was taken as evidence that the respondent contributed to the family livelihood, even if they did so only on an irregular or even occasional basis.

This exercise suggested that standard labour market measures under-count the size of the working population by around 14 per cent, with 17.5 million conventionally employed and an additional 2.4 million people contributing in some way to the family business. The under-count is more pronounced for some groups than for others. Women's labour market participation, for example, is under-recorded by around a third compared to a more modest 5 per cent for men (Abrera-Mangahas 1993: table 1). A count was taken of all those who worked at, from or nearby their home (ibid.: 65) – once again, a much broader conceptualisation than any of the categories we propose. In 1989 this comprised some 7.9 million people (39.5 per cent of the workforce). Of these, 5.1 million were working at or within the grounds of their homes and 2.8 million were working from

Table 4.5 Taking a count in Asia

Estimator	Counts	Data source
Philippines Abrera-Mangahas (1993)	Almost 8 million (39.5 per cent) persons performed work 'basically in the home ... in either self or paid employment or who contribute to the family livelihood' (p. 63). Of these, 5 million (25.8 per cent) were completely housebound and 2.5 million (13.7 per cent) worked from home.	National Survey of Homeworkers, Autumn 1989
India Dholakia (1989)	In 1981, there were 7,710,920 'household industry' workers defined as 'an industry conducted by the head of the household himself/herself and/or by the members of the household at home or within the village in rural areas, and only within the precincts of the house where the household lived in urban areas' (p. 37). These represented about 3.5 per cent of the Indian workforce. Of these, around 4,400,000 (2 per cent) were said to be particularly 'exploitation prone'.	Census of Population, 1981
Hong Kong Wong (1983)	Growth in numbers of 'individuals who are free to take their work wherever they choose and are not constrained to working physically in the firm' (p. 1). These rose from 0.34 per cent of women workers in 1971 to 5.05 per cent of women workers ten years later.	Census of Population, 1961, 1971 and 1981
Lui (1994)	Numbers of employees said to be free to take work home or anywhere they like (pp. 7–8) rose from just under 11,000 (0.9 per cent) in 1961 to almost 56,000 (2.4 per cent) in 1981 before falling back to around 49,000 (1.8 per cent) in 1986.	Census of Population, 1961, 1971 and 1981
Japan Suzuki (1993)	Homeworkers (as defined in Chapter 2) declined from 1,811,200 in 1970 to half that figure (977,700) in 1988. Recent data from the same source suggest numbers have fallen to 549,000 in 1995.	Annual General Survey of Home-Working, October, various
Statistics Bureau (1995)	In 1994 persons doing 'piecework at home' (p. 30) were estimated to number 650,000 compared to 930,000 in 1988.	Labour Force Survey, various

home. However, the proportion involved shrinks dramatically if one adopts a stricter definition more in line with our conceptualisation of home-located wage labour. On this basis, the Filipino study suggests that there were 587,000 such workers in 1989, representing about 2.9 per cent of the working population (ibid.: tables 7 and 9).

India

One might expect to find estimates at least of a similar order of magnitude in India but, in point of fact, official estimates appear to be surprisingly low. This may be because official data sources are restricted in scope (see Table 4.5). Of greater interest to us, however, is that estimates based on the Census figures have been cognisant of some of the conceptual issues outlined in Chapter 2, most notably those constructed by Dholakia (1989). He develops a hierarchy of different types of home-located production, ranging from the broadest to the narrowest. At each step in the hierarchy, groups are clearly defined and delineated from one another. The size of each group is subsequently estimated. Dholakia (1989) in particular aims to identify those who carry out work at home, using capital assets they do not own, taking raw materials from suppliers of work and continuing to work under these circumstances for a 'fairly stable' length of time. These he regards as especially 'exploitation prone' (ibid.: 1989). The size of this group was estimated at 4.4 million workers, or 2 per cent of the Indian workforce. However, this estimate is notably at odds with others, some of which put the figure for the 'beedi' (cigarette) rolling industry alone at 2.25 million (Bhatt 1987: 29). We therefore have great doubts about the accuracy of these estimates. Nevertheless, the analytical framework Dholakia (1989) applies to the data at his disposal has much to commend it.

Hong Kong

Hong Kong also has some official estimates of the number of people working at home. These are based on the Census of Population and its rather loose and all inclusive definition of the phenomenon (see Table 4.5). This refers to anyone 'who is free to take his [sic] work home or anywhere he [sic] likes' (quoted in Lui 1994: 7–8). This should, in principle, cover a wide spectrum. However, somewhat surprisingly, they are estimated to make up a relatively small proportion of the working population. In 1961, for example, they accounted for just under 1 per cent of all workers. By 1981, the proportion had risen to 2.4 per cent, although by 1986 it had fallen back slightly to 1.8 per cent (ibid.: 53). Given the broad conception used, it is surprising that the proportions are so low. Even more striking is the finding that over nine-tenths were in manufacturing and that only one in five were men (ibid.: 1; Wong 1983: table 3). In other words, such a broad definition which would elsewhere in the world capture a wide range of different types of worker and jobs, when adopted in Hong Kong appears to generate a narrow and relatively homogeneous group. One interpretation of these data is that working at home in Hong Kong is heavily confined to manufacturing industry and women workers in particular (see Chiu and Lui 1996).

Japan

In Japan, data collection is limited to a particular form of home-located production more akin to our concept of homeworking (see Table 4.5). There are two official series from which to draw – one conducted annually by the Bureau for Working Women in the Ministry of Labour and the other based on the Japanese Labour Force Survey. Both come up with similar estimates, but from different starting points. The former captures the number of homeworkers that employers report using to local state officials. This is a requirement laid down by the 1970 Industrial Homework Act. This legislation enshrines a definition of homeworking close to ours except that it is limited to the manufacture or processing of goods (Suzuki 1993; Kamio 1995). These estimates chart a decline from 1.8 million in 1970 to just over half a million in 1995. The LFS estimates, on the other hand, are derived by asking respondents to characterise their employment status. 'Doing piecework at home' is given as an option. While, in principle, this is likely to pick up a range of different occupational groups, in practice only those in manufacturing are included in the count. As a result, the estimates produced for the same year are roughly comparable to one another. In 1994 the LFS counted 650,000 people doing piecework at home, representing a decline from the figure of 930,000 in 1988.

Conclusion

Counting home-located production in its various guises is far from easy. There is little discussion, let alone agreement, on the concepts to be measured. In some countries there are few data sources – official or otherwise – to draw on. In others researchers have a much wider choice. Nevertheless, even where data are plentiful, there are many technical problems and conceptual differences that make comparison within and between national counts highly problematic.

A *theoretical* typology can go some way to help by separating out economic and social actors who occupy different positions within the social relations of production. A major and recurring theme of this book is the need for conceptual clarity and rigour in the application of such definitions and their use. In particular, we have argued that it is essential to distinguish carefully between different categories of people who work at home. It is imperative *conceptually* to compare like with like. Without an anchor of this kind, it becomes impossible to make any sense of the counts from around the world. Hence, one of our objectives has been, as far as possible, to map these estimates onto our conceptual framework.

However, in the course of this exercise, it has become increasingly apparent that there is another serious obstacle confronting those who wish to count home-located producers. In addition to conceptual minefields there is a formidable array of *technical* traps and pitfalls. Many of the official estimates reviewed in this chapter are based on wildly contrasting technical decisions about measurement. They can serve to narrow or to widen the focus and hence diminish or raise overall counts. This is one of the main reasons that estimates vary so widely within a single country. Thus, for example, one estimate has it that almost one-fifth of Americans are home-located producers while another puts the proportion at one-fiftieth. This difference can be accounted for in terms of the relative inclusiveness of the measurement devices adopted.

It is, then, *technically* critical to compare like with like. This chapter has identified several key aspects of the technical variations between counts that can be summarised under three headings (see Table 4.6). First, counts vary according to the *forms of employment* that are deemed eligible for inclusion. These can, at one extreme, refer to main jobs only or, at the other, to any commodity production undertaken whether paid or not. Various positions are taken in between. Second, *time thresholds* required to trigger inclusion of an individual in a particular count can range from a small fraction of the working day to exclusive and total commitment around the clock. Thus some counts include people who do both a few and many hours of work at home, while others only include those who make a full-time commitment. A third source of technical variation concerns *location of work*. Here, too, eligibility can vary widely. Counts may incorporate a broad range of definitions, stretching from a loose interpretation encompassing any paid work connected in some way with the home, to a more specific and narrow interpretation.

One aim of this chapter has been to make the reader aware of technical problems of interpretation, comparison and reconciliation of estimates within and between nations. Table 4.6 presents the issues in a schematic form. On the left-hand side are displayed dimensions of variation in the ways in which counts are operationalised. They are grouped together under the three headings identified above. On the right-hand side, selected examples of official data sets are listed – all of which have been discussed in this chapter – from which published counts have been derived. This table has two purposes. First, it provides a framework for understanding and differentiating the many technical issues that we have raised. Hopefully, it enables the reader to progress from recognising the differences between specific estimates towards a broader appreciation of the overall issues. Second, the examples listed graphically illustrate the problems of comparison – as well as the scope some data sets offer. Put simply, data sets differ in what they count.

Our plea is that published counts from official data sets take on board the need to standardise and regularise the technical and conceptual bases on which calculations are made. In the absence of such rigour their value is greatly reduced – and indeed may simply serve to add to the widespread confusion and misunderstanding. It would be nice to think that the adoption of the ILO Convention and Regulation on home-located wage labour marks the beginning of a new era as the provision of basic data is one of its requirements (ILO 1996: 7–11).

Table 4.6 Published counts from around the world*

Operationalising definitions	Examples
Forms of employment	
Any commodity production (paid and unpaid)	Indian Census 1981; Philippines NHS 1989
Main job plus other jobs	Australian LFS 1989, 1992 and 1995; UK LFS 1992 onwards; England and Wales NHS 1981; EC LFS 1992 onwards
Main job only	British Census 1991; US Census 1980 and 1990; UK LFS 1992 onwards; US CPS 1985 and 1991; Canadian Census 1991 and 1996
Time thresholds	
Any	US CPS 1985 and 1991; Australian LFS 1989, 1992 and 1995; Philippines NHS 1989; EC LFS 1992 onwards; Indian Census 1981; Canadian SWA 1991 and 1995
Some	Philippines NHS 1989; US CPS 1985 and 1991
Mainly	British Census 1991; Australian LFS 1989, 1992 and 1995; US CPS 1985 and 1991; EC LFS 1992 onwards; England and Wales NHS 1981; US Census 1980 and 1990; Philippines NHS 1989; UK LFS 1992 onwards; Canadian Census 1991 and 1996
Location of work	
At home plus from home plus same grounds and buildings as home	US Census 1980 and 1990; US CPS 1985 and 1991; Indian Census 1981; Canadian Census 1991
At home plus same grounds and buildings as home	British Census 1991; Philippines NHS 1989; UK LFS 1992 onwards; Canadian Census 1996
At home plus from home	EC LFS 1992 onwards; England and Wales NHS 1981
At home	UK LFS 1992 onwards; Australian LFS 1989, 1992 and 1995; US CPS 1985 and 1991; Philippines NHS 1989; England and Wales NHS 1981

Note

* Data sets have been located in this table on the basis of published evidence which is not always wholly clear about the collection and compilation strategies adopted. In some cases survey questions, in principle, allow disaggregation of variables but published data do not always reflect this capacity. This table only refers to *published* counts.

Nevertheless, the counts which do currently exist are intrinsically interesting. They suggest that working at home is a global phenomenon not confined to the less developed nations of the world. Large numbers of home-located producers are found in the US, Australia, Canada and Europe. One US estimate suggests that 20 million Americans (or 18.3 per cent of those employed) are doing some of their work at home as either part of a formal arrangement or, more usually, as an incidental addition to their normal routine (Deming 1994). Moreover, the number of Americans working *formally* at home have risen dramatically in the 1990s – almost doubling between 1991 and 1997 (Bureau of Labor Statistics 1998). The picture is much the same elsewhere. A quarter of Australians (or 2.1 million of those in work) are estimated to be doing some of their work at home (McLennan 1996). Even more cautious estimates from Canada and the European Union put the figure at around one in ten. This amounts to over a million Canadians and 18 million people across Europe who use their home as their workplace for some of the time (Eurostat 1996; Akyeampong 1997).

The reader can be forgiven for finding the technicalities revealed in this chapter to be intellectually challenging – they have certainly given the authors a headache for some time! The crucial point to grasp, however, is the one made at the beginning of the chapter; that is, there is no one correct count only many different ways of counting. Leaving aside errors and omissions, each of the counts reviewed here is correct within its own terms. Nevertheless, the totality of the evidence strongly suggests that home-located production in all its various forms is not an anachronistic left-over from an earlier period; rather, it is an important part of the modern economic life which merits close scrutiny.

Chapter 5

Revealing diversity

The traditional homeworker is no longer a lady badly paid for piecework – knitting jumpers, filling envelopes or cutting out patterns – while she looks after the children. The telephone answering machine and desk-top copier have cleared the way for a more ambitious type of non-commuting person. Mr Insurance man works from home, as does a high powered literary agent friend and a very organised woman who manages the professional affairs of several musicians.

(*The Times*, 31 October 1983: 9)

Introduction

The aim of this chapter is to identify the social characteristics of those who work at home, providing profiles of different types of home-located producers. It will evaluate the relative importance of a series of variables in determining the likelihood of individuals engaging in these kinds of work. This will be achieved by reviewing the quantitative data on the correlates of working at home and by examining the reasons given by individuals themselves. An international focus will be maintained throughout, drawing on a wide variety of sources of information from around the world.

Statements such as those at the top of the chapter have sparked an intense debate. Battle lines have been drawn around two stereotypes (Phizacklea and Wolkowitz 1995; Stanworth 1996). On the one hand, there are those for whom the typical image is of a woman tied down by the needs of her family, often from an ethnic minority community, exploited by her employer, with few or no skills and working for low wages on tedious, repetitive tasks. On the other hand, there are those for whom working at home evokes a quite different picture: one in which workers, often men, have the ability to exercise choice over their employment options, working in high level non-manual occupations, possessing advanced qualifications and working at home by choice. We shall unpick the elements of these stereotypes and subject them to empirical assessment. We begin by examining the sexual composition of home-located producers, and thereafter proceed to look at ethnicity, education, age, marital status and parenthood.

Sex

One of the main features of the stereotypes referred to above is the assumption that 'traditional homeworking' is the preserve of women whilst those who work at home in managerial and professional jobs are predominantly male. In this section, we will consider whether the research evidence supports these assertions. We begin by examining the gender of participants engaged in home-located production. This is the broadest category in our framework and hence covers anyone engaged in production for exchange carried out at the place of residence. Many national studies generate results that approximate to this category – although the reader should be aware of the difficulties involved in mapping data sets against our theoretical framework (see Chapter 4).

The data suggest that in many countries participation in home-located production is the preserve of neither women nor men. In most cases, there is a roughly equal split (see Table 5.1). There is a slight tendency for women to outnumber men, although in Canada and the European Union the reverse is the case with women accounting, in both instances, for 47 per cent of those engaged in home-located production. However, it should be noted that different ways of designing and executing surveys sometimes produce a range or spread of results for any one country. In Britain and the United States, for example, some data sets suggest a gender balance in favour of women, while others suggest the opposite.

In some countries there is evidence of differential rates of growth in home-located production between the sexes. In Canada, for example, the number of women working at home has increased more quickly than the number of men. Between 1981 and 1991, female participation increased by 69 per cent, compared with 23 per cent for men (Nadwodny 1996: 17). Similarly, in Britain over the last decade the number of women engaged in home-located production rose by 56 per cent compared with a rise of 44 per cent for men (Pugh 1984: 5; Pugh 1990: 134; Felstead and Jewson 1995: 96). In the US, however, the trends appear to be going in the opposite direction with numbers of men involved in home-located production increasing more rapidly than numbers of women. The 1980s saw a rise of 50 per cent among women versus 63 per cent among men (Silver 1989: 116; US Department of Commerce 1998b).

Although there appears to be rough parity between the proportions of male and female home-located producers, there is greater imbalance among the different categories of people who work at home. Some positions in our typology of home-located production are more feminised than others. Regrettably, there are some notable gaps in the available empirical evidence. Few countries, for example, publish data which singles out home-located employers. The South African data come closest (SEWU 1995: 19). They suggest that men in South Africa are twice as likely as women to work at home, employing others, but are less likely to be involved in home-located production in general. Men are also more likely to be home-located petty commodity producers than women.

Table 5.1 **Gender profile of home-located production by country**

Country	Proportion of home-located production undertaken by women (%)
Argentina[1]	50
Australia[2]	51–70
Britain[3]	45–73
Canada[4]	47
European Union[5]	47
Finland[6]	71
New Zealand[7]	62
Philippines[8]	56
South Africa[9]	60
United States[10]	40–54

Notes
1 Marshall (1992: 54–58).
2 Walker (1987: 20) and McLennan (1996: 5).
3 Felstead and Jewson (1995: 96), Foster *et al.* (1995: 56), *Labour Market Trends* (1996: LFS32) and Hakim (1987a: 43).
4 Nadwodny (1996: 17).
5 Eurostat (1996: 144).
6 Salmi (1996: 148).
7 Loveridge and Schoeffel (1991: 11) and Loveridge *et al.* (1996: 15).
8 Abrera-Mangahas (1993: 69).
9 SEWU (1995: 6).
10 Heck (1993: 17), Horvath (1986: 32), Deming (1994: 15–16), Silver (1989: 116) and Horvath (1986: 34).

Secondary data from different countries around the world allow us to profile various types of home-located production identified in our schema, but few, if any, offer a complete account. In Britain, for example, the National Homeworking Survey (Hakim 1987a) provides a picture of home-located production and home-working but little on those who work at home under other social relations of production (such as home-located wage labour). Filipino and South African studies (Abrera-Mangahas 1993; SEWU 1995) also break down the concept of home-located production, but only as far as home-located wage labour and not beyond. For other countries this disaggregation process is only possible by drawing on separate pieces of research. These may adopt different methodologies and be conducted several years apart. The New Zealand data on home-located production, for example, are taken from the travel-to-work question contained in the 1986 Census of Population (Loveridge and Schoeffel 1991; Loveridge *et al.* 1996), while data on home-located wage labour are taken from a survey of 2,000 randomly selected New Zealand workplaces carried out in 1991 (G. Anderson *et al.* 1994). The data presented here for Canada and Argentina are based on a similar mixture of Census results and other special surveys. The resulting contrasts can, therefore, only be illustrative of a particular pattern. None the less, the pictures produced are compelling.

Table 5.2 **Gender profile of home-located wage labour by country**

Country	Proportion of home-located wage labour undertaken by women (%)
Canada[1]	66
New Zealand[2]	87
Philippines[3]	59
South Africa[4]	Over-represented

Notes
1 Siroonian (1993: 51).
2 G. Anderson *et al.* (1994: 237).
3 Abrera-Mangahas (1993: 105).
4 SEWU (1995: 7).

Table 5.3 **Gender profile of homeworking by country**

Country	Proportion of homeworking undertaken by women (%)
Argentina[1]	88
Australia[2]	67
Britain[3]	82–92
Japan[4]	93

Notes
1 Marshall (1992: 57).
2 McLennan (1996: 13).
3 Felstead (1996: 230), Felstead and Jewson (1996: 25) and Hakim (1987a: 44).
4 Ministry of Labour (1995: 9).

Best estimates suggest that when we shift the focus from home-located production to home-located wage labour we find more women involved (see Table
5.2). In Canada, around a half (47 per cent) of home-located producers are
female but women comprise two-thirds (66 per cent) of home-located wage
labourers. Figures show a broadly similar pattern for New Zealand and the
Philippines. However, when one focuses on homeworking (as defined conceptually in Chapter 2) women begin to dominate the picture. In the case of
Argentina, Japan and Britain around nine out of ten homeworkers are women
(see Table 5.3).

When we turn the spotlight on homeworking, as we have defined it, the evidence from around the world is unequivocal. From Argentina to Australia, Britain
to Japan women dominate this kind of employment (see Table 5.3). This emerges
as a robust finding from a range of different data sets and research strategies,
deploying a variety of techniques in searching for subjects. In the case of Britain,
for example, it is confirmed by estimates based on official data sets, doorstep interviews and sift surveys. An equally robust finding, however, is that homeworking

is not the exclusive preserve of women. Across the world, surveys and research studies consistently find a minority of male homeworkers.

Perhaps surprisingly in these circumstances there is little research which *compares* male and female home-located producers. This is because, contrary to the evidence, homeworking is commonly regarded as an exclusively women's issue and a wholly gendered form of employment. As a result, gender comparisons are ignored and neglected. A further consequence of this emphasis is that it is sometimes assumed or implied that *all* home-located production is conducted by women.

Such assumptions sometimes appear to have influenced academic research. For example, Allen and Wolkowitz (1987: 1) initially pose a series of research questions, which include investigation of the male–female balance among home-located wage labourers. However, after only a few pages they appear to assume rather than demonstrate that such work is an almost exclusively female activity (ibid.: 5). The organisation, experience and reward structure of home-located wage labour is then analysed, interpreted and explained in terms of the economic position of women in the labour market and the dynamics of gender-based household relationships in Britain. It would appear that there are no men in their sample, although this is never explicitly spelt out. None of their research effort appears to be devoted to uncovering men who do this type of work or to a systematic comparison between the sexes.

Phizacklea and Wolkowitz (1995) are similarly hamstrung in this regard. They utilise a combination of techniques in searching for subjects, generating over four hundred replies to a direct appeal in a popular women's magazine. These methods produced an almost exclusively female sample and, in any case, the authors decided to exclude the few male respondents they had recruited. They base their argument that homework is a feminised form of employment on this evidence.

Other researchers, too, have focused exclusively on women. Christensen (1988), for example, carried out a survey of women's experiences of home-located production. Readers of *Family Circle* – a magazine read by around 19 million women in the US – were invited to complete a postal questionnaire. Although the questionnaire did not preclude men from replying, their responses were excluded from the published results (Hirshey 1985). Similarly, some Australian research has focused specifically on women involved in home-located production to the exclusion of men. O'Donnell (1987), for example, gathered data on 224 women who worked at home in a range of occupations and employment relationships, drawn from ethnically diverse backgrounds. Dawson and Turner (1989: 8) adopted a similar women-only focus by examining the working conditions and experiences of 20 Melbourne women who, at the time of interview, were paid to do clerical work at home, using 'new' technology. Other research which takes a women-only focus includes studies by Benería and Roldán (1987) of home-located industrial workers in Mexico City and ILO-sponsored investigations of home-located workers in South East Asia (see Lazo, 1992a–c, 1993a–c; Wirutomo 1993).

Some studies, such as Presser and Bamberger (1993), have explicitly excluded men from the analysis despite their presence in relatively large numbers in the data set under scrutiny. They focus their attention solely on women who work at home, even though the data set – the 1985 US CPS – on which their analysis is based contains results for both sexes. The justification given is that there is 'minimal research on men who do paid work at home, but the current debate about its practice focuses mostly on women' (ibid.: 815).

Other research is skewed by the techniques adopted in searching for subjects. Reliance on media appeals for respondents to come forward are inevitably influenced by the channels adopted. In the case of Huws (1984), these appeals were made via the Equal Opportunities Commission (EOC) Press Office and were predominantly picked up by newspapers, magazines, TV programmes and radio broadcasts with a particular interest in women's issues. Just four of the 78 homeworkers surveyed were men and no separate analysis of their circumstances was carried out. However, unlike other researchers, Huws (1984) did not remove them from the overall picture simply on account of their sex. A similar methodology was adopted by Richards (1994) in Ireland. An article appeared in the national press and an appeal for respondents was made on national radio. However, both were couched in terms of women's participation in this type of work. The results are based on a women-only sample of 19 which, as far as we can detect, approximates to our narrow definition of homeworkers.

Gender differences in the lives of home-located producers and homeworkers are extensively discussed in Chapters 7, 8 and 9. In this chapter, however, we confine ourselves to quantitative issues. In summary, we have seen a more complex picture than is portrayed in the popular stereotypes. National data sets, local studies and studies of particular employers and industries suggest that men and women are present in roughly equal numbers in what we call home-located production. They also suggest that women predominate in homeworking, as we have defined it. However, the data show that a not insignificant minority of homeworkers are male. There is very little hard evidence about the gender composition of other types of home-located production, but there is at least some reason to believe that men are present in larger numbers among high discretion home-located wage labourers, home-located petty commodity producers and home-located employers. Hence, gender stereotypes of home-located producers are not wholly wrong but they do oversimplify. The evidence reveals a more diverse picture.

It is apparent that the major pieces of research reviewed so far provide very few opportunities for a comparative analysis of male and female home-located producers or for making estimates of the proportions. In order to cast light on these issues we are forced to turn elsewhere. Several national data sets, local studies and studies of particular employers and industries reveal that men are *more* likely than women to be doing certain types of home-located production. The gender profile does, however, change for each type under scrutiny. This finding goes some way to reconcile the two gendered stereotypes with which this chapter began.

Ethnicity

The issue of ethnicity has excited heated debate. Many argue that migrants and members of ethnic minorities are over-represented among the most disadvantaged types of home-located production, while others regard ethnicity as of little consequence. Authorities such as the ILO make forthright statements:

> In several industrialised countries home work [*sic*] is concentrated in industrial regions and in large urban areas where recent immigrants (often illegal) and ethnic minorities are concentrated. Immigrant women most often do not even look for formal employment because of language barriers, low levels of formal education and fear of discrimination. Often they literally want to remain invisible and work in their homes. This phenomenon has been observed in districts of London, Paris, Boston, New York, Los Angeles and many other urban centres.
>
> (ILO 1989: 7)

Those on the ground, such as local campaigning groups, make similar claims. In Britain, many bluntly state that they deal with 'groups within the community who cannot find alternative employment and for whom the pay, however inadequate, is of economic necessity . . . a significant proportion of whom are from Black and minority ethnic groups' (Birmingham City Council 1993: 3). Much the same picture has been painted for many of Britain's cities (Elwin 1994: 8; Huws 1994: 5; Phizacklea and Wolkowitz 1995).

Assertions of this kind have been corroborated by independently conducted research. London's homeworking labour force, for example, includes several ethnic minority groups, although different parts of the capital draw upon different communities (Hope *et al.* 1976). The ethnic make-up of the homeworking labour force varies substantially from borough to borough. In Haringey, for example, the Cypriot community is a ready source of labour (Burdett 1980). In other parts of the capital, Asian communities in general and Bangladeshis in particular provide a major part of the labour pool from which homeworking employers draw (Shah 1975; Mitter 1986b; Mitter *et al.* 1993). This leaves little doubt that at the local level, at least, the connection between homeworking and ethnicity is a strong one, often associated with the clothing trade.

Our own research (Felstead and Jewson 1996) tends to confirm this view. One of the aims of the survey commissioned by the Employment Department was to skew our sample towards ethnic minority homeworkers, about whom relatively little is known (see Chapter 1, pp. 9). We therefore targeted particular wards in several selected areas in Britain where ethnic minority communities were known to live and in which anecdotal and Census evidence suggested that homeworking was relatively commonplace. Particular attention was directed to the composition of the local research teams, which were recruited so as to include people with a wide range of ethnic backgrounds and language skills. Over half of our in-depth interviews were conducted with members of ethnic minority communities engaged in homeworking (181 respondents or 54 per cent of the sample). It included people who identified themselves as White (157), Indian (54), Bangladeshi (38), Turkish (27), Pakistani (22), Kutchi (14), Black Caribbean (12), Black African (5) and Others (9). The research underlined the association of ethnic minority homeworking with the clothing trade. Thus, under one-third (31 per cent) of White respondents were involved in sewing but the vast majority of ethnic minority homeworkers were engaged in these activities (96 per cent of Turkish homeworkers, 93 per cent of Kutchis, 80 per cent of Indians, 66 per cent of Bangladeshis and 64 per cent of Pakistanis).

This picture is not confined to Britain. In the US, the apparent resurgence of interest in homeworking in the 1980s was sparked not only by the disclosure of its persistence in traditional industries, but also by a series of reports that documented its rapid growth and estimated that thousands were illegally working at home in New York City and elsewhere (Faricellia Dangler 1989: 149). Many have proved to be recent migrants (some illegal) from neighbouring countries such as Mexico and Cuba. They have provided a ready source of homeworkers from which employers can easily draw. As a consequence, an indelible mark has been left on the ethnic make-up of the homeworking labour force in many US cities – see, for example, the Hispanic-dominated clothing industries of Los Angeles and Miami (Fernández-Kelly and García 1988).

Urban areas in Australia, Canada and France are replete with similar examples of migrant homeworkers working for long hours and for low wages. Many of the homeworkers in Wollongong – a city south of Sydney – are drawn from non-English-speaking countries around the world (Illawara Migrant Resource Centre 1984). In Toronto many Chinese-speakers are found among the ranks of homeworkers (Cameron and Mak 1991; Dagg and Fudge 1993). In Paris homeworkers are often of North African origin (Varesi and Villa 1986: 32; Morokvasic 1987).

However, despite the evidence of local studies, official data does not always reveal the importance of home-located production for particular ethnic groups. Sometimes this is because the relevant data appear not to have been compiled. In Canada, for example, the published Census and Survey of Work Arrangements (SWA) results do not enable researchers to test whether home-located production is an especially important source of employment for the Chinese-speaking section of the population (Akyeampong and Siroonian 1993; Siroonian 1993; Nadwodny 1996; Akyeampong 1997). Even when the relevant data are collected, however, ethnic groups are sometimes not adequately detected in large scale official surveys.

One of the most startling conclusions of the 1981 National Homeworking Survey (NHS) of England and Wales (Hakim 1987a, 1987b) was the suggestion that members of ethnic minorities were marginally less likely to be working at or from home in any capacity than their national presence would suggest . However, the survey did not contain any direct information on ethnic background. Due to an oversight, the relevant data were not transferred from the 1981 LFS data (Hakim 1987a: 45). As a result, Hakim uses information on language problems as a proxy for ethnicity. Only 1 per cent of the sample experienced difficulties in speaking English. It appears to be on the basis of this crude indicator that Hakim makes her statements about ethnic minority involvement. Even so, as Hakim disaggregates her data from the broad definition of those who work at or from home, the picture changes. The proportion reporting language difficulties grows fourfold to 4 per cent when the focus is on 'manufacturing homework' (which approximates to our definition of homeworking), rising by half as much again to 6 per cent when the further condition of working for a single employer is added (ibid.: table 4.1).

Official surveys elsewhere also fail to detect a substantial ethnic minority presence. The 1991 CPS in the US, for example, found that a far higher proportion of White respondents worked at home (3.6 per cent) than Black (1.3 per cent) and Hispanic respondents (1.7 per cent) (Deming 1994: 16). In the European Union, too, there is little official evidence that home-located production is especially prevalent among ethnic minority and migrant communities. The Eurostat data suggest that only 1.6 per cent of people working at home are born outside of the Union.

Similar findings are evident from more recent analysis of the UK Labour Force Survey (LFS) for Spring 1994 (Felstead 1996: 230–231). It suggests that ethnic minorities are relatively under-represented in the homeworking labour force – as we have defined it – compared to their presence in employment more generally. Around 4 per cent of the workforce are from ethnic minority communities, while they make up around 3 per cent of homeworkers. However, there is good reason to suspect that the LFS substantially under-represents ethnic minority homeworkers. For example, the LFS fails to pick up any Bangladeshis despite local studies which suggest their presence. Research in areas such as the East End of London, West Yorkshire and the Midlands highlights the difficulties of making contact with Asian homeworkers, particularly those in the Bangladeshi community (Mitter *et al.* 1993; West Yorkshire Homeworking Group 1990; Felstead and Jewson 1996). It is, therefore, hardly surprising that an official survey conducted in English – on a face-to-face basis in a fifth of cases and on the telephone in the remainder – elicits such a poor response among ethnic minority homeworkers, who may feel apprehensive and vulnerable when responding to any kind of survey (see Chapter 3).

Having said this, analysis of the available LFS data suggests that ethnic minority homeworkers tend to be concentrated in a narrow range of occupations and industries. Around 70 per cent of female Pakistani/Bangladeshi homeworkers in the sample are in textile, clothing and footwear occupations doing activities such as sewing, machining, seamstressing and clicking. The remaining 30 per cent are in other craft related occupations. Two-thirds of Black women homeworkers are recorded in textiles and the remaining third in secretarial jobs. Indian women homeworkers appear to be wholly confined to secretarial work. None of the ethnic minority men in the LFS sample are reported to be homeworking in any of these occupations (Felstead 1996: 236).

In Australia official data paint a somewhat different picture. They suggest that around 12 per cent of people who work at home originate from non-English-speaking parts of the world (McLennan 1996: 8). This is broadly in line with their participation in the Australian workforce. However, as soon as this category is broken down a different pattern emerges. An examination of the Australian 1981 Census, for example, reveals that most of the women reporting that they worked at home in the textile, clothing or footwear industries were born overseas, mostly in Italy, Greece or Yugoslavia. Furthermore, over half spoke English less than 'very well' (Walker 1987: 36). Studies of these industries in Australia reveals a similar pattern of reliance on immigrants with limited English language proficiency (e.g., Brosnan and Thornthwaite 1997). For example, one survey found that almost four out of every five clothing homeworkers had poor or no skills in spoken English, whereas none of the journalists and only a few of the childminders who worked at home reported similar problems (O'Donnell 1987: 29, 45, 53).

In summary, then, local research studies that target migrant and ethnic minority respondents show that homeworking is prevalent in their communities. This is sometimes associated with the involvement of ethnic minority entrepreneurs in the garment and other traditional industries. In contrast, national official data sets tend to portray ethnic minority homeworkers as a small proportion of the total homeworking labour force. In part, these differences probably reflect the respective strategies in searching for subjects adopted by these two types of study (see Chapter 3). However, it is also important to realise that their findings are not necessarily mutually exclusive.

Education

Data on educational qualifications can provide a useful analytical tool for those interested in revealing the social characteristics of those who work at home because they provide a proxy for the extent to which individuals are able to wield economic power in the marketplace. The stereotypes, which we are evaluating, would have us believe that home-located producers are divided into two segments – a highly qualified male group and a poorly qualified female group. What, then, does the evidence show?

Only a few of the countries covered in this book have published data – national, local or otherwise – capable of offering answers to this question. Fewer still allow one to disaggregate. The British, and to some extent, the New Zealand, data provide us with the best opportunity of shedding light on each of the types of home-located production identified earlier (see Chapter 2), although even here the picture is incomplete.

In many countries these data are not compiled at all. The Australian LFS, for example, does not appear to gather and publish educational data on 'persons employed at home', yet the survey collects a raft of information on other characteristics (McLennan 1996). Educational data is also noticeably absent from several other country sources, including Japan, the Philippines and South Africa (Ministry of Labour 1995; Abrera-Mangahas 1993; SEWU 1995).

The National Homeworking Survey of England and Wales contains within its remit categories we would call home-located production as well as ones more akin to our definition of homeworking. As a result, from this source we can compare the educational profile of these two groups, albeit only for 1981. The first thing to note is that over two-thirds of home-located production was carried out by individuals who possessed educational qualifications of some sort, compared to only half of the entire labour force. Moreover, almost one-third had a degree or equivalent higher educational qualification, double the figure for the labour force as a whole. Furthermore, both men and women engaged in home-located production were found to be more highly qualified than their counterparts in the workforce generally, men being especially well qualified (Hakim 1987a: tables 4.5, 4.6). However, within this group there were marked differences in the educational profile of those doing different types of work. For example, the group described as 'manufacturing homeworkers' – a category close to our definition of home-workers – were well below the national average in terms of educational qualifications. Far fewer possessed degrees or equivalent and those with no qual-ifications at all were over-represented (ibid.: table 4.1).

More recent national evidence broadly confirms this picture. The British Household Panel Study (BHPS) found a higher percentage of people working at home who had a degree compared to others in employment. This was especially the case for men. They were twice as likely as women working at home to have these qualifications and twice as likely as other men to be qualified to such a level (Laurie and Taylor 1995: tables 7.3, 7.4). Joeman's analysis (1994) of the Spring 1992 LFS found that home-located producers were more qualified than the workforce as a whole, but that this was entirely due to higher level credentials held by male home-located producers. Female home-located producers had a similar distribution to the workforce as a whole. In the US, Canada, Finland, Argentina and India those engaged in home-located production are educated to much the same level as the workforce as a whole (see US Department of Commerce 1998b; Gerson 1993; Marshall 1992; Nadwodny 1996; Salmi 1996; Dholakia 1989).

Gender differences also appear to be significant in the distribution of educa-tional qualifications among homeworkers, as we have defined them. Felstead's (1996) analysis of the Spring 1994 LFS produces some interesting findings. He finds that at the higher levels of qualification (degree and above) British home-workers are less well qualified than the workforce as a whole. This is true of both male and female homeworkers, although males are more likely than females to have a degree. At intermediary levels – such as vocational and post-secondary – homeworkers are equal to or better qualified than the workforce as a whole. This is true of both male and female homeworkers, although once again men outstrip women. At the bottom end of the hierarchy there is little difference between homeworkers (male and female) and the workforce as a whole (ibid.: table 1).

Available evidence in New Zealand offers an interesting comparison. When home-located production is examined in its entirety, little difference is detectable between those who work at home and those who work elsewhere. According to the 1986 Census there is just one percentage point difference between the proportions who have a post-compulsory qualification of one sort or another. However, the picture becomes more diverse when analysed by gender. In the general workforce, men are more likely to have post-compulsory qualifications than women (42 per cent compared to 35 per cent), but the gap widens for those working at home (53 per cent compared to 35 per cent) (Loveridge and Schoeffel 1991: 19–23). Regrettably, no data are available in New Zealand for our narrower category of homeworkers.

In summary, the evidence is not extensive and does not consistently point to one conclusion. However, in general, it would appear to be the case that male home-located producers, as we have defined them, are better qualified than females. Moreover, homeworkers – both male and female – have considerably lower qualifications than the workforce as a whole. Interestingly, though, male homeworkers appear to have significantly better educational qualifications than female homeworkers at the higher and intermediary levels. Once again, we find that the stereotype picture is not wholly inaccurate but that it oversimplifies.

Age

The age profile of those involved in home-located production is remarkably similar across the world, and, unlike some of the other dimensions considered in the course of this book, changes little whatever type of home-located production is put under the spotlight. This is even more remarkable when one considers the different methodological approaches and conceptual tools adopted by researchers around the world.

Typically studies show that the average age of people working at home tends to be late thirties or early forties (Kraut and Grambsch 1987: 414; Gerson 1993: 232; Deming 1994: 6; Laurie and Taylor 1995: 11; Lui 1994: 114; Wong 1983: 3; McLennan 1996: 6). This is higher than the workforce as a whole. Average age for men outstrips that for women by several years, reflecting the fact that women tend to start working at home earlier than men – often in their twenties. Another approach is to examine the proportions of each age group who work at home. This shows that the likelihood of working at home is greater among older age groups. In Canada, for example, those aged 65 and over are more than twice as likely to work at home than those ten years younger and more than six times as likely as those in their early years (Nadwodny 1996: 18). This pattern is repeated in many countries, the only difference being one of degree. A variety of explanations have been put forward for this pattern. Mandatory retirement and ageist recruitment policies, for example, may encourage older workers to find a job which enables them to work at home or to start a home-located business of their own. Older workers generally are more likely than younger people to have the knowledge and capital necessary to become self-employed. Working at home may appeal to some older workers because of the extra income and the flexibility that this work arrangement can provide. Some may choose to work at home as a way of easing themselves into retirement, while still contributing to their organisation or company.

The published evidence suggests that homeworkers, as we define them, have a slightly younger age profile than other types of home-located producer. Allen and Wolkowitz (1987: 75), for example, found many home-located wage labourers in their sample to be in their late twenties or early thirties. Our own study of home-working (Felstead and Jewson 1996: 26) found much the same: two-fifths of our respondents were in their thirties, one-fifth were in their late twenties. Very few were retired. The only notable exception to this pattern is in Japan, where home-workers are more likely to be in their forties. Moreover, the age profile of Japanese homeworkers has tended to rise over time as more and more young women have instead taken part-time work in factories and offices (Suzuki 1993: 3; Kyoto Labour Standards Bureau 1994: 14).

The age profile of home-located producers – especially that of women – is often assumed to reflect their marital status and childcare responsibilities. Accordingly, it is to these variables that we turn next.

Marital status and parenthood

A relatively uniform picture of home-located production and its constituent types can also be painted as far as marital status is concerned. Study after study has shown that around three-quarters or more of men and women who work at home – in whatever capacity – are married or cohabiting (Christensen 1989: 185; McLennan 1996: 7; Siroonian 1993: 50; Felstead 1996: 231; Hakim 1987a: 43; Phizacklea and Wolkowitz 1995: 74; Huws 1994: 4). This is higher than the rate for the workforce as a whole.

Given the older age profile of those who work at home and the greater the like-lihood that they are living with a partner, it comes as little surprise to find that they are more likely to be parents than others in the labour market. Moreover, women in all categories of home-located production are more likely than their male counterparts to be parents. This is corroborated in study after study in many parts of the world and for all types of home-located production. The data suggest that working mothers in particular are more likely to work at home while their children are of pre-school age (e.g., Akyeampong 1997: 49: Deming 1994: 17; Felstead and Jewson 1996: 26). It is largely based on these findings that the stereotype of the woman working at home with her children at her heels has assumed its prominence.

For many writers the heart of the gender issue concerns childcare. It is very often argued that women take up what may be regarded as a disadvantaged form of employment because of their pressing need to combine earning an income with looking after a young family. Indeed many interviews with respondents elicit such a response. This is assumed to be the reason for the presence of women particularly among lower paid forms of home-located production such as homeworking. There are, however, various problems with these arguments. First, they do not appear to provide an explanation for the presence of men in this kind of work. Second, it does not explain why some women *without* young children become home-located producers. The numbers of these are not inconsiderable. In the US, for example, the Current Population Survey found that around four-fifths of home-located producers do not have pre-school children living with them (Deming 1994: 17). US Census data on those doing white-collar work at home suggest much the same (Kraut and Grambsch 1987: 37). Even American magazine surveys produce remarkably similar results (Christensen 1989: 185). In Britain official data suggests that around half of all those working at home have no dependent children (Laurie and Taylor 1995: 42). Figures for homeworkers, as we define them, are of a similar magnitude. Felstead's (1996: 231) analysis of the Spring 1994 LFS data revealed that 48 per cent of female homeworkers did not have dependent children. The number of male homeworkers without children was greater at 67 per cent. Even the National Group on Homeworking (NGH) survey (Huws 1994), which appears to have generated a sample among some of the most deprived homeworkers, found that a quarter of their respondents had no children (94 per cent being female). Hakim (1987a: 21, 54) found that one-third of homeworkers in manufacturing (roughly equivalent to our category of homeworking) did not have children (91 per cent being female).

In summary, the points we have made about age, marital status and parenthood both confirm and contradict the stereotypes of those who work at home. The likelihood of being a home-located producer increases with age but a high proportion of homeworkers are in early adulthood (twenties and thirties). This is often explained by their responsibility for childcare. Parenthood is also commonly seen as accounting for the gender composition of homeworkers. However, remarkably enough, quantitative evidence from many different sources shows that a high proportion of home-located producers in general and homeworkers in particular do not have young children living with them at home.

Probability of working at home

So far, the discussion has sought to profile types of home-located production in terms of the characteristics of those engaged in it. From these pictures, more refined inferences can be drawn about which kinds of people are likely to be involved. One way of extending this analysis is to carry out multivariate analysis on the quantitative statistics reported earlier. This technique isolates the impact that each independent variable (such as sex, age and education) has on the probability of someone working at home, holding all other factors constant. It can, for example, determine whether a woman is more likely than a man to do particular types of home-located production even though in all other respects they are identical (i.e., same age, education level, etc.). Alternatively, one can isolate whether certain characteristics have different effects on the probability of men or women working at home – the presence of children, for example.

The technique, then, promises much. However, in practice its role is circumscribed in several ways. First, it is restricted to data sets which contain information on those working at home as well as on those working elsewhere, so that comparisons can be made. In the main, this criterion means that the only data amenable to multivariate analysis are those contained in official surveys such as population censuses and labour force surveys. Other studies which focus on various types of home-located production often do not contain comparator groups of workplace-located individuals. Second, there are currently only a few multivariate studies from which to draw. These have been carried out in the US, New Zealand and Hong Kong. What makes this all the more surprising is the availability of similar data sets in many of the countries covered in the course of this book. This certainly presents a research opportunity that others may wish to pursue.

Another problem is that data sources, definitions and foci vary. Take the US studies, for example (Kraut 1988; Presser and Bamberger 1993). Kraut (1988) bases his work on the 1980 US Census and the Microdata, while the Presser and Bamberger (1993) study is based on the 1985 Current Population Survey (CPS). This leads to a series of technical differences in the way in which information is operationalised and analysed. The foci of the studies differ in other ways too. Presser and Bamberger (1993) focus on women only. Kraut (1988) analyses both sexes but examines men and women separately. Another difference is that Presser and Bamberger (1993) examine working at home in its broadest sense (i.e., home-located production), while Kraut (1988) only looks at those working in white collar occupations (a sample which cuts across our typology).

Despite these differences the results generated by these two American studies are broadly in line with one another. Both found the odds of working at home rose with age. The presence of children, particularly pre-schoolers, had the expected effect of raising the probability of women working at home, but made little difference as far as men were concerned. However, the findings did not support the popular view that poorly educated women are more likely to work at home. The results suggested that working at home – either fully or partly – is more likely among better qualified women, holding all other things constant. These studies also question the suggestion that ethnic minorities are more likely to participate in this type of work. Indeed, the findings suggest the complete opposite. One should, however, be cautious of accepting these particular findings at face value. After all, Presser and Bamberger (1993) and Kraut (1988) examine a category of employment which approximates to home-located production. They do not focus on homeworking where clusters of disadvantaged groups of workers are more likely to be found.

The New Zealand study (Loveridge *et al.* 1996) – based on the 1986 New Zealand Census – demonstrates the importance of disaggregating broad categories that capture home-located producers of all kinds. The results show that the odds of working at home change with an individual's characteristics and the type of work they undertake. Thus, in New Zealand women are five times more likely to be working at home in manufacturing jobs than men, six times more likely to be doing so if they do not possess post-compulsory qualifications and ten times more likely to be working at home in this industry if they are wage earners (ibid.: table 3). Although not directly comparable to our conception of homeworking, these results approximate to it. They suggest that poorly educated women are the more likely individuals to engage in homeworking.

By focusing exclusively on women who work at home in manufacturing (which again approximates to our definition of homeworking), the Hong Kong study suggests why this might be the case (Wong 1983). It shows a tendency for some mothers to switch from working as on-site workers to become 'manufacturing homeworkers' when their children are young, and then gradually switch back as their children get older. In other words, this is consistent with the image of homework as an intermediate option between on-site working and not working at all, thereby allowing mothers to combine caring for their children while not giving up paid work.

In summary, it must be emphasised that multivariate analysis reveals *probabilities* and *likelihoods*. It does not preclude other possibilities. Therefore it should not be regarded as detracting from the picture of diversity that has emerged in earlier sections of the chapter.

Conclusion

Those wishing to trumpet the virtues of working at home typically paint a rosy picture. They emphasise the liberating experience of being able to reintegrate work with home life, the savings made by doing away with the daily commute and the environmental benefits of reduced pollution levels and the like (e.g., Toffler 1980: 204–217). Diametrically opposed to this image, is that of the mother of small children toiling over a sewing machine in the front room of a terraced house. Those seeking to protect and improve the conditions of the most vulnerable homeworkers have portrayed them as women hemmed in by childcare responsibilities and with little option but to work at home to support their families.

What this chapter has shown is that both images contain an element of truth. This is because home-located production is a heterogeneous form of employment. Different types of home-located production involve different kinds of people. The gender, ethnic and educational make-up of those engaged in home-located production *as a whole* should not, therefore, be taken as a guide to the social characteristics of those engaged in a particular type.

In addition, a further important lesson has emerged from the analysis contained in this chapter. Among those engaged in each type of home-located production are to be found individuals who are not typical of the group as a whole. We have seen, for example, that – depending on which data set is used – between a fifth and a half of all female homeworkers in Britain do not have young children, that a fifth of all homeworkers are male and that a minority are highly qualified. In short, there are substantial numbers of homeworkers who defy simple categorisation and challenge well established explanations for their behaviour. It is true that certain kinds of people are more likely to take up this kind of employment – as multivariate analysis suggests – but there remain many who simply do not fit the stereotype.

Our review of quantitative data from around the world has revealed, therefore, significant contrasts within and between different types of home-located production. Our conclusion, then, is that homeworking in particular – and home-located production in general – is characterised by greater diversity than is commonly recognised.

Chapter 6

Documenting the grim realities

The economic condition of their [homeworkers'] labour is extremely serious. It is only occasionally that an approximate living is earned. For the
most part the weekly wages are monstrously small, and the hours of work
cruelly long . . . In short, the economic conditions are as bad as they could
be, and entail immense suffering upon a great number of persons . . . with
no means of organising their labour and no voice to reach the authorities.
But, besides this, home work and out work involve dangers, not only to the
health of the workers but to that of the whole community.

(Smith 1902: 461–462)

The picture of homeworking is in many ways a profoundly depressing one.
Homeworkers in Britain today are clearly experiencing such immense problems of low pay, isolation, insecurity and health hazards that it may be
tempting to some commentators to suggest that this form of employment
should be outlawed altogether.

(Huws 1994: 36)

Introduction

The aim of this chapter is to document and interpret existing research findings on
the working conditions of home-located producers in general and homeworkers
in particular. As we have seen in previous chapters, measuring the extent of home-
located production and identifying who actually does this type of work are not
easy tasks to undertake. Without a conceptual framework it is difficult, if not
impossible, to reconcile the conflicting estimates and pictures presented in the
existing literature since the focus of investigation changes from study to study (see
Chapters 4 and 5). However, analyses of working conditions have, with only a few
exceptions, a much narrower focus; in fact, one much nearer to our conception of
what constitutes homeworking. As a result, many more 'like with like' comparisons can be made. Not surprisingly, therefore, the picture presented is more
consistent. In short, it is one characterised by low pay, hidden costs, health hazards and the absence of benefits. Where there is debate it concerns how bad
conditions are.

What is surprising is how little appears to have changed over more than a century. Many of the conditions reported at the beginning of the twentieth century are much the same as those of today. It would appear that the lot of the homeworker has changed little with the passage of time. The examples of poor conditions are endless and not confined to a particular point in time nor to a few isolated countries in the world (Council of Europe 1989; ILO 1989). These have been described by media stories and campaign groups. The pictures presented by research studies are remarkably consistent despite being conducted at different historical moments in time, in different countries and using different research techniques. Their main findings will be summarised in this chapter under the headings: pay and conditions, health and safety, legislative regulation, and organisation and protection.

Pay and benefits

There are two senses in which homeworkers may be said to be disadvantaged as far as pay and conditions are concerned. First, they comprise some of the lowest paid workers in the entire labour force. Hence, in terms of any *absolute* measure of poverty, they are among the worst off. Second, the terms and conditions of homeworkers are often poorer than those of their workplace-located counterparts. In this regard, they may be described as disadvantaged *relative* to their peers. The pattern of relative disadvantage may well be characteristic of home-located production in general. Thus, professionals and managers who work at home in high discretion occupations typically earn more than homeworkers (Hakim 1987a). However, their remuneration may fall below that of office-located colleagues and their career opportunities may be narrower. It has to be said that there is far more hard evidence about absolute levels of deprivation than about relative disadvantage *vis-à-vis* comparable others. Nevertheless, some researchers have sought to explore the full range of inequalities faced by home-located producers (Kraut and Grambsch 1987). Others may follow in their footsteps.

The association of homeworking with low pay and poor conditions of employment is commonplace. The research evidence in support of this view has rarely come from official national data sets since many of these do not collect usable information on issues such as pay (e.g., censuses in several countries). Instead figures are largely drawn from smaller scale surveys, some of which have a local focus, which have searched for subjects by techniques such as door-knocking, direct appeals and chasing known points of contact (see Chapter 3, pp. 29–40).

Without doubt, pay rates are headlined by researchers and those who lobby on behalf of homeworkers. Survey after survey has shown that pay is low, both as measured against workers doing similar jobs and against standard indices of low pay. For example, in toy manufacturing, it was found that 82 per cent of homeworkers in Britain earned less than the statutory minimum rates in force at the time (ACAS 1978b: 45). A survey of wages in the clothing industry found eight times as many homeworkers as on-site workers with rates of pay below the minimum specified for the industry (Hakim and Dennis 1982). Some surveys have uncovered very low rates of pay indeed. For example, Brown (1974: 8–10) gave an example of a homeworker crocheting baby boots and another knitting Aran sweaters for just one-twentieth of the average hourly rate of pay for manual work at the time. This finding is corroborated by studies using a range of *different* ways of searching for subjects. These include radio appeals (Brown 1974), adverts in the printed media (Crine 1979; Huws 1984; Bisset and Huws 1984), publicity campaigns (Yorkshire and Humberside Low Pay Unit 1991) and doorstep surveys (Hope *et al.* 1976; Allen and Wolkowitz 1987; Felstead and Jewson 1996, 1997). Similarly, the National Homeworking Survey of 1981 found that almost seven out of ten (69 per cent) of those working at home in manufacturing were low paid according to a definition used at the time (Hakim 1987a: 106).

The picture presented by our survey (Felstead and Jewson 1996) is much the same. However, before discussing these findings it is important to outline how these data were collected. Homeworkers themselves often do not consider their income in relation to the time it takes them to complete the work. Our estimates of the hourly rate of pay were, therefore, derived from three sources. First, a minority of respondents were paid on an hourly basis and were able to indicate an hourly rate. Second, those who were paid by the piece were asked to indicate how much they were paid per item and to provide information about their pace of work so that an hourly rate could be calculated. However, while some homeworkers could state how much they earned per week and how much they received per item, they were decidedly vague about how much time they spent doing the work. In these cases, a third method of calculation was used. Here, the rate was derived by dividing average weekly pay by average weekly hours of work. We were unable to collect data on hourly rates of pay in around one in seven cases, due to either a flat refusal by respondents to answer questions on their wages or an inability to provide sufficient information. Occasionally homeworkers revealed that wages were paid in kind by their employer, such as buying toys for the children. Nevertheless, the study was able to derive an hourly rate of pay for 287 homeworkers out of the 338 successfully interviewed in the August 1994 to January 1995 period.

To give our figures meaning, it is important to compare the hourly rates homeworkers receive with various indices of low pay for the period. The Council of Europe's decency threshold, pitched at 68 per cent of full-time average earnings, was equivalent to £5.88 per hour in 1994. The Low Pay Unit's definition is set at two-thirds of median male earnings, which, in 1994, was £5.53 per hour. Another often used definition sets the threshold at half median male earnings – £4.16 per hour in 1994 (Low Pay Unit 1995: 1). The average pay of homeworkers falls well below all of these thresholds. According to our results, they receive on average £3.03 per hour. Moreover, the vast majority of homeworkers surveyed were low paid: 93 per cent earned less than the Council of Europe's threshold, the same proportion earned less than the Low Pay Unit's definition and 84 per cent earned less than half the hourly rate of pay of median male earners. Even adopting a lower threshold, many would still be deemed low paid. A level of £3.60 – the UK National Minimum Wage figure for 1999 – would capture just over three-quarters of all the homeworkers we surveyed. Legislation to protect workers from low pay might, therefore, help to raise the income of the vast majority of Britain's homeworkers.

This picture is remarkably similar to that revealed by Allen and Wolkowitz's (1987) survey of home-located wage labour in West Yorkshire in the late 1970s. Their study showed that 92 per cent of home-located wage labourers earned less than the commonly used definitions of low pay of the time (ibid.: 99). Not surprisingly, the proportion deemed to be low paid falls as soon as the type of home-located production under focus is widened. Nevertheless, in the Autumn 1997 UK Labour Force Survey, a third of home-located producers who describe themselves as employees had rates of pay below £3.60 per hour (President of the Board of Trade 1998: 42, 141).

Some of the homeworkers we interviewed received extremely low rates of pay indeed (Felstead and Jewson 1996). Around one in eight were paid less than £1 an hour. These were doing a range of activities and were drawn from a cross-section of the working population. For example, our sample included a White mother who earned £3.50 for every 100 bows she made from ribbon supplied by her employer. Despite having long-standing experience, she was only able to complete an order every six hours. She then had to count, pack and bag up the completed work before returning it to the factory. Another woman with a similar background painted ornamental cottages of various sizes for eventual sale in several well known high street stores. Each cottage required the application of 14 separate colours, with drying time required in between. Even by painting several cottages simultaneously, each took between one and a half and two hours to complete. The piece rate ranged from 65p to £1.00 per item, working out at less than 50p per hour. Some homeworkers reported still lower rates of pay, including those whose products were eventually destined for well known companies and even trade unions. For instance, one female homeworker reported being paid 5p for each advertising folder she assembled from a printed piece of card. The process entailed scoring, folding and gluing (sometimes re-gluing) the appropriate parts together. After this, the folders had to be counted, bundled up, placed in a box and sealed with masking tape ready for collection by the agent. She estimated that, at best, it was possible for her to make-up five folders in an hour, equivalent to an hourly rate of 25p. This did not include the time spent packing the folders for collection.

Men, too, were represented among some of the poorest paid homeworkers we surveyed. In one case, a White married man with two young children was packing nails. This entailed bagging up into packs of 100, sealing the plastic bags with a hot press and putting 10 bags into a box for collection. He was paid 13p for each box completed and was able to do six boxes in an hour. This worked out at less than 80p per hour.

Ethnic minority workers were also represented among the poorest paid homeworkers we surveyed. For example, we discovered a case of an Indian woman cooking vegetable and meat samosas at home for a local restaurant. Her piece rate was £1.50 for 200 samosas. She estimated that each batch took her two hours to complete, thereby making her rate of pay 75p per hour. Also included within our sample was a Bangladeshi woman who spoke no English at all (our interview with her was conducted in Bengali) who was paid 14p for each garment overlocked. She claimed to complete 5–6 garments in an hour. On this basis, her hourly rate was, at best, 84p. Another Bangladeshi woman, who also spoke no English due to her recent arrival in Britain, earned 60p per hour for pairing, folding and labelling socks – her piece rate was 10p per dozen. Rates of pay for this type of work, however, varied substantially, and so, too, did homeworkers' productivity.

In our survey the lowest rates of pay were not the *sole* preserve of homeworkers with particular social characteristics, as the examples above serve to illustrate. Nevertheless, it is the case that *average* rates of pay differed markedly according to homeworkers' gender, ethnicity and locality (cf. Phizacklea and Wolkowitz 1995, who claim that home-located production is also racialised and gendered). In the sample as a whole, male homeworkers received an average hourly rate of £3.91 (N=18) compared to just £2.85 (N=264) for women. Differences were also apparent by ethnicity. Hourly pay rates varied from £3.36 for White respondents (N=135), £3.31 for Indians (N=50), £2.57 for Bangladeshis (N=30), £2.39 for Black Caribbeans (N=12), £1.64 for Kutchis (N=13) and £1.53 for respondents of Turkish origin (N=24). What is more surprising, though, is the finding that pay rates varied markedly by local area. Pay rates ranged from £2.64 and £2.77 per hour in two areas renowned for their use of homeworking to much higher rates of pay in the two areas with less of a historical legacy (£3.26 and £4.19).

The recent work of the National Group on Homeworking (NGH) suggests that wage rates are even lower (Huws 1994). Their average figure is £1.28 an hour – less than half that of our survey (ibid.: 20). Inevitably, this prompts the question of why there is a discrepancy between these figures, especially as the findings are so close in many other respects. Here, we offer some possible explanations.

First, the studies were conducted during different time periods. The NGH's survey was carried out over a two-year period beginning in 1991, whereas our survey was carried out over a six-month period beginning in August 1994. The time lapse accounts for some of the difference, although growth in earnings was relatively modest at around 4 per cent per annum. A related point is that while our sample comprised currently active homeworkers or those who had been doing homeworking during the previous 12 months, a third of the NGH's sample consisted of lapsed homeworkers (Huws 1994: 16). The more retrospective the data, the lower rates of pay are likely to be.

Second, there were differences in the character of the locations studied in the two surveys. The NGH interviewed 175 homeworkers in traditional homeworking locations – Leeds, Rochdale, Oldham, London, Nottingham, Birmingham, Manchester, Leicester, Wakefield and Calderdale. All of these are predominantly urban areas served by local campaigning groups, as is readily acknowledged by the author (Huws 1994: 2). Our survey suggests that this is likely to reduce reported wage levels. If one focuses on the two traditional homeworking areas in our survey, the hourly rate of pay drops to £2.68 – although this is still substantially above that of the NGH.

A third factor may be differences in techniques adopted in searching for subjects. In the case of the NGH, interviewees were selected from those with whom local campaigns had been in contact, whereas over four-fifths of our sample had had no contact at all with local homeworking campaigns or support groups. Instead our sample was generated by a range of techniques including doorstep surveys, 'snow-balling', various proactive community based approaches, a mail-shot to selected institutions and a diverse collection of advertising strategies. The NGH sample was, therefore, more likely to contain homeworkers who sought help from support organisations in coping with the worst excesses of homeworking.

Fourth, there may be differences in the methods of calculation and the proto-cols adopted in the two studies. Regrettably, it is by no means clear how the NGH survey arrives at a figure of £1.28 per hour. It is simply reported without expla-nation. Given the widely acknowledged difficulties in making such a calculation in the context of homeworking, this omission is indeed glaring (see Hope *et al.* 1976). It leaves several crucial questions unanswered. Does the NGH rate take into account unpaid work? This might include tasks such as counting, bagging up, folding, separating different sizes into bundles/boxes, folding and packing fin-ished goods, trimming and ironing. Over two-fifths of our respondents (43 per cent) said that they were expected to undertake additional unpaid work of this kind. Inclusion of this in calculating an hourly rate of pay would close the gap between our figure and that reported by the NGH. Homeworkers may also incur a variety of costs in carrying out work in their own homes. Do the NGH's figures take these costs into account? These include the provision of a work environment, expenses entailed in arranging or collecting goods, the costs of running and maintaining equipment and materials consumed in the process. Our survey sug-gests that homeworkers routinely meet such costs, including lighting (78 per cent), heating (73 per cent), telephone calls (62 per cent), electricity for running machines (58 per cent), materials used in the work process (e.g., cleaning mate-rials, needles, cotton, etc.) (39 per cent), repair of machines (38 per cent), purchase of machines (32 per cent), travel (e.g., to collect work) (23 per cent), workbench (13 per cent), postage (12 per cent), protective equipment (e.g., gog-gles, masks, overalls, gloves, etc.) (12 per cent), rental of machines (7 per cent) and other (9 per cent). Incorporation of these costs in calculating the hourly rate would also narrow the gap between the two estimates.

Problems in deriving pay rates are not confined to Britain. Much the same story can be repeated for many countries around the world, although there are techni-cal and conceptual problems in interpreting their research results. The Australian example is typical. Australia can boast several studies of home-located working. However, only a handful collect any pay data at all, and of these only a few focus on people we would define as homeworkers. To make matters worse, the pay data are sometimes quoted without an appropriate comparator set alongside – and hence have little meaning to an international audience. For example, three separate studies carried out in the late 1980s collected data on women who did clerical work at home, yielding a range of pay rates from A$7 to A$45 per hour (Cummings 1986: 25; Dawson and Turner 1989: 30; Probert and Wacjman 1988b: 442–444). The absence of a comparator group, or an indication of average pay levels at the time, makes it difficult to assess the extent to which these figures should be greeted with alarm. Other studies, though, do suggest that the pay of homeworkers (as we define them) is relatively low. For example, O'Donnell (1987: 7) cites a report which suggests that many clothing homeworkers earned between A$2 and A$3 per hour in 1985, while their factory counterparts received treble that amount. More recently Brosnan and Thornthwaite's (1997: 12) study of a Queensland furniture manufacturer suggests that homeworkers get substantially less than their factory counterparts for the same type of work – A$5 and A$8 per hour respectively.

Other problems beset the official national data sets on which we have drawn in previous chapters. Many simply do not collect pay data; for example, the US Current Population Survey. Hence, none of the published results are able to compare rates of pay according to work location (cf. Horvath 1986; Deming 1994). Only recently have income questions been added to the LFS in Britain. This, coupled with questions on work location (re-introduced in 1992), has provided researchers with an opportunity which has yet to be fully explored. The same goes for the periodic Canadian Survey of Work Arrangements, with the initial results of the 1995 survey being published only recently (Akyeampong 1997). More progress has been made using the Australian LFS which already reports weekly incomes by industrial sector (McLennan 1996: 13). Similarly, not all censuses collect pay data: for example, New Zealand (Loveridge et al. 1996), Britain (Felstead and Jewson 1995) and India (Dholakia 1989). Those that do include Canada, the US and Australia.

According to the Canadian Census people working at home generally earn less than those who work outside the home. Self-employed people working at home full- or part-time, as well as paid employees who worked at home full-time, were less likely than their counterparts who worked outside of the home to earn C$20,000 or more in 1991. More specifically, some 29 per cent of self-employed women who worked at home full-time earned C$20,000 or more, compared with 44 per cent of those who worked outside the home. Paid employees working at home part-time, however, earned more than part-timers outside the home. This was true for both men and women (Nadwodny 1996: 19).

These findings must be tempered by the knowledge that those who work at home do so in different occupations and possess different personal characteristics than their workplace-located counterparts. Work on the US Census has taken these differences into account (Kraut and Grambsch 1987; Kraut 1988). The focus of this research has been on a particular occupational slice of those who work at home – white-collar work. These jobs include lawyers, accountants, computer analysts, bookkeepers and secretaries, irrespective of whether in our terms they are wage labourers, petty commodity producers or home-located employers. In other words, the focus is not on homeworkers as we would define them, but on home-located producers who happen to do white-collar work. The findings reveal that those who work at home in white-collar jobs tend to be older, more likely to have some kind of disability and less likely to live in urban areas. It might be argued that these factors could negatively affect income levels to a greater degree than work-place location. By using multiple regression, it is possible to assess the effect that workplace location has on income while holding all other factors constant. Such an analysis suggests that those who work at home in white-collar jobs earn as little as two-thirds of the income of conventional workers (Kraut 1988: 41). This result is achieved after controlling for variables such as: age, whether the home is in an urban or rural area, ethnicity, years of schooling, self-employment, family structure variables, the presence or absence of disability, and some of their inter-actions. In other words, spatial location matters.

Another interesting facet of this US study concerns the incomes of people in different jobs. Some 17 occupations were included, spanning the spectrum of white-collar work. In all but three, they earned less. For example, lawyers work-ing at home earned just over half (51 per cent) the income earned by their office-based counterparts, while accountants fared little better getting 63 per cent of the income their office-based colleagues received (Kraut 1988: table 2.4). It is possible that these income differences reflect subtle variations within occu-pations. In other words, lower paid specialities – like conveyancing or doing the company accounts of a small family firm – may be done at home, while higher paid specialities – like corporate law or auditing the accounts of a large, multinational corporation – may be done in a conventional office environment. None the less, the results suggest that home-located producers of all types suffer *relative* disad-vantage compared to their workplace-located peers. Indeed, this disadvantage may be greatest among otherwise affluent groups of individuals such as lawyers and accountants. Further research is required here.

The Australian Census results have also been analysed, if only patchily, for insights into the link between pay and working at home (Walker 1987: 32–37). This suggests that working at home in textiles, clothing and footwear is associated with lower income than working in more traditional premises. Moreover, the dis-advantage may be even greater than the data reveal. First, the Census collects data on income which may include social security payments as well as earnings from a job. Second, the relationship between hours worked and income may be distorted, since working at home in these industries is often characterised by an irregular work flow. Income data is collected on a yearly basis, whereas the hours of work data refer to the week immediately before the Census day. Third, to the extent that home-workers work longer unpaid hours than their factory counterparts, their incomes will be overestimated. Fourth, the likely bias of the sample towards those working at home 'on the books' will tend to raise recorded incomes.

So far, this chapter has assembled fragmentary pieces of evidence from around the world. Nevertheless, a remarkably consistent story emerges. Our survey of the literature has revealed that the lowest rates of pay tend to be concentrated among those who come closest to our concept of homeworkers, although all those who work at home – in whatever capacity – appear to 'pay for the privilege'. However, home-located producers are penalised in other ways too. For example, in the US Gerson and Kraut (1988: table 3.1) found that compared to their office-located counterparts, secretaries working at home were half as likely to receive company-sponsored health benefits or social security contributions and only an eighth as likely to have paid holidays. Fringe benefits were rarely offered to those home-workers we surveyed in Britain (Felstead and Jewson 1996: 74). Very low proportions of our sample received sick pay (7 per cent), holiday pay (6 per cent), retainer whilst not working (2 per cent), redundancy notice (6 per cent), redundancy pay (1 per cent), maternity pay (5 per cent) and access to a company pension scheme (1 per cent). Australian data suggests a similar pattern, with 28 per cent of those who work at home entitled to sick pay, 29 per cent eligible for holiday pay and 58 per cent covered by superannuation provided by their current employer (McLennan 1996: 3–4).

Health and safety

Historically, the health and safety of homeworkers has been of special concern for several reasons. Modern homes, unlike factories and offices, have rarely been designed and built with work in mind. As a result, the home is unlikely to incorporate features which provide a safe working environment, such as extractor fans, machine guards, specialised storage facilities for hazardous substances and temperature control. Furthermore, working and living in the same space means that work materials and equipment have to compete with household furniture, children's toys, the washing and even food. Any hazards which result are more likely to affect other household members than when contained outside the home. Children, the elderly and the infirm are particularly at risk. Another source of concern stems from the dispersed nature of homeworking activity and the tendency for those involved to conceal it from view. This makes it difficult for information about safe working practices to be passed onto homeworkers who might not otherwise be aware of how to minimise the risks and hazards.

Against such a background it is not surprising that many surveys report that homeworkers are exposed to serious health and safety hazards. Our survey asked homeworkers whether they or any members of their household had suffered accidents, injuries or ill health caused by work done at home. A fifth (21 per cent) of the sample reported that they had experienced difficulties of this kind. Probably the most common accident reported by our interview respondents was injury to fingers or hands from sewing needles. In a number of cases these required hospital or other medical treatment. The next most common complaints were backache, pains in the joints, aches and pains in the shoulders and arms. Respondents related this to the poorly designed or improvised workstations which they used. Cuts to the hands were also a familiar hazard, as were a variety of respiratory problems – particularly asthma. Smaller numbers of respondents referred to specific problems associated with particular kinds of work. These included fumes, skin allergies, noise induced hearing problems, burns, headaches and sickness due to fumes. In addition to injuries sustained by homeworkers themselves, a number of respondents referred to accidents affecting their children. These comprised two main problems: cuts and injuries sustained from machinery, and respiratory problems (particularly asthma) caused or aggravated by dust, fibres and other materials (Felstead and Jewson 1996: 61–64). Homeworkers may also encounter a series of specific nuisances and problems associated with working and living in the same space. According to our survey the most common of these was the competition for space (60 per cent), closely followed by dirt (59 per cent), excessive noise (34 per cent), unpleasant smells (23 per cent), fire hazards (19 per cent) and electrical dangers (11 per cent) (ibid.: table 9.2).

Surveys based on different methodologies and conducted at different times corroborate this picture for Britain (e.g., Bisset and Huws 1984: 31–32; Huws 1994: 24–30). There is also evidence that similar problems confront homeworkers world-wide. In Italy and Spain, the public authorities are reportedly concerned about the introduction of hazardous materials and processes into the home without environmental controls and monitoring, particularly in the leather and textile trades (Council of Europe 1989: 23). These concerns have focused around the toxic fumes given off during the processing of hides and leather. Similar concerns are in evidence elsewhere. For example, 'beedi' (cigarette) rolling – a common homeworking activity in India – carries the risk of nicotine poisoning contracted through the skin from repeated and prolonged exposure to tobacco. In the Philippines, the concerns centre around reports of hand injuries and other wounds sustained by rattan (cane) workers. These injuries come from handling sharp rattan poles and also from the constant and prolonged sanding and finishing of furniture parts (ILO 1994: 24).

More recently, Australian evidence suggests that homeworkers are more likely than their factory counterparts to face health and safety dangers. A comparison of 100 factory workers in the garment trade with 100 similarly placed homeworkers found that homeworkers were more than three times as likely as their factory counterparts to suffer injury. This can be attributed to the combination of low pay, which led to very long working hours, and the pressure placed upon them to meet tight deadlines (Mayhew and Quinlan 1998).

Legislative regulation

Despite these relatively poor terms and conditions of employment, homeworkers often have little means of redress, legislative or otherwise (see also pp. 168–170). The ILO examined the legislative provisions of some 150 member states and identified those applicable to homeworkers (ILO 1989). Legislative regulation comes in three forms. First, some countries have specific legislation. For example, Japan, Argentina and the Netherlands have laws governing the use of homeworkers. This group also includes countries which have legislation relating to certain industries or activities where homework traditionally occurs. Examples here include the Indian regulations on 'beedi' and cigar manufacture, and the Portuguese regulation of embroidery homeworkers on the island of Madeira. In all, 21 countries come into this category.

The second group of countries are those whose labour law includes explicit references to homeworkers. According to the ILO (1989: 31), 17 countries still have regulations of this sort, including many in Latin America, Scandinavia and Britain. So, for example, minimum rates of pay for homeworkers in Wages Council industries in Britain were part of the wage setting framework below which wages were not (legally) allowed to fall. Similarly, under the Factories Act 1961 employers were required to register homeworkers, as specified in the Homework Orders 1911–1913 and 1929, with the local authority. Both these protections have since been repealed – the Wages Councils were abolished in 1993 and the registration requirements under the Factories Act were repealed in 1995. However, explicit reference to homeworkers has recently surfaced once again – this time in the National Minimum Wage legislation.

The third and most numerous group of countries are those which make no specific reference to homeworking in either dedicated legislation or as part of their overall legal framework. The ILO report suggests that around 110 countries fall into this category. Here, the nature of the employment relationship becomes ever more critical since only by proving employee status is it possible to access the protections commonly accorded to employees by national labour law.

In all three types of national regulatory regimes, however, the issue of employment status remains problematic and contentious. Typically the self-employed have far fewer protections than employees. Legal status, therefore, assumes great importance in many countries of the world, irrespective of the existence or otherwise of protective legislation. This can only be determined by examining the nature of the employment relationship. However, it is frequently the case that homeworkers find their employment status is confused, ambiguous, uncertain and fraught with legal difficulties. In order to illustrate the issues this raises, we concentrate on the arguments used in British case law as well as the results of our survey. The discussion serves to highlight the contradictions surrounding the employment status of homeworkers in Britain and elsewhere (Roxby 1984).

The importance of these legal decisions cannot be overemphasised. According to our survey around a third of homeworkers regarded themselves as self-employed and a similar proportion believed their supplier of work regarded them as such. A further 15 per cent were unable to describe their employment relationship and 20 per cent did not know how they were regarded by their supplier of work. In other words, about half of the homeworkers we surveyed were labelled as self-employed by one party or other to the relationship (Felstead and Jewson 1996: 72). Left unchallenged this leaves them excluded from employment protection offered to employees. These protections include redundancy pay, minimum notice of termination, guaranteed lay-off pay, maternity pay and maternity leave, protection from unfair dismissal and minimum pay rates.

In Britain, when homeworkers have turned to the law to clarify their employment status, three issues in particular have been examined by the courts: supervision, continuity and ancillary support. One of the grounds on which to mount a claim to employee status revolves around the extent to which the homeworking labour process is supervised by the employer (e.g., *D'Ambrogio* v. *Hyman Jacobs Ltd* [1978] IRLR 236 IT). In this particular case, it was the degree of control exercised by the clothing firm over the trouser machinist that was the deciding factor. The regularity of the employer's visits was taken as evidence of control over the labour process deemed sufficient for a contract of service to be established. According to our survey of homeworkers in Britain a fifth are visited daily. Even though the 'control' test is no longer considered paramount, because of the greater autonomy employees now commonly enjoy at work, it is still sometimes considered. Moreover, homeworkers who are not visited regularly are unlikely to achieve (or sustain) employee status through this particular test.

The issue of continuity was raised by *Airfix Footwear Ltd* v. *Cope* [1978] ICR 1210 EAT, one of the most celebrated homeworking cases in Britain. Here the court accepted that although the relationship between employer and homeworker was sporadic, it was sufficiently regular to establish continuity of employment. Empirical studies suggest that most homeworkers have similarly long-standing relationships with their current supplier of work. One study estimates that three-quarters of homeworkers have been with their current supplier of work for over two years (Felstead 1996: 234), while another puts the figure at around a half (Felstead and Jewson 1996: 41).

Another celebrated case – *Nethermere (St Neots) Ltd* v. *Gardiner and Taverna* [1984] IRLR 239 CA – concerned two homeworkers who were supplied with variable amounts of work and could, in theory, fix their own hours of work, take time off when they wished and vary how many garments they were willing to take on any particular day or even take none at all on a particular day. However, in practice, both homeworkers worked 'whenever needed', rarely refused work and told the company well in advance when they planned to take a holiday. The court held that well-founded expectations of continuing homework by the regular giving and receiving of work over periods of a year or more constituted continuity and that each party had an irreducible minimum obligation to the other. The importance of this decision for homeworkers more generally is that it raises the odds of being able to claim (or sustain) employee status. Only a third of homeworkers actually have *specific* minimum work loads (Felstead and Jewson 1996: 45). Furthermore, homework is often seasonal or irregular – recent evidence suggests that over half of homeworkers are engaged in this type of work (ibid.: 45). *Nethermere* provides a precedent for linking stints of work provided they form part of a 'lengthy course of dealing', which in this case the provision of machinery was also taken to indicate (see also *Industrial Relations Law Bulletin* 1995; Adkin 1994).

The importance of ancillary support in defining employment status was high-lighted by *Bradley and Roberts* v. *Herrburger Brooks Ltd* (unreported) [1981] 4987/81–4988/81 IT). Here the tribunal considered a number of facts, but most crucially the case turned on the help the homeworkers received from their families in carrying out the work. This was taken as indicating that they were free to choose to do the job themselves or get others to do it on their behalf and hence could be deemed employers themselves. On this basis, those who regularly receive help from whatever quarter are prima facie less likely to successfully claim (or defend) employee status in IT cases than those who do not. The existing evidence suggests that many homeworkers fall into this category. For example, Hakim found that a quarter (27 per cent) of 'manufacturing homeworkers' had made use of assistants to carry out their work (1987a: 135). A similar proportion (30 per cent) of the homeworkers we surveyed said that they had been assisted by others, most of whom reported getting help occasionally or frequently. A majority said that a partner or spouse (57 per cent) was among those who offered assistance, followed by those who mentioned children (32 per cent), relatives (14 per cent) and friends (11 per cent). Most helpers did not receive payment for this work (Felstead and Jewson 1996: 37, 46–47). Allen and Wolkowitz's (1987) study came up with much the same picture – 39 out of 90 reported using the help of others, with husbands being the most common source, followed by children and other adult relatives (ibid.: 131).

These and other cases illustrate that much confusion still remains in British law about the legal status of homeworkers. Decisions by different courts often appear to be contradictory. This is best illustrated by the case of a homeworker who was defined by the High Court as self-employed for tax and National Insurance pur-poses, but was an employee – according to an Industrial Tribunal – when it came to redundancy pay. The case involved the *same* homeworker doing the *same* work under the *same* conditions (*Patel* v. *HM Inspector of Taxes* (unreported) [1995] CD; *Patel* v. *Map Textiles Ltd* (unreported) [1996] 48637/95 IT).

Organisation and protection

Conventional trade unionism has made few inroads into the homeworking labour force; according to our survey only 5 per cent were members (Felstead and Jewson 1996: 55). Other studies have reported much the same. ACAS, for instance, found little evidence of trade unionism among homeworkers in toy manufacturing (ACAS 1978b: 48). Allen and Wolkowitz (1987: 142–146) found that some West Yorkshire home-located wage labourers saw unions as uninterested or unable to do anything for them. Trade union penetration is little better among home-located producers, where trade union density was 10 per cent in 1981 compared to a figure of 45 per cent for the working population as a whole (Hakim 1987a: 245). Recent Australian data tell much the same story. In 1995, around 4 per cent of those working at home, irrespective of their employment status or occupation, were trade union members compared to a third of the employed workforce (Lafferty et al. 1997: 154).

Those who work at home present organisational difficulties for trade unions, which have been almost exclusively concerned with mobilising workers at the factory or office level. Homeworkers are dispersed physically and rarely, if ever, meet together. They are often recruited by word of mouth and are unlikely to know more than a handful of others working for the same supplier of work. It is easy for suppliers of work to switch production among different homeworkers. Any who are difficult, critical or inefficient can be easily by-passed – this could apply to particular individuals or even entire neighbourhoods. Consequently, homeworkers are in a weak bargaining position. Whether real or imagined, many homeworkers are intimidated by fears that close inspection by the authorities might not be in their interest and hence they may deliberately maintain a low profile. The fact that homeworking takes place in the domestic context may also present further organisational dilemmas. For example, female homeworkers may have to engage in struggles with patriarchal members of their own households as well as with suppliers of work. Senior male household members may negotiate with suppliers of work, owe favours to suppliers or confiscate the wages women homeworkers earn. More generally, domestic roles may limit the availability of female homeworkers for meetings and union duties.

Another obstacle to effective organisation is that many homeworkers are at the end of a pyramid of subcontracting chains. Intermediary companies are locked into chains of dependency with large organisations which do not themselves employ homeworkers. Big companies are, therefore, able to wash their hands of the employment practices of those with whom they trade. Small employers have their profit margins squeezed by the larger companies further up the chain. As a result, many homeworkers are employed by firms which have minimal room for manoeuvre.

However, despite these obstacles there have been some notable efforts to organise and protect homeworkers. A unifying characteristic of these has been the use of innovative strategies of mobilisation not typical of conventional ways of organising and protecting workers. Moreover, post-Fordist capitalism – and late modern society generally – offers a range of opportunities to exercise influence and achieve improvements which may ensure that homeworkers become 'invisible no more' (Boris and Prügl 1996; Mitter 1994: 31).

Many of the major firms standing at the apex of subcontracting chains are household names. As retail organisations they rely on their high public profile. They spend vast sums of money, not only in marketing products but in establishing a more general image for themselves relating to style, fashion, good value and reliability. Customers buy lifestyle or cultural associations when they shop in such outlets, thereby making these organisations vulnerable to attacks on their image (Littlefield 1996). Examples might include retailers who identify themselves with the environmental movement or financial institutions that are keen to describe themselves as equal opportunities employers. As a result, a small but effective lobbying and publicity group can have a major impact.

One tactic adopted is to 'name and shame' retailers into taking responsibility for the working conditions of their subcontractors, many of whom use homeworkers.

This has been successful in Canada and the UK. For example, in 1992 the names of designers and clothing companies in Canada using poorly paid homeworkers were released by campaigners. Among these were three prominent Canadian designers, the most famous being Alfred Sung. Simultaneously, postcards were printed urging the three main Canadian clothing retailers to re-evaluate their buying strategies to ensure that their garments were being produced under decent terms and conditions. The public were urged to send in these postcards. Over the course of the campaign, which lasted about a year, retailers received over 10,000 cards from across Canada. Since March 1993, the campaign has taken a further twist with the launch of the Clean Clothes List. This was designed to promote the 'more decent employers in the clothing business at the same time as highlighting the particularly bad ones' (Dagg 1996: 249). The List divided trade names and designer labels into various categories according to their record as an employer. These were, in descending order: 'dazzling', 'decent', 'dingy' and 'dirty'. However, one of the difficulties of the campaign – apart from defining these categories – was that some firms offered significantly different terms and conditions to different groups of homeworkers. Consequently, some garments might be produced under 'dazzling' conditions, whilst others – or other components of the same garment – might be produced under poorer conditions. Furthermore, it was often difficult to trace the actual producers of 'own label' garments (Dagg 1996: 249–250).

A similar campaign was recently mounted in the UK by the charity Oxfam. Launched in May 1996, the Clothes Code Campaign called upon high street retailers to ensure that minimum workplace standards were met among their suppliers. The charity targeted C&A, Burton, Marks & Spencer, Next and Sears who collectively account for over half of the UK clothing market. Consumers were urged to send in postcards printed by Oxfam calling for the adoption of ethical production along the supply chain. During the course of the campaign the companies each received thousands of postcards. As a result, C&A published a code ensuring that workers making garments destined for its stores would have decent working conditions. Existing and potential suppliers are contractually required to follow this code, and to guarantee that their subcontractors and other third parties do likewise. Next and Sears also promised to re-examine their buying policies (*Financial Times*, 3 October 1996; *Sunday Times*, 24 November 1996).

Elsewhere, the power of the consumer has been harnessed with similar effect. For example, the Rugmark Foundation was set up in 1994 in India with the aim of stamping out the use of child labour in India's 'carpet belt' in the north-eastern state of Uttar Pradesh. Before the advent of Rugmark, 300,000 children were estimated to be involved, many of whom were working at home. A 'smiling carpet' label is the Rugmark stamp of approval: no exploited child has woven the carpet to which the label is attached. A third of all Germany's imported carpets now carry this label, while importers in Canada, the Netherlands, Switzerland and the United States are moving in this direction. Licences have been issued to over a hundred exporters with 13,000 looms. Spot checks are carried out by inspectors and those found to be using child labour are decertified with immediate effect. The cost of inspections is borne by exporters (who pay 0.25 per cent of the value of the rugs they export) and importers (who pay 1 per cent) (Christian Aid 1997: 22).

Another tactic is to organise homeworkers themselves. The difficulties encountered are well demonstrated by the efforts of the Homeworkers' Association (HWA) in Canada (Dagg 1996: 250–256). This type of organising has a long lead time, demands many resources and takes a great deal of effort. Recruiting outside factory gates or offices is not possible for obvious reasons. The HWA, therefore, targeted Chinese and Vietnamese homeworkers in Ontario, Canada. Various methods were adopted to organise homeworkers. The most effective included establishing a profile in the community, via ethnic minority newspapers, other media and a hotline telephone link. However, above all, word-of-mouth recommendations proved to be the most productive. These, in turn, depended on being able to do something positive for homeworkers. Recruiting strategies here included the organisation of social events, prescription drug and sickness provision, the hosting of courses and seminars on relevant topics such as marital relations, leadership skills, negotiation techniques and legal rights. The HWA, therefore, functioned more as a community focus or mobilisation point than as a traditional union. The office acted as a drop-in centre for members of the community, with crèche facilities available for those who needed them. It also offered a counselling service and made referrals to other agencies in respect of legal issues. To raise its profile further the HWA made links with other Chinese community institutions. Throughout, the HWA sought to couch its appeal in terms of the lived experience and needs of homeworkers themselves.

Probably the best known example of an innovative approach is that of the Self-Employed Women's Association (SEWA) in India. SEWA specifically caters for women's demands. It is not confined to homeworkers but organises all types of home-located producers and beyond, and undertakes a wide range of activities in addition to negotiation with employers. It was set up in 1972 and is based in Ahmedabad, the largest city in Gujerat (Rose 1992; Jhabvala 1994). Although often referred to as a trade union, it incorporates a much more broadly based conception of labour organisation than is usual in the West. SEWA has an all-female membership, recruited from among women engaged in a wide range of different types of economic activities and work relationships. Its membership consists of three main categories: women who work at home; women who sell their labour to employers; and women who act as street vendors or hawkers carrying out a myriad of trades. They receive income in various ways, including sales to clients, piece-rate payments, wages or barter. SEWA deliberately chose the term 'self-employed' to describe this diverse collection of labour market participants in order to counter the negative connotation of so many of the terms used in the literature – such as 'informal', 'unorganised', 'marginal' and 'peripheral' workers. Even the SEWA acronym conveys a positive image – meaning 'service' when pronounced. It had around 200,000 members in 1994 – over 75,000 in Gujerat alone (Oxfam 1996). The range of services offered is more extensive than those conventionally associated with trade unions. In addition to negotiating with employers, SEWA provides credit facilities, low cost loans, legal advice, medical care, maternity support, crèche facilities, advice and training with respect to social issues, and help with literacy. It even supports activities designed to transform the employment relationship of its members via the creation of cooperatives, 70 of which it has helped to set up (Oxfam 1996).

Based on the SEWA experience, Jhabvala (1994) argues that trade unions in India must go beyond the Western model of organisation, 'where labour is composed mainly of wage earners working for large scale manufacturers or enterprises' (ibid.: 116), to embrace the self-employed who have no employer to negotiate with. The self-employed comprise a large proportion of India's workforce, many of whom are women. Jhabvala argues that if trade unions are to play a major role in developing countries, they must, therefore, find ways to represent the interests of 'the millions upon millions of self-employed landless labourers, small farmers, sellers, producers and service workers' (ibid.: 116). It is interesting to note, therefore, that in India SEWA conceives its mission as that of protecting, promoting and encouraging self-employment. In contrast, homeworking groups in the West have often been engaged in lobbying for the extension of employee status to those whom they represent. In Britain, for example, this was the explicit purpose of the Homeworkers (Protection) Bills of 1978 and 1981, as well as the Homeworker Bill of 1991.

However, Western organisations have learnt from the SEWA model. In particular, they have sought to help and support homeworkers in their daily lives rather than simply launching traditional trade union recruitment drives. For example, several local campaigning organisations in Britain – such as the Leicester Outwork Campaign – have built on the SEWA experience in this way. Their strategies have included providing homeworkers with free information packs detailing their employment, welfare and other rights. Telephone hotlines on which homeworkers can get free advice have also commonly been provided. Newsletters have also been produced and circulated to existing contacts as well as community and advice centres. The more developed and well resourced groups are able to print both Fact Packs and Newsletters in several languages, thereby expanding their reach. In addition, some local groups have, on occasion, run training programmes designed to give homeworkers the self-confidence to progress to other programmes and possibly escape from homeworking altogether (Hopkins 1992; Tate 1994b). However, all this activity is contingent on accessing local resources, often provided by friendly local authorities and, therefore, subject to the vagaries of the political process. The effectiveness of local campaigns in Britain has been enhanced by the networking efforts of the NGH, which has operated as a long-standing national coordination and lobbying group.

Elsewhere other organisations have taken up the issue of homeworking. In the Netherlands, for example, the Vrouwenbond van de Fderatie Nederlandse Vakbeweging (FNV) – a women's trade union affiliated to the Federation of Dutch Trade Unions – aims to stand up for specific groups not protected by other unions. These include domestic helpers, women returners, voluntary work-ers, housewives and, since 1979, homeworkers (Tate 1993, 1994c; *Labour Research* 1993). It set up a number of Homework Support Centres across the Netherlands. The first was established in 1985 in Hengelo – an area renowned for homeworking – followed by others in Tilburg, Amsterdam and The Hague. Each aims to provide both an over-the-telephone and a drop-in advice and information service to homeworkers in the area. They also organise regular meetings on a range of topics, usually relating to legal rights and benefits. The centres also act as bridges between traditional unions and homeworkers by encouraging trade unions to include homeworkers in collective bargaining, urging unions to adopt reduced membership schemes for homeworkers, and building contacts between homeworkers, the organised factory workforce and the relevant trade union.

Recently some traditional trade unions have launched novel recruitment drives of their own. In Australia, for example, during the 1980s the Clothing and Allied Trades Union (CATU) abandoned its traditional cry for the abolition of home-working in the industry and sought to extend the scope of collective awards to include homeworkers (Ellem 1991). This entailed attempts to enrol non-factory labour and ensure that the terms of the award were upheld irrespective of where the work was carried out. Their tactics included the following: the preparation of a multilingual handbook for homeworkers outlining their rights; a publicity cam-paign aimed at ethnic minority homeworkers in particular; the distribution of information through ethnic and community channels; training union officials on how to deal more effectively with homeworking issues; and the setting up of a telephone hotline to deal with enquiries from homeworkers. Some doubts have been raised about the success of the campaign (Ellem 1991: 110). However, the Australian experience serves to underline the point that homeworkers cannot be organised and protected in the same way as workplace-located workers. Instead, different strategies and techniques need to be adopted.

Conclusion

This chapter has highlighted some of the grim realities of working at home. The worst conditions are experienced by those we would define as homeworkers. They often receive extremely low rates of pay, are exposed to health and safety dangers and are poorly protected by traditional workers' organisations. To make matters worse, their employment status in national law is often ambiguous and few countries have specific laws to protect them. The result is that many homework-ers are denied rights commonly accorded to employees.

Given the poor working conditions under which homeworkers labour, it is unsurprising that international organisations such as the European Union (EU) and the International Labour Organisation (ILO) are making efforts to improve their plight. For example, the ILO recently voted to lay down basic employment rights for home-located wage labourers backed up by international law. These include minimum pay, freedom of association, collective bargaining, health and safety protection, and social security coverage. If the ILO Convention containing these rights is ratified by national governments they may then be translated into national law, thereby ensuring that all workers have the same rights in the labour market. However, enforcement will bring the issue of the organisation of home-workers to the fore again.

This chapter has shown that organisation is possible, but only by adopting innovative and novel strategies. The importance of 'brand names' and their associated images offer campaigners a potent lever with which to 'shame' employers into making improvements in homeworkers' conditions. Similar strategies might have to be adopted to ensure that any future regulation proposed by the ILO or by individual national governments is enforced. Traditional ways of organising homeworkers via trade unions have, in the past, been disappointing. However, specialist campaigns and specific homeworking groups have had more success and, therefore, offer much more promise for future attempts at regulation and protection.

The emphasis on homeworkers' conditions has often left those of others who work at home relatively unexplored. The scant evidence available offers some interesting insights which future researchers might wish to pursue. Foremost among these is the finding that home-located producers – the broadest category in our schema – appear to be paid less than their workplace-located colleagues. Moreover, even after holding all other variables constant – such as age, ethnicity, place of residence, years of schooling and family structure – those who work at home earn significantly less. This prompts a further research agenda. Is the *relative* gap in pay, earnings and benefits similar for all types of home-located producer? Or is the differentiation wider at the top end of the occupational and income hierarchy than at the bottom? There is little existing evidence on which to answer these questions.

Chapter 7

Struggling for control

> The self is not merely *enabled* to choose, but *obliged* to construe a life in terms of its choices, its powers, and its values. Individuals are expected to construe the course of their life as the outcome of such choices, and to account for their lives in terms of the reasons for those choices. Each of the attributes of the person is to be realised through decisions, justified in terms of motives, needs and aspirations, made intelligible to the self and others in terms of the unique but universal search to find meaning and satisfaction through the construction of a life for oneself.
>
> (Rose 1990: 22; our emphasis)

Introduction

In this chapter, and the two which follow, the focus of attention is shifted to the meaning and experience of home-located production; that is, what it feels like to make a living at home, how home-located producers make sense of their situation and the ways in which they seek to manage it. This chapter addresses a long-standing debate concerning the choices and constraints experienced by home-located producers in general and homeworkers in particular. We will argue that their lives are best understood as an ongoing struggle for control.

In empirical research, these issues have often been explored obliquely by asking respondents what they perceive to be the advantages and disadvantages of working at home. The chapter will begin by briefly reviewing some of these findings. However, we shall then go on to explore a somewhat different approach. We will focus on the social and psychological construction and reproduction of the times and places of employment within the context of the home. We argue that this necessarily involves all home-located producers in distinctive social, emotional and cognitive processes that are central to the meaning and experience of making a living at home.

Perceived advantages and disadvantages

A number of studies have attempted to explore the choices and constraints faced by home-located producers by asking them what they take to be the advantages and disadvantages of making a living at home (e.g., Christensen 1988; Huws 1994; Huws *et al.* 1990; Haddon and Lewis 1994; Felstead and Jewson 1996; Hakim 1987a: 196–199; Salmi 1996). These investigations have often generated mixed, or even contradictory, responses. Advantages and disadvantages described by respondents often bear close similarities. It seems that the very attributes of home-located production that appeal to those who undertake it also bring with them drawbacks and problems. Thus, for example, home-located producers often report that the opportunity to work in close proximity to children and partners, to construct their own working environment, to manage their own working times and to be close to their work are both major attractions and pose serious problems (see, for example, Felstead and Jewson 1996; Huws *et al.* 1996; Armstrong 1997).

Our own survey of British homeworkers produced results that are typical (Felstead and Jewson 1996: 49–55). The opportunity to look after children whilst doing paid work was easily the most widely cited advantage, being mentioned by two-thirds of respondents to our in-depth interviews. They commonly referred to picking up children from school, looking after children in the holidays, taking time off when children fell ill and scheduling daily routines around the unpredictable requirements of baby care. Other advantages mentioned by our respondents included flexibility (33 per cent), being in the home environment (31 per cent), convenience (20 per cent), opportunity to do housework (18 per cent), autonomy (24 per cent) and, quite simply, the money (26 per cent). For some the income from homeworking, though low, made a crucial contribution to household income. Many commented that at home they could work at their own pace and in their own way – stopping and starting at will, wearing the clothes that suited them, eating or not eating when convenient, playing music of their choice, watching favourite TV programmes and generally working in a familiar environment under their control. They also valued the absence of minute by minute surveillance by a boss. For many respondents, home represented a secure environment. Ethnic minority homeworkers in particular commented on the opportunity to meet religious and cultural requirements, such as repeated daily prayers, whilst in the home. Others remarked upon the racism or language difficulties they encountered in workplaces. Throughout, they emphasised the need to deploy self-management skills in making a living as a homeworker – a theme to which we shall return in this and the next chapter.

The major drawbacks mentioned by our sample were mess (42 per cent), unpredictability and unreliability of payment (31 per cent), isolation (29 per cent), stress (16 per cent), irregular hours (11 per cent), health and safety problems (10 per cent) and inconvenience (10 per cent). The problems of mess commonly related to the use of solvents and dirty machinery, the need to store materials, and the impact of dust and fumes. The particular problems encountered reflected the details of the labour processes involved, which varied from area to area and job to job. Some respondents saw homeworking as undermining the 'homeliness' of the home, others commented on the implications for entertaining friends and family (cf. Bulos and Chaker 1993). Lack of communication with other adults and lack of external stimulation tended to generate a sense of isolation.

Ironically, for a number of respondents the presence of children in the home – their motive for taking up homeworking in the first place – also proved a major obstacle. They were caught between feeling guilty about neglecting their children and feeling pressurised to meet their production deadlines. These findings are similar to those of a number of other studies (Christensen 1988; Costello 1988; Gerson and Kraut 1988). These problems were sometimes exacerbated when suppliers presented 'rush jobs' or there was a sudden surge of work. Other disadvantages experienced by home-located producers in general, and homeworkers in particular, are failure by family and friends to recognise their toil as 'real work'. Many feel trapped in the same environment day after day. Finally, in common with most other studies, many of our respondents commented bitterly on their low pay and poor terms and conditions (see Chapter 6, pp. 90–91).

A number of studies, including our own, suggest that men and women tend to cite different advantages and disadvantages of making a living at home (see, for example, Salmi 1997b; Felstead and Jewson 1996; Huws *et al.* 1996). Men appear to regard the major benefit as enhanced flexibility, thereby offering opportunities for self-expression, personal liberation and the reconciliation of work and leisure. Women also rate flexibility highly but seem to perceive it as a chance to combine employment with the demands of the household, especially childcare. Isolation, absence of support and lack of teamwork are all seen as disadvantages by both men and women. However, there is a tendency for males to emphasise isolation from the social relations of work itself, including colleagues and work culture, whereas women tend to refer to a more general sense of personal detachment. These gender differences in the perceived advantages and disadvantages of working at home are also reflected in the spatial and temporal organisation of work regimes, discussed further in Chapters 8 and 9.

Survey questions about the advantages and disadvantages of home-located production tell us something about what it feels like to make a living at home but, nevertheless, represent an essentially descriptive and partial account. This chapter will adopt a rather different approach. It is our contention that the meaning and experience of home-located production are shaped by a distinctive set of social and psychological challenges that are inherent in its spatial location. These, in turn, call forth a distinctive socio-psychological disposition or attitude which, to some degree, is characteristic of *all* home-located producers, notwithstanding the differences in their social relations of production. To explore these issues we shall turn to a closer examination of the much-vaunted 'flexibility' and 'autonomy' of home-located production.

The myth of autonomy

As noted in Chapter 5, in academic and popular literature there have been two contrasting interpretations of the situation and experience of home-located producers in general and homeworkers in particular (Gerson and Kraut 1988; Ahrentzen 1992; Shamir 1992; Haddon and Silverstone 1993; Salmi 1996; Huws *et al.* 1996). One version has it that home-located producers are a peculiarly advantaged group who have freely chosen a lifestyle that maximises flexibility and independence. They are portrayed as autonomously constructing their own work schedules, integrating domesticity and employment, and shaking off workplace controls (e.g., Toffler 1980; Gutek 1983; Young and Willmott 1973: 285; Bailyn 1988; Stanworth 1998). This stereotype has been particularly influential in portrayals of so-called 'teleworkers' (Armstrong 1997: 2).

In contrast, another interpretation presents homeworkers in particular as among the most downtrodden and exploited members of the labour force, with minimal autonomy (see Chapter 5; also Allen and Wolkowitz 1987; Bisset and Huws 1984; Berch 1985). According to this view, homeworkers suffer from low wages, an absence of benefits, intense work pressures, occupational dangers and poor-quality working conditions. Far from exercising choice, they are presented as a group driven into harsh and poorly paid employment by brutal economic necessity. They are seen as exploited by suppliers of work and further oppressed by the burdens of domestic work and family care.

We suggest that both these perspectives are misleading – or, more precisely, that each offers a partial truth. Our argument is that home-located producers are both subject to powerful sources of regulation *and* engaged in a distinctively self-driven process of defining crucial aspects of their working lives. In short, they are neither wholly free nor wholly downtrodden. Rather, they are engaged in an active struggle to exert control over social relationships within the labour market and household.

In order to develop this point we will first examine the arguments of one of the leading critics of the view that home-located wage labour offers an autonomous way of making a living. Allen and Wolkowitz (1987), in their pioneering book, challenged what they describe as the 'myth of autonomy'; that is, the myth that home-located wage labourers (as we define them) enjoy levels of freedom, autonomy and flexibility denied to factory and office workers. In contrast, they argue that those who work at home are typically hemmed in by a range of pressures that, in reality, leave very little room for manoeuvre. They note that all labour processes for profit entail a system of control or management. For home-located wage labourers, they assert, this control lies with suppliers of work who utilise various indirect mechanisms to regulate performance and output. As a result there can be 'an appearance of autonomy which is more apparent than real' (ibid.: 113).

Allen and Wolkowitz (1987) argue – and we also accept – that the extent of the power and control exercised by home-located wage labourers within the management process depends on the nature of their social relations of production and, to some degree, the nature of the work tasks. However, they suggest that a series of managerial strategies enable employers and suppliers of work to compensate for low levels of face-to-face surveillance (see also Olson and Primps 1984; Haddon and Lewis 1994; Hendry 1994). Piece rates – often subject to variation over time or from job to job – are commonly used as a means of driving up levels of output. Quality is often maintained by rigorous inspection by suppliers of work who reject – and refuse payment for – sub-standard output. Stringent and tight deadlines coupled with seasonal or irregular supply frequently leave those who work at home with minimal control over the allocation of working time and the length of their working day, which may unpredictably break into other family and social appointments. Furthermore, it is not unusual for suppliers to take on more wage labourers than are needed but to keep them 'on the books' by supplying a trickle of work. This enables the supplier to switch production among the most compliant, preventing dependence on a few and providing a way of rewarding 'good workers'.

Another commonplace tactic of managerial control is that of establishing personal and paternalistic ties. This is made easier by the absence of contact with other workers in a similar position. Suppliers may sustain and manipulate personal relations by promising real or fictitious 'favours', such as allocating easier jobs, maintaining a steady flow of work, paying wages promptly, or extending deadlines. Ties of dependence are further enhanced when they coincide with those of kinship, community or ethnicity. A sense of obligation and loyalty to what is perceived to be an 'understanding employer' can result in a willingness to be reliable, trustworthy and compliant.

Allen and Wolkowitz (1987) also suggest that a further range of constraints are generated by the social relations of the home, which may well further undermine autonomy. They conceptualise these as basically the same in all households. For women these constraints primarily include the regular demands of domestic work and childcare, imposed by the sexual division of labour. Such pressures frequently make it difficult to combine domestic and work routines, resulting in 'harassed coping strategies' (ibid.: 123). These may include working late into the night, when the children are asleep, as well as sacrificing social and leisure time. Pressures are further enhanced because the work is always present and any hour is, in principle, a potential working hour.

For all these reasons, it is suggested, the picture of autonomy conjured up by some apologists for home-located wage labour is misleading. Instead, it is argued, those who work at home are caught between the twin pincers of management control strategies and the demands of the domestic division of labour. This has been referred to as 'the autonomy paradox' by Huws *et al.* (1996: 72). The promise of more leisure, self-control and family contact turns into the reality of long hours, unpredictable workloads and family tensions.

Choices and constraints

While accepting much of Allen and Wolkowitz's (1987) argument as a starting point, we wish to develop a wider interpretation that incorporates additional elements and perspectives. This includes giving prominence to the opportunities for resistance to and struggle against the many limitations encountered by those who work at home. Moreover, we want to emphasise that, although homeworkers are not autonomous, in common with all home-located producers they are *relatively self-directed*. All the types of home-located producers that we identify in Chapter 2 are routinely called upon to exercise a greater degree of self-management than others in comparable workplace employment. This is because they are required to construct for themselves critical aspects of their working lives:

- they must decide *when* to work and *where* to work;
- they must, in the absence of a supervisor or manager on site, *monitor and police* their own working schedules;
- they must establish and maintain the *interface* between these work routines and the life of the household.

Thus, whilst we fully recognise that homeworkers are not free agents, we wish also to highlight the *self*-discipline, *self*-motivation and *self*-organisation inherent in their everyday lives and work routines. The difference between their lives and those of workplace employees is in some ways analogous to the contrast between the academic regimes and study skills required of school pupils and university students. In short – precisely *because* of the need to cope with the many constraints and pressures upon them – homeworkers must manage and police themselves. They are routinely required to achieve this to an extent and in ways that are not characteristic of those who earn their living in workplaces. As we shall argue, the management of many workplaces is increasingly moving in a direction that calls for attitudes and skills from employees that have similarities with those intrinsic to home-located production. However, home-located producers remain distinctive in the origin and maintenance of a day-to-day working regime (Haddon and Silverstone 1993; Haddon and Lewis 1994).

> Thus, what is important about autonomy is not so much the independence in the work itself, but the autonomy in putting together the different pieces of everyday life and coping with the different daily time patterns . . . This independence is not only about freedom to choose the working methods, hours or pace of work, but, and most importantly, it is about better chances to form the structure of one's everyday activities oneself.
>
> (Salmi 1997b: 113)

We wish, therefore, to argue something slightly different from both those who portray home-located producers as free spirits and those who see them as weighed down by social constraints. Rather, we suggest that they are engaged in a distinctive type of struggle, on a routine basis, to define and to bring into being aspects of their working lives that workplace producers rarely if ever encounter. It is the processes of the management of the self that are the bedrock on which the meaning and experience of home-located production rests.

Forms of managerial control

All paid employment involves a process of management; that is, the organisation of work tasks and the monitoring of their successful completion. This routinely entails recruiting and mobilising labour, planning and implementing the overall work process, allocating tasks, maintaining the intensity of work, measuring the quantity and quality of output, exercising discipline over the labour force, imposing sanctions and distributing rewards. In short, management entails a process of 'policing'. This is typically achieved by a combination of *external* controls exerted by others (such as supervisors and company agents) and *internalised* ways of acting, thinking and feeling – the emotional and cognitive dispositions of the worker.

Whilst both external and internal sources of management are always present in capitalist labour processes, the balance between them may shift over time. It has been argued, for example, that the rise of factory-located production was not simply dictated by technological considerations but also reflected the determination of employers to exert greater external managerial control over unruly and unpredictable workers (Marglin 1974). This typically entailed an increased degree of control by specialist managerial and supervisory staff over the working time and space of company employees (Reid 1976; Thompson 1967; Whipp 1987). Foucault has explored the ways in which processes of external discipline and surveillance within institutional contexts in general, not just workplaces, have contributed to shaping the internalised emotional sensibilities typical of modernity (Foucault 1977). Although his account arguably leaves insufficient room for processes of resistance or for the growth of counter-cultures among the oppressed, it does highlight the way in which power relations constitute, rather than simply mould, patterns of human feeling, thought and desire.

In the late twentieth century the advanced capitalist societies witnessed a further shift in the relationship between external and internal constraints associated with new strategies of management. It is beyond the scope of this book to explore the debates that have surrounded the precise extent of the development of such techniques and their implications (see, for example, Wood 1989; Kumar 1995; Sayer and Walker 1992; Thompson and Warhurst 1998). Nevertheless, there appears to be evidence, in a range of employment contexts, of a general trend in organisational governance away from the external imposition of bureaucratic rules and regulations towards the internalisation of norms, values and attitudes through the manipulation of organisational culture (see, for example, Donzelot 1991; Casey 1995; Du Gay 1996a, 1996b; Noon and Blyton 1997; Flecker and Hofbauer 1998).

The values of entrepreneurialism – and an ideological construction of the entrepreneurial personality – have become the dominant practices, organisational forms and personal identities that public and private sector firms seek to encourage (Rose 1990; Casey 1995). The discourses of this strategy emphasise *inter alia* empowerment, participation, self-motivation and self-control. These practices have often been presented as a liberation from external constraints. They have, in fact, often been accompanied by massive increases in employee surveillance; for example, by the application of information technology to the policing of employees (Sewell and Wilkinson 1992). Moreover, constraints in the form of internal markets provide constant 'bottom line' pressure to perform. Nevertheless, the rhetoric and, to a degree, the practice of management have shifted towards an ostensibly 'high trust' model that prioritises internalised constraints and the execution of work tasks outside the immediate presence of management or supervisory staff (Giddens 1991; Fox 1974; Rose 1990). Productivity is maximised, compliance secured and innovative flexibility enhanced by shaping and mobilising the individual psychological dispositions of employees.

Attempts have been made to introduce such entrepreneurial modes of organisational governance not only in private sector businesses but also in the public and voluntary sectors and in government (Burchell 1993; Flecker and Hofbauer 1998). Such a mode of organisation is characterised by employees who are required to meet externally set production targets by taking responsibility for their own output through the development of innovative, self-directed and creative problem-solving techniques. The capacity to make decisions, to switch tactics, to innovate, to take control is mobilised as the organisational ideal (Casey 1995). This is to envisage a novel subject; that is, a person who has to invent their own job, career, qualifications, biography, and ultimately themselves. They are expected to become entrepreneurs of the self (Gordon 1987; Mulholland 1996; Du Gay 1996a, 1996b). Management has in part become a calculated process of generating emotional and intellectual dispositions among staff that further the formal objectives of the institution (Rose 1990: 56).

Home-located production and self-management

All home-located production incorporates elements of the entrepreneurial mode of governance and self-management in three key respects.

First, the nature of home-located production requires producers to organise their own time and space in getting the job done within a deadline – the organisation of work. Of course, this is not to deny that many market and household constraints impinge upon home-located producers. Such restrictions are greater in some types of home-located production than others, and probably greatest of all for homeworkers. Nevertheless, it is inherent in all home-located production that producers can and must make choices about the environment, hours, pace, location and milieu of work. They have to invent for themselves and sustain the work ethic. It is true that their decisions may well be manipulated, or even pre-empted, by the supplier of work; for example, the supplier may refuse to take on someone who does not have a telephone link or even a separate room in which to work. Nevertheless, within these parameters, home-located producers of all kinds have to create their own work routines by defining and organising the time and place of their labour.

Second, having established a locale and timetable for work, home-located producers have to maintain their commitment to this routine – or else invent new plans and develop contingency arrangements. Home-located producers take on board key aspects of policing performance, output and quality. Again, suppliers may seek to use various devices for monitoring work effort which reduce the discretion and need for self-management. In some cases, for example, attempts have been made to measure electronically the hours that information technology workers spend at their workstation and the number of key-strokes made (Haddon and Lewis 1994; Sennett 1998: 58–59). However, at present, relatively few of those who earn their living at home face such draconian managerial intrusions into their domestic space. Most home-located producers must motivate, drive and police themselves in order to get the work done. Rarely are supervisors present. The psychological contortions and emotional tussles that self-motivation and self-policing can entail should be familiar to all students and academics. Indeed, research (including our own) suggests that home-located producers themselves believe that certain personality traits – such as self-confidence, self-discipline and self-motivation – are advantageous (Huws 1993; Huws *et al.* 1996; Haddon and Lewis 1994).

Third, home-located producers are required to manage the interface – or interfaces – between the times and spaces of making a living and those of the rest of the household. This involves managing relationships with other family members; for example, fitting in home-located production with the demands of domestic labour and childcare. This may well call for flexibility, communication and negotiation skills and the capacity to manage ambivalent feelings. Since domestic labour is profoundly gendered, so too is the management of this interface. As men and women experience and participate in domestic labour in different ways, it is inevitable that they will also find different meanings in home-located production. In addition, however, it should be recognised that all home-located producers, both male and female, face a potential confrontation between two of the most powerful sources of meaning and identity – home and work. There is a potential collision of values, ideas and roles. These circumstances require home-located producers to become entrepreneurs of the self. They must judge in what ways and to what extent they will draw the lines between relations of production and social reproduction in their lives. They must invent a landscape for themselves, with few cues or support from elsewhere.

Technologies of the self

Home-located production thus incorporates a mode of governance of the self that is congruent with the general direction of contemporary business management. The social construction of time and space, the policing of performances and the management of the interface between domestic and paid labour are typically achieved by home-located producers through the generation of a series of 'technologies of the self'. The concept of technologies of the self has been developed by a number of writers, most notably Michel Foucault, particularly in his later work (Foucault 1979, 1987, 1988, 1990; see also Burchell 1993; Gordon 1987; Martin *et al.* 1988; Rose 1990; Sennett 1998).

Gordon (1987: 295) has described technologies of the self as 'cultural practices dedicated to the formation and transformation of the self by the self'. They refer to ways in which people, more or less consciously and reflexively, mobilise and organise their attitudes, practices and feelings in the course of their everyday lives. Rarely are these fixed or closed attributes of behaviour that constitute an integrated intellectual system. They are better thought of as capacities and processes that may be more or less vulnerable, contradictory or fractured. They enable individuals to conceive of themselves as autonomous, sovereign authors of their lives, capable of freely choosing their own destinies. Ironically, however, these very sensibilities are based on self-inspection, self-criticism, self-monitoring and self-regulation – that is, internalised restraints learned in a range of social contexts. They may, moreover, mask the broader social origins of the challenges and pressures that call forth such techniques of self-direction.

Technologies of the self are, therefore, part of the reflexive project of the self (Giddens 1991). They are the means by which self-identity is constituted through conscious ordering of narratives and accounts of the past, present and future. They achieve their effects not by terror or threats of violence but by stimulating deep-rooted desires and anxieties about identity and self-worth. They are, therefore, relations of power.

Technologies of the self encompass three broad aspects of subjectivity (Rose 1990: 241):

1   *A body of knowledge and beliefs,* with their own assumptions, concepts, theories, facts, methodologies, techniques and lines of enquiry. These are also frequently imbued with diffuse moral and ethical significance. In the case of home-located producers, these may include knowledge and belief about matters such as wage rates, payment systems, market opportunities, labour processes, occupational skills and health and safety risks. It may also include more general understandings about the predictability of work loads, the likelihood of meeting deadlines, times and places available within the household, 'difficult' and 'easy' jobs, 'good' and 'bad' employers and the personalities of other household members.

2   *A collection of normative rules,* which identify what is permissible and forbidden, normal and exceptional, fair and unfair. In the case of home-located production this will cover such matters as the behaviour of suppliers of work, the legitimacy of demands by other household members, notions of acceptable standards in domestic labour and evaluation of the needs of children.

3   *An attitude to the self,* adopted by individuals, which concerns a reading which each person makes of their own identity, character and the esteem in which they are held by various others. It implies techniques of presentation and management of the self. In the case of home-located production this may

concern matters such as the extent to which individuals see themselves as reliable, honest, hardworking, generous, selfish or moody. It also entails the ways in which they manage these perceived character traits.

The aspect of technologies of the self featured in this and, more especially, later chapters predominantly concern the ordering of time and space. In particular, we focus on ways of coordinating the activities entailed in earning a living at home with those entailed in being a member of a household. The home is an environment of domestic labour, leisure, family, kinship, child-rearing and personal intimacy. Technologies of the self deployed by home-located producers are the practices entailed in introducing a set of work processes associated with paid employment into this context. They are directed, therefore, at managing the juxtaposition of the social relations of production and reproduction. Among the most interesting and insightful discussions of these processes are those provided by Haddon and Silverstone (1993), Bulos and Chaker (1993), Beach (1989) and Ahrentzen (1992, 1990).

Household dilemmas

Home-located production potentially problematises the social relations of the household. As a result, there may develop a raised awareness of the significance of home and the private domestic sphere of life (Bulos and Chaker 1995). Reaching decisions about how to accommodate work in the home may force household members to articulate principles and beliefs about domestic time and space that have not previously been expressed in an explicit and direct form. Ingrained and taken-for-granted habits and practices may thus evolve into conscious decision-making.

The process of constructing temporalities and spaces in a fluid and demanding situation is a difficult one and the meanings so created can be complex and diverse. They may sometimes be contradictory or full of conflicts, reflecting divisions of interest and interpretation among household members. The particular demands of the labour process or the configuration of the home may mean that households are forced to adopt solutions that run contrary to their preferences, tastes and desires. There is a constant need to police and reproduce established temporal and spatial boundaries. As a result, it is common for home-located producers to feel that they could do better – or to experience a partial or total breakdown of the order they wish to establish. Moreover, their isolation – coupled with unrealistic images and expectations of home-located production – may lead them to attribute an absence of enhanced personal fulfilment to their own failings rather than to structural circumstances. These were indeed themes among a number of the qualitative interviews that we conducted, discussed further in the next chapter. Self-management by home-located producers is, therefore, frequently vulnerable to disruption or self-doubt. For some there may be a periodic oscillation between different temporal and spatial arrangements, depending on circumstances and immediate pressures. In short, the spatial location of home-located production makes it *inherently* problematic. Moreover, space and time in the home involve personal values and identities. Hence, struggles typically have symbolic as well as utilitarian dimensions. Furthermore, home-located production often calls forth a degree of self-conscious invention of technologies of the self because many of those who make their living at home do not have established traditions to draw on or culturally prescribed role models to emulate. For people from certain backgrounds – such as small shopkeeping or smallholding – this may not be the case. Nevertheless, many home-located producers literally have to make it up as they go along. All have to fit making a living into their particular household relations.

This conceptualisation thus allows for the possibility of ambiguity and uncertainty. It avoids perceiving home-located producers simply as helpless victims but also recognises that they are subject to many limitations beyond their control.

Employer dilemmas

Home-located production potentially problematises the managerial control that employers seek to exercise within the social relations of production. Relatively little research has been conducted on employers' perspectives and strategies (see Huws 1993; Smith and Anderson 1992; Judkins *et al.* 1985; Hendry 1994; Olson and Primps 1984; Olson 1989; Shamir 1992; Hamblin 1995). The main benefits which employers anticipate are increased numerical and functional flexibility, increased productivity, lower overhead costs and lower expenditure on factory or office space. However, the available evidence suggests that home-located production is also perceived by many as posing problems. The use of home-located workers has financial advantages, particularly when production schedules fluctuate dramatically or the costs of office and factory space are significant. However, as noted in Chapter 2, the distance in time and space between supervisor and home-located producer raises doubts about the productivity, honesty, reliability and standards of work of those who earn a living at home.

Those who work at home may seem to be beyond the scope of the 'moral fabric of the office' which reinforces respect for authority and the work ethic (Shamir 1992). They are outside the panoptican of the workplace. The very attributes of self-direction and self-organisation that are inherent in technologies of the self deployed by home-located producers may be interpreted as repudiations of, or threats to, managerial authority (cf. Flecker and Hofbauer 1998). This is ironic given, as we have argued, that the trend of workplace-located management is towards high-trust models of management. However, these are combined with extensive surveillance and the manipulation of corporate culture via the relationships, symbols and rituals embedded in the workplace. Trust is equated with presence. Concerns about the potentiality for loss of control may be one of the factors that inhibits employers from further commitment to home-located production (Olson 1989).

Employers may respond by seeking to impose enhanced bureaucratic and rule-bound controls over home-located wage labourers (Shamir 1992; Sennett 1998: 58–59). This may, for example, take the form of tightening procedures, instituting additional quality controls or using electronic means of surveillance in the home to monitor work activities. It may encourage them to restrict the kinds of work tasks they make available to home-located producers to the relatively low discretion jobs (see, for example, Huws 1993). It may even encourage them to perceive home-located producers as not really part of the company at all (Hendry 1994) – reflected in a tendency to resort to temporary contracts or recruitment through outsourcing agencies.

As Huws (1993) notes, the effective incorporation of home-located producers into the workplace of an organisation requires a different approach to management, rather than the mere extension or adoption of traditional practices. Jobs may have to be redesigned, so that the tasks of both home-located and workplace-located employees are suited to their spatial locations. Managers may well have to learn to focus on the outputs of workers rather than their inputs in terms of hours and effort (Hamblin 1995: 481). New patterns of communication and information flows may have to be devised (Smith and Anderson 1992). If managers fail to rise to these challenges, the use of home-located production may be perceived as inherently problematic.

Conclusion

Allen and Wolkowitz (1987) have been pivotal in emphasising the exploitative nature of home-located wage labour. Whilst accepting much of their analysis, in this chapter we have argued that it has partly obscured a full appreciation of the ways in which regulation and control are achieved.

We have focused on the creation of the subjectivity of home-located producers. It is our contention that they routinely exercise forms of self-direction and self-control that are distinctive and mark them out from others in workplace-located employment. These are *inherent* in the coping strategies necessitated by the spatial location of home-located production. In the words of Rose (1990: 227), quoted at the beginning of the chapter, home-located producers are obliged to choose. The management of these choices necessitates the generation of self-discipline and self-surveillance, reflected in a distinctive emotional and intellectual disposition. Such a mentality confers powers that home-located producers may deploy in struggling for control over others and themselves.

Chapter 8

Managing the self

> Everything I do I have to generate myself. Decide myself I'm going to do it. And that sometimes is very wearing . . . I have to drive myself to make myself do it, even though I find it very hard.
> (Henrietta; home-located petty commodity producer interviewed in authors' qualitative research study)

Introduction

This chapter will explore specific features of a series of 'technologies of the self' characteristic of home-located producers, including homeworkers. They are all concerned with defining and controlling time and space in households where processes of production and consumption – capitalist labour and domestic labour – are juxtaposed and coordinated. The discussion contained in the previous chapter may have painted a somewhat abstract or nebulous picture of technologies of the self. Here we show that, in reality, they comprise day-to-day routine practices and regimes.

The central focus will be on the ways in which temporal and spatial boundaries between various activities are generated, maintained and policed. The material in this chapter is derived from the interviews undertaken in our qualitative research study (see Chapter 1, pp. 10–11). It is, therefore, based upon the accounts, reflections and descriptions offered by respondents. These interviews were not confined to homeworkers (as we have defined the term), but included a wide spectrum of home-located producers. Brief descriptions of the occupations and backgrounds of the sample can be found in the Appendix. Our respondents were selected to provide examples of each of our conceptual categories of home-located production. All respondents are referred to by pseudonyms.

Constructing the times and spaces of home-located production involves the management of boundaries both *within* the household and *around* the home separating it from the outside world (cf. the concepts of 'grid' and 'group': Douglas 1973).

Technologies of the self devoted to managing divisions *within* the household include:

- *marking* or the identification of boundaries around the temporalities and localities of employment and domestic relationships;
- *switching* or movement between the temporalities and localities of employment and domestic relationships;
- *defending* or the management of invasions into employment times and places by other household relationships and commitments;
- *intruding* or the management of intrusion into household times and places by employment relations and activities.

Technologies of the self devoted to regulating the interface *between* the household and the outside world are concerned with:

- managing social and geographical *isolation* from colleagues, supervisors and subordinates experienced by home-located producers;
- managing *encroachments* by suppliers, employers, business associates and clients on the times and spaces of household members;
- managing the unpredictability and *variability* of work loads, and hence of flows of material, stock and income across the divide between the home and the outside world;
- managing the *invisibility*, and reduced status, of home-located producers compared with workplace peers, resulting in problems surrounding perceived credibility.

It is not suggested that this list is definitive. These are, however, the themes which were prominent in our qualitative interviews.

Managing divisions within the household

Marking

One of the principal challenges faced by home-located producers is that of defining and constructing boundaries around times and spaces dedicated to different activities and functions – and ordering relationships between them. Salmi (1997b), echoing a phrase used by Giddens (1991: 71), has aptly described this process as 'holding a dialogue with time' – although we would wish to add a dialogue with space as well. Marking temporal boundaries involves identifying – on a daily, weekly and longer-term basis – divisions between working and non-working times, such as the length and distribution of blocks of working time and the length and timing of breaks. Marking spatial divisions involves deciding where in the home work will be conducted and the degree of permanency and exclusivity of these places. This may involve decisions such as the location of workstations, storage of raw materials and stacking of finished product.

For a variety of reasons, different kinds of home-located producers exercise varying levels of discretion and flexibility in generating their temporal and spatial regimes. Nevertheless, even the most pressurised have to mark out for themselves a work regime. Indeed, a wide range of our respondents – including homeworkers – emphasised the flexibility that home-located production offered. For a number of those interviewed, entry into home-located production represented an attempt to utilise this perceived flexibility in order to redraw and reconcile the boundaries of family and work. This was particularly the case among our female respondents, but a number of male interviewees also mentioned the aim of reconciling parenting and employment. Thus, for example, male and female respondents commented that working at home enabled them to reschedule timetables so as to go shopping, attend a school play or go to a child's sports day. The corollary of this much vaunted flexibility, however, is that home-located producers are required to create the temporal and spatial boundaries of their work routines. Some of our respondents regarded their self-imposed time boundaries within the household as inflexible, to be protected at all costs. Others had fewer problems in adjusting to contingencies. Typically, however, all were conscious that they had devised temporal and spatial regimes which they strove to reproduce.

Research suggests that there are different patterns here for men and women (Haddon and Lewis 1994; Salmi 1997a, 1997b; Salmi and Lammi-Taskula 1998; Probert and Wacjman 1988a, 1988b). Men tend to say that they value flexibility in order to coordinate work time and free time, to escape the control of workplace authority and to enhance working efficiency. Women, on the other hand, are more likely to seek flexibility in order to combine a number of different work demands, such as housework, childcare and paid employment. Consequently, for women flexibility may have more to do with juggling different kinds of work loads than in combining employment and leisure (Haddon and Lewis 1994). 'Juggling' was indeed a term used extensively by one of our female interviewees. It is not surprising, therefore, that female home-located producers of all types who participated in our qualitative interviews typically organised their work times around the demands of their children and other household members. As a result, their working days tended to be broken up into smaller time segments than those of their male counterparts:

> I can never have anything planned, I just have to wait for an opportunity . . . and just do it pretty quick . . . before I get disturbed by the little one, or the other one wants to come in and play with pee-wee bear or something . . . I just have to play it by ear . . . it just all depends on the kids, really. You know, if they're quiet then I can do the work, if not, then . . . I just have to stop, wait for maybe later on in the day, when they're asleep in the afternoon and then get down to it . . . I just play it by ear and the work gets done anyway.
>
> (Chantelle; homeworker)

> You could do about ten jobs at the same time, really . . . yeah whatever comes along, then you do have to interrupt your working day, but . . . it does fit in, you know, it has to, really.
>
> (Maureen; home-located petty commodity producer)

> If I was on my own, it might be a bit different but I've got other people's routines to take into account. I've any number of balls in the air at any one time. I'm a wife, I run a house, I've got a dog . . . my daughter to take to school and collect and then I've a business to run, so it's juggling.
>
> (Isobel; home-located employer)

Our male respondents more often sought, and succeeded, in constructing working routines that mimicked those of the workplace. They also tended to emphasise the *extra* hours of working time available to them at home – which suggested their schedules were not dominated or disrupted by routine domestic labour. This was most strikingly apparent in the case of a couple we interviewed, both of whom were working at home. Charles worked a nine to five day, with extra hours at weekends and evenings if necessary. His wife, Sarah, threaded her work in and out of her domestic commitments, creating a hectic 'chequer board' working pattern which mingled different domestic and employment demands, similar to that described above. Her husband succinctly summed up the contrast between his own working day and that of his wife:

> Obviously she has to get meals and this sort of thing . . . My wife basically has more flexible hours because obviously she has to blend in with the cooking and cleaning side irrespective of work hours really.
>
> (Charles; home-located petty commodity producer)

Some female respondents had weighed up the problems involved in reconstructing their working hours in ways similar to conventional industrial time and – although attracted by the prospect – had concluded it was not acceptable to other household members and was more trouble than it was worth:

> I am happy enough with it where it is, really. I've been through this thinking bit – thinking one ought to work from nine to five and shut the door on it. But that's a whole new lifestyle and it would obviously cause a big upheaval in this house if I decided to work nine until five. That's a serious amount of aggravation.
>
> (Barbara; home-located petty commodity producer)

Nevertheless, some female home-located producers whom we interviewed – particularly those capable of high earnings – had opted to buy in, or otherwise arrange for, childcare in ways which enabled them to adopt an unbroken working day.

Home-located producers construct spatial as well as temporal boundaries within their homes. They lay claim to and mark out space within the home for the purposes of making a living. Options we encountered included: taking over a spare room; conversion of a marginal space within the home (e.g., loft, garage, shed, corridor or outhouse); construction of purpose-built extensions; arrangement of furniture or screens to seal off an area within a room; closing of doors and

windows surrounding working areas; display of 'do not disturb' signs; and invest-
ing spaces with an office or business-like atmosphere by means of decor. All of
these entail the construction of physical and/or symbolic markers within the
home around spaces dedicated to home-located production.

Some of our respondents made use of temporary spaces that reverted to other
functions at non-working times. Others, in contrast, insisted upon the creation of
spaces permanently dedicated to home-located production. Among the latter,
some were prepared to share these localities with other household members whilst
others kept them strictly for one purpose only. Whatever the strategies involved,
respondents typically could talk at length about the negotiations and trade-offs
involved in reaching these decisions. The following extracts illustrate some of the
sensitivities, calculations and principles involved:

> I can't work in the front room, 'cause we try and keep the front room . . .
> nice. And then you've got somewhere to go, you know, if anybody comes
> unexpectedly or anything. And rarely upstairs, because you can't hear people
> knocking at the door and you feel like you're isolated upstairs. We've got no
> spare rooms anyway . . . and in the kitchen's inconvenient, obviously, with
> cooking and everything, so . . . I got an old dining room table that I've got
> up against the window. So I mean, I've got daylight, you know, while I'm
> doing my work and then I've got a table lamp for working at night-time. I'm
> just tucked away in the corner.
>
> (Elizabeth; homeworker)

> I don't bring any work in the room . . . We just don't like to bring work in
> the room. If, like, there's collars or that, then we'd bring it in the room, just
> little bits, but not the whole work . . . And we don't even put bags in the
> room, because I think that's a bit untidy . . . I just cover it up and I just put
> the chair on top of the machine . . . Saturday afternoons I do that, after I've
> finished the work and then just Hoover up and that, so it looks all neat
> and tidy.
>
> (Meena; homeworker)

There may be a feeling of unease when spatial boundaries of the home associated
with other domestic and family functions are crossed. Such transgressions may be
of nominal practical significance but have symbolic importance:

> The only bugbear really, is that you've got boxes, you know, in the dining
> room. I mean, it's not a messy job that I do, but you've just got, like, perhaps
> one box or two boxes full of socks and there's nowhere else really that I can
> put the boxes . . . So . . . I just feel as if the dining room's cluttered all the
> time.
>
> (Elizabeth; homeworker)

You have to make the dividing line and so I've actually eliminated all the filing cabinets to the garage . . . all I work with here is a fax and a telephone and a desk and it's very neat, very tidy and everything gets put away at night. That's the other thing, put it away, so you don't sit down to eat your dinner in the dining room, looking at a pile of files.

(Lorna; home-located petty commodity producer)

Options adopted clearly will reflect *inter alia* the income of the household and of the home-located producer, the nature of the home-located production process, the size and age of the accommodation and the disposition of rooms. Residential houses are rarely designed or constructed with work processes in mind. Some aspects of the improved general facilities of the housing stock in the twentieth century – such as installation of electric power and telephones – make working at home more feasible. On the other hand, newer houses may offer fewer chances of physically separating home and work because many are built to smaller specifications, incorporate open plan areas and have fewer bedrooms. Moreover, standards of decor and expectations of domestic comfort also have risen, heightening resistance to disruptions.

Some research, including our own qualitative interviews, found that women tend to claim less space (for example, smaller and less desirable rooms in the house) than male home-located producers. They are also more likely to work in areas that are, more or less regularly, used by other household members. This may reflect a tendency for the paid work done by female home-located producers to be more 'invisible' than that of males, because the home is seen as the 'natural' place for wives and mothers to be located (Haddon and Silverstone 1993; Miraftab 1996; Michelson and Lindén 1997).

One of the ways of attempting to cope with the juxtaposition of domestic and work life within the home is that of synchronising working times and spaces with those of others – including partners, children, friends and other network members. This involves an attempt to avoid conflicts over spatial and temporal resources by scheduling home-located production around the demands of domestic, household and family life:

You can't ignore the family so you really have to work around the family.

(Bella; home-located petty commodity producer)

For many home-located producers this entails a process of constant alternation between domestic labour and home-located production (Haddon and Lewis 1994; Miraftab 1996; Rangel de Paiva Abreu and Sorj 1996). Domestic tasks are woven into and between the times and spaces of home-located production. This may entail, for example, breaking off from paid work for a few moments – possibly even under the guise of resting – to set a domestic task in motion, only to return to home-located production shortly thereafter. This strategy can be very taxing but also quite invisible – particularly for women who are expected to get domestic work done if they are physically in the home. It is probably more often characteristic of female home-located producers than male, although our own interviews would suggest that the level of earnings is also crucial:

> For me particularly, I can go and put the washing machine on, then go back to work and then put the washing out. And the same with food, I can put a meal in the oven and then go back to work again.
>
> (Henrietta; home-located petty commodity producer)

> If I've got something for the house I need to do or someone's coming to service the Aga, or I've got someone coming in to do some work, they can be here and I can be here and I can still be working. I haven't got to leave the key with someone or spend half a day at home sitting around twiddling my thumbs . . . I'm here all the time and it saves me time if I've got little household jobs I need to do . . . Like I wanted to do a special meal for tonight I can nip out there, I could do something for half an hour and come back in . . . I used to sit outside the school in the car, sewing. Everywhere I went I took some sewing with me. If I had an appointment anywhere I would take sewing with me and would sit and sew whilst I was waiting.
>
> (Isobel; home-located employer)

Synchronisation with the timetables of other household members may result in working late, early or at other unsocial hours. Women, in particular, tend to avoid the times when partners and children demand their attention. At least one of our respondents had refined the process of synchronisation by developing a joint diary for the whole household which all members filled in. This enabled her to identify domestic commitments, spot potential clashes and plan ahead to cover the problems.

A contrasting approach to synchronisation is that of segregation. It entails establishing, and demanding recognition for, a work schedule in the home that mirrors the temporal and spatial patterns of conventional employment in office or factory (Haddon and Lewis 1994). This tactic requires the domestic life of the household to accommodate to times and spaces determined by the employment needs of home-located producers. There is research evidence which suggests that this approach may be more typical of male than female home-located producers (Haddon and Silverstone 1993; Salmi 1996), although both male and female respondents in our interviews adopted this strategy:

> I always keep to hours. If you don't keep to hours then it becomes more of a relaxation as you might say . . . basically it's from 9 o'clock to 1 o'clock and then we have lunch and then obviously after that from about 2 o'clock I work through until 5.30/6 o'clock.
>
> (Charles; home-located petty commodity producer)

This introduces the greatest possible spatial and temporal division between home and work life. One of our respondents, who did his work in an outhouse, even spoke of 'going home' at the end of his allotted work time.

Switching

So far our discussion has focused around establishing spatial and temporal boundaries in the home. Once in place, however, home-located producers must become adept at crossing backwards and forwards between different times and places. Technologies of the self concerned with this process we have called 'switching techniques'; that is, those involved with the process of changing, or switching, between the practices and expectations of the household and those of employment. They include, for example, the means employed by home-located producers to get themselves up and running at the beginning of a work session as well as those deployed in winding down at the end (Michelson and Lindén 1997). These cues or prompts are concerned with processes of discipline, effort and motivation that in many workplaces rest, to a significant degree, with management and supervisors. They are, therefore, focused on self-motivation and self-control.

Our respondents indicated that home-located producers use various devices to signal the start of a working session to themselves and to others in the household. They may go through familiar routines and rituals. Some employed domestic timetables as cues and markers (e.g., meal times or coming back from taking the kids to school). A number paced themselves against the timetables provided by the media, although others saw these as temptations to be avoided. Some even spoke of getting 'dressed up' as if to go out to work. Shamir (1992) reports that in the US it is possible to purchase commercial products that simulate the background noise of an office environment as a stimulus for those who work at home!

Having started, home-located producers need to stay switched on long enough to get the job done. This also requires self-imposed discipline. Various techniques were mentioned, such as working up to a preset time limit, promising oneself treats at the end of the work session, reproducing familiar timetables for continuity, varying work timetables for a change, combining work with other amusements or consciously avoiding distractions. Some respondents regarded TV and radio programmes as a useful aid in this regard, others saw them as a hindrance. Indeed, avoiding temptations was a familiar theme:

> It doesn't make any difference where you put your desk, it makes no difference whatsoever, because you will still have the temptation. As long as it's nowhere near a TV – and I definitely will never switch the music or the radio on. I won't do it.
>
> (Lorna; home-located petty commodity producer)

An experience very commonly reported by all types of home-located producers is difficulty in putting down the work. The task is continuously present in the immediate locality of the home and, as a result, sometimes feels like a looming presence during non-working hours. It requires self-discipline to stop work – and to stop thinking about work – as well as to start. Sometimes technologies of the self may not be adequate to cope with the reproach of unfinished tasks:

> Well, I can't actually see the work, but it's still on my mind, I don't leave it behind . . . It's a headache which hangs over my mind, really. I have to think about the fact that the work has to be done, that the boss is going to want the work and I won't be able to do it, so there is that constant worry.
>
> (Vikash; homeworker)

> It's there all the time. It totally absorbs you and you never get away from it. Not that you want to all that much, but there are times it would be better for you to just walk away and close the door. You never seem to be able to do that.
>
> (Henrietta; home-located petty commodity producer)

Where home-located producers are not sufficiently adept at developing switching-off techniques, there is a danger of becoming a 'workaholic' (Probert and Wacjman 1988a, 1988b; Ahrentzen 1992; Haddon and Silverstone 1993; Armstrong 1997; Salmi 1996, 1997b). Some home-located producers report that they cannot stop thinking about work issues and sneak back to put in extra time. Their whole lives can become consumed because the cues and prompts that forced them to 'go home from work' are not operative. As a result, the home-located producer may be in the home but not of it – living a life dominated by work and cut off from the rest of the household. In this context, the workstation itself may become a 'second home' or 'home in the home' – a 'little bolt hole' as one of our respondents described it – which absorbs time and interest outside of working hours:

> Yes, you could shut the door, it's very easy for me to come in. Too easy for me to come in and say I'm just going to do a bit of work.
>
> (Isobel; home-located employer)

It might be argued that the risk of becoming a 'workaholic' is greater for men than women. Men are used to their daily lives being ruled by fixed and continuous working hours. As we have seen, they are more accustomed to doing one task at a time rather than switching backwards and forwards between multiple roles. In addition, their gender roles may offer greater legitimacy when resisting interruptions or pleas to stop working from partners and children. However, in our qualitative interviews both males and females recognised this pitfall.

Home-located producers may respond to these pressures by insisting on creating leisure – or at least non-work – times. This may take the form of defending holiday times or other leisure times at all costs. Another way of facilitating switching off is to reduce or limit work loads; for example, by deliberately restricting the amount of work taken on. One of the temptations of home-located production can be taking on more work than can be completed. This may be encouraged by the variable nature of work loads, leading to a determination to grab all that is available. Switching, therefore, means defending both work and non-work times.

Whatever the techniques adopted, however, those who work at home commonly need to teach themselves to relax and to leave some tasks unfinished:

> You have to learn to switch off and think: 'Well, you know, I can't do that, because I haven't got time and I'll do that tomorrow.' And you just have to . . . get your priorities. You know what needs to be done, really, and then you try and fit the rest in round . . . it is difficult, but you just juggle it around, you know.
>
> (Maureen; home-located petty commodity producer)

Defending

The boundaries of time and space within the home characteristic of home-located production are rarely formalised or totally unambiguous. They tend, therefore, to be inherently fragile, problematic and in need of monitoring and policing. On the one hand, employment activities may cross their legitimate boundaries within the home – wherever these are drawn – and disrupt the wider life of the household. On the other, the demands of family and home may gobble up times and spaces home-located producers need in order to function in the labour market. Home-located producers generate technologies of the self which detect and address these eventualities.

Some techniques are intended to deter or neutralise the effect of invasions into working times and spaces by other household members, such as children or partners. These we have defined as defending techniques. Disruptions may take many forms – such as distracting noise, enquiries about domestic matters, demands for personal servicing, more or less insistent requests to socialise, routine visits to the home by friends and family, household emergencies, and pleas for assistance:

> Basically you are here at everybody else's beck and call . . . You end up trying to please everybody else and losing track of where you're going – because you're always on call. And the children say: 'Oh well, so and so can't take us to choir today because they're at work – so you can take us can't you Mum?' And you end up doing all the runs because everybody else is at work. Then you end up working at night to make up. And sometimes you wonder if it's totally fair.
>
> (Barbara; home-located petty commodity producer)

There are sort of headaches of working at home as well. Like, you know, the little girl comes into this room and she says, 'Oh papa, I want to go out somewhere.' And then she touches the machines . . . And that is not very good and

I get worried about it, you know. Her hand could go in the machine and that is dangerous. So that is a bit of a headache. And there are people coming in here to see me. So all that is kind of a hassle.

(Vikash; homeworker)

The thing that used to irritate me more than anything when they were here was when they would come in and say: 'What's for tea?' – which made me feel as if I was neglecting them.

(Diane; home-located employer)

Male home-located producers may find it easier than females to assert their right to defend themselves against invasions into their working space and time. Indeed, some – though not all – of our male respondents described the home as a quiet place to work, free from the disruptions of office and factory:

You don't get any distractions. There are no big company irritations, like meetings, office work, board meetings, things of that nature.

(Daniel; home-located petty commodity producer)

Women are more vulnerable to being seen primarily as housewives and, therefore, regarded by other family members as available and eligible for interruption. Female home-located producers may even face invasion of their very thoughts by their continuing responsibility for domestic labour, heightened by their presence in the home:

I tend to be the one that organises everything. In a way men have it a lot easier. Because he goes out to work and he focuses on his business, right, and that's all he has to worry about. He doesn't have to worry whether his shirts are clean, what he's having for dinner, who's doing what, who's picking Justina up unless I ask him to – but I have had to organise everything. It doesn't bother me but I think women do have to have the ability to be very, very well organised and self-disciplined. And time management, I think we're much better at it . . . I couldn't afford for my time-keeping to be terrible because everything has to slot in otherwise I wouldn't be efficient at what I do. I think working women have to be a lot more organised and have to be able to have a brain that can think of lots of things at once.

(Isobel; home-located employer)

Responses to domestic and other household interruptions can be ambiguous, reflecting both irritation at the loss of production and guilt over perceived neglect of household duties (cf. Huws *et al.* 1996: 45–46):

I'm getting a bit laid back about it now but before, when I was doing contract work, it was extremely difficult . . . it felt that everyone felt they were more important than my work. And whereas my work was adding a quite considerable amount to the household budget and nobody seemed to take that into consideration . . . I'm trying not to worry about it because I think I did get to fever pitch over it and had it carried on I wouldn't have been worth knowing – so it came to the fact that something had to give . . . Basically I've had to draw up a list of priorities and my work has got to come at the bottom. The family has to come first and my husband's job contributes a lot more to this household than I do so you know – you've got to put it into perspective and work accordingly.

(Barbara; home-located petty commodity producer)

Domestic invasions of working time may be headed off by teaching children early on not to cross symbolic or physical thresholds. Alternatively, counter attractions and entertainment may be arranged:

Sometimes I just say to Justina: 'Look I can't have you in here I need to concentrate, I've got to make a 'phone call.' . . . Because she's grown up with me working I'm not like a lot of the other mothers; she knows that I have other priorities. I'll give her time but it's likely planned in and she won't ask to have it because she knows that she can't. It doesn't bother her, it's just the way it's always been. So we're not going out on a lot of trips and stuff and she doesn't have loads of friends round for me to entertain.

(Isobel; home-located employer)

My daughter's known since when she was little that you don't go into the workroom with drinks or anything like that.

(Sarah; home-located petty commodity producer)

They just entertain themselves . . . I mean, they're not far, they're either in the front room, while I'm in the dining room, or they play in the bedroom or . . . they sit and watch telly or a video or they just entertain themselves.

(Elizabeth; homeworker)

Sometimes the invasion of household life into work may take the form of social visits by friends and neighbours, who may have to be 'cooled out' if they arrive during working hours:

I work from home but they don't see me trolling around the village, they think I'm a bit odd . . . In the day, they go past the window and they all know that should they knock the door [I'll say]: 'I'm sorry, I'm busy.' 'Cause when I first moved . . . ladies all used to knock the door: 'Oh, would you like coffee?' Can't do it! . . . You can't, because if you started that . . . it's not serious . . . I'm known as a bit of a recluse.

(Lorna; home-located petty commodity producer)

It should be emphasised that not all our respondents experienced such visits as a problem. Some, particularly those engaged in homeworking, found the presence of friends sometimes broke the monotony. They often continued to work during such episodes or might even give their visitors work to do. For others – particularly those with high discretion or creative jobs – such interruptions could not be sustained.

Intruding

Just as household relations may invade the times and places of work so, too, may the routines of home-located production become an intrusion into the home. It should not be assumed that the presence of a production process in the home is always intrusive – farm houses, for example, have traditionally blended home and work. Moreover, the degree of intrusiveness will depend on the type of work, size of the house and lifestyle of the occupants. Nevertheless, home is widely regarded as a private and personal place. The introduction of a labour process can lead to the feeling that it has been opened up to strangers – such as suppliers, clients and customers – as well as machinery and materials that have no place in a domestic setting. Common problems concern lack of space, smells, noise, electrical or mechanical hazards, the presence of unsightly machinery in the home, and storage of working materials (see Chapter 6, pp. 96–97). Home-located producers may find themselves involved in domestic disagreements and conflicts over the use of household space, which call for techniques of negotiation, adjudication and legitimation.

One of the invidious features of being in work at home is that intrusions into domestic life are likely to be presented – by both home-located producers and other household members – as one-off contingent events whereas, in reality, they are often intrinsic and regular features of home-located production. The variability and unpredictability of work loads makes it all but inevitable that working schedules and regimes will be subject to last minute alterations. This is further compounded by managerial strategies that entail a 'feast and famine' distribution of work. Individual home-located producers may cope by negotiating piecemeal concessions from other family members on a 'just this once' basis. Home-located producers may make these promises in good faith, only to discover later that they repeatedly have to renegotiate domestic commitments. This may result in them being perceived by other household members as inefficient, incompetent or not sufficiently dedicated to family life. Our interviews suggest that there are a range of responses to these pressures. Domestic labour may be reduced in volume, organised more efficiently, delegated to others or replaced by market-based alternatives:

> Well, the domestic timetable tends to go rather doesn't it . . . I don't do anywhere near the amount of housework and cooking that I used to when I wasn't so busy. Things do tend to slide quite a lot . . . We do have to pay

other people to do things for us sometimes. There is a guy decorating the outside of the house now, and in the past we would have done that ourselves. And a guy comes and does the garden.

(Henrietta; home-located commodity producer)

Occasionally, well, my mum actually lives in Yorkshire, but she does come down, perhaps every couple of months, she'll come and have a week with me and she'll sort of . . . spring clean!

(Maureen; home-located petty commodity producer)

I cook a meal every evening but then I may do a bulk meal at the weekend and therefore I put a lot of stuff down in the freezer. I don't get stuff out of packets very often. It's usually stuff I've cooked and planned. I would say I'm very well organised, you have to be well organised otherwise it would just be chaos . . . Shopping – I usually do most of it on Friday, ready for the weekend and I usually fit it in with what business commitments I have on that day . . . I always think of time, because time to me is very, very precious . . . I try to do it at the beginning or at the end of a day so I'm not itsy bitsy.

(Isobel; home-located employer)

It may well be that different members of households have contrasting perceptions of the intrusiveness of home-located production. We certainly found, when we interviewed couples in the same household, that male and female partners often had strikingly different estimates of the impact of home-located production on domestic labour and routines.

Managing boundaries around the household

In the previous section we explored techniques concerned with the construction and reproduction of divisions of time and space *within* the home. In this section, we shall turn to the management of boundaries *around* the home which mark it off from the wider world. Such boundaries have acquired great significance since the separation of home and work, the privatisation of sexual and family ties, the construction and celebration of childhood, and the growing emphasis on the home as a locus of personal identity and ontological security based on consumption choices. Home-located production represents a potential threat to the encapsulation of family and home (Saunders 1990; Dupuis and Thorns 1998). It opens up domestic time and space to the encroachments of the labour market. Such disruptions may be exacerbated by the variable and unpredictable flow of work into the home experienced by many home-located producers.

There is, moreover, an ironic twist to attempts by home-located producers to maintain boundaries between their households and the labour market. Home-located producers often feel that their isolation from the opportunities and sociability of the office and factory may disadvantage them in the race for pro-motion, bonus payments and recognition. They fear that they are under-valued and under-rewarded compared to their peers in conventional workplaces (see Chapter 6). However, they are also often under pressures, of various kinds, to keep their homes as 'homely' as possible. Such pressures emphasise the divisions between home-located producers and other groups in the labour market. It is, thus, possible to detect an ambivalence or duality in the techniques of the self employed by home-located producers in defining and managing boundaries around the home. On the one hand, they seek to combat the effects of isolation and lack of credibility. On the other, they seek to maintain the integrity of the home against outside encroachments. We turn now to consider various elements of this dilemma.

Isolation

Our qualitative interviews, and other research studies, demonstrate that by no means all home-located producers object to the solitude of their work. Nevertheless, a common complaint is that of isolation and detachment from others, including colleagues, clients, advisers, friends and neighbours (see, for example, Christensen 1988; Beach 1989; Ahrentzen 1992; Haddon and Silverstone 1993; Haddon and Lewis 1994; Felstead and Jewson 1996; Huws et al. 1996). Isolation is very commonly cited as a major disadvantage of home-located production of all kinds – even by those who also say they value not having to deal with the petty routines of office politics or the 'rat race' of commuting:

> The isolation problem. It is one of the biggest problems that teleworkers face. If you are in a house on your own on a very quiet estate like this, you could very rapidly get into feeling very isolated and withdrawn.
> (Stephen; home-located petty commodity producer)

> I've noticed with me being at home now with the kids, you don't seem to socialise as much as you used to at work . . . it just seems . . . now, working from home, even though it's part-time . . . you're very isolated.
> (Chantelle; homeworker)

> Loneliness, nobody to bat things off . . . no support, if somebody sort of drops a ton of bricks on you . . . nobody's there to buoy you up.
> (Lorna; home-located petty commodity producer)

Isolation techniques are the ways in which home-located producers cope with these circumstances; that is, manage to retain motivation and enthusiasm during long periods of absence of contact from colleagues, superiors or juniors. One approach, mentioned by our respondents, involves deliberately creating moments of human contact during the working day:

> I probably still look for some social interaction during that working day. So I'll actually come out with the excuse of getting a coffee, to see whether there's anyone around in the house who I can talk to. So I still look for that sort of social contact, being amongst other people.
>
> (Bill; home-located petty commodity producer)

Others deliberately created interruptions to their working day to relieve their sense of seclusion:

> When you're on the computer you just have to take breaks because you just get boss-eyed . . . If you worked in an office you would tend to go out and have a cup of coffee with people – natter on the stairs, go for a walk to go and see someone. You build breaks into your pattern of work. I build them in by just doing things around the house.
>
> (Stephen; home-located petty commodity producer)

Other respondents commented that they broke up the isolation by deliberately spending part of their day or week in contact with clients, whether by fax, phone or at personal meetings:

> What I try to do is to compensate . . . by having periods when I'm out working with people, going to meetings, running around all over the place. And it's a very nice package because I can sit here and I can shift a lot of work that needs to be done at home in a quiet situation and the rest of the time I can go out and work with people. So I get the best of both worlds.
>
> (Stephen; home-located petty commodity producer)

Encouraging visits by friends and relatives can relieve the loneliness but create other problems, as is indicated by the ambivalent comments of one of our respondents:

> So they sit here and they talk to me while I carry on working. They'll stay for a while and then they go, but sometimes I do mind them being here, because I know that the work has to be done and them being here slows me down. And then the work has to be completed on time and the boss will want it. But none the less, you know, it's nice to have a little bit of company. So I do mind and I don't. And then there are days when I don't see anyone at all . . . So I do have friends. It is difficult but if I don't then I'd be very lonely. So I do like to have friends, but sometimes I do wish they'd go, so I can get on with my work.
>
> (Vikash; homeworker)

Another option open to some home-located producers is to create virtual networks and contacts via email bulletin boards and chat rooms. This was a tactic heavily developed by one of our respondents – Stephen – also leading to subsequent face-to-face contacts in conferences, training courses or career development ventures.

Encroachments

One of the ways in which the isolation of home-located producers is most likely to be broken is by contact with suppliers of work and clients. However, these interactions are often problematic in themselves, calling for techniques of encroachment management. Such visits may pose a variety of potential problems. The supplier of work might call at inconvenient times during family or social events or disrupt intimate leisure occasions. Furthermore, clients, colleagues or business associates who drop in might not be impressed by 'homely' surroundings or the unruly behaviour of other household members:

> The biggest problem is that you've got to try and sound professional when people 'phone the house . . . if you have a business customer with this number, and they 'phone the house and they hear a screaming kid in the background or a dishwasher whirring or whatever, it's not on. So you have to keep the business front, as though it was business.
>
> (Lorna; home-located petty commodity producer)

Our respondents coped with these pressures in various ways, including forestalling such visits altogether, scheduling them for times when there was least likely to be a collision with other household members, or even creating separate entrances and spaces for business-related visitors (cf. Armstrong 1997, 1999; Christensen 1988).

Further problems may arise if the home-located producer needs to expand and take on employees:

> I would feel difficult employing someone to come and help me in the business if it was a complete stranger. It would be difficult having a stranger come to the house and go upstairs and work with you. I'd have to use outworkers.
>
> (Henrietta; home-located petty commodity producer)

> But if I wanted to employ someone I would have a problem. I did where we used to live, employ someone to work on back-up work and I just didn't like it. It was someone coming into my home and it's really funny. If I had an office that was attached to the house with a separate entrance and self-contained I don't think it would bother me. But I didn't like the idea if I wasn't here – although I know you can trust people, because I've got a cleaner who comes in and out when I'm not around.
>
> (Isobel; home-located employer)

Variability of work loads

Home-located production in general and homeworking in particular are notori-
ous for the variability of work loads. Much homeworking is inherently seasonal or
market sensitive. Moreover, suppliers of work may switch production around
among various homeworkers as a deliberate managerial strategy. Piece rate payment systems mean, of course, that variations in work intensity result in income
variations. All these characteristics also pose challenges to self-organisation and to
negotiated arrangements with other household members (Haddon and Lewis
1994; Huws *et al.* 1996; Felstead and Jewson 1996).

A number of our respondents emphasised that coping with unpredictability
called for careful planning and self-discipline. It may mean being prepared to
handle disruption or cancellation of family events, with possible consequences for
relationships with other household members. It can also involve working unsocial
hours and generally dealing with great stress.

> I think I cope with it quite well. I don't mind being in that situation. I don't
> think it would suit a lot of people because sometimes, if I'm tired, I some-
> times think 'I can't cope' and I go into a mad panic and have to go and sit
> down and think: 'It's not too much of a problem.' I just have to think about
> it. I think you are either like that and can cope with it, or you can't. I thrive
> on it.
>
> (Isobel; home-located employer)

Several respondents were acutely aware of the danger of becoming overstretched
by taking on too much work:

> You're inclined to panic when there's no work coming in. You can then
> overbid and if they all come in you can't do it.
>
> (Bella; home-located petty commodity producer)

It may be necessary to develop the confidence to refuse or postpone work – and
the wisdom to pick the right jobs to decline.

> I had to turn something down last week. She's one of my old clients, she'll
> just wait until I can do . . . If I can't do it, I can't.
>
> (Sarah; home-located petty commodity producer)

> People who come to me now – it's mainly through word of mouth and
> they are recommending me on my quality of work and not the speed at
> which I do it. If they have to wait a couple of months or longer – they
> don't tend to mind. They come to me because I'm good and they're pre-
> pared to wait. Most of them say: 'Well, do it when you've got time' because
> they know I've got other commitments . . . if people don't like it I tell

them they can take their fabric elsewhere because I'm not going to worry about it now.

> (Barbara; home-located petty commodity producer)

Another tactic adopted by one of our respondents in ironing out variability in work loads was that of cultivating contacts with the supplier of work and learning to manage this relationship:

> When I first started, I mean, I used to think, 'Oh, I need to finish the work off, he's dropped the work off, I've got to finish it.' I'd sit at night to finish it off. But it's different now, like, because I know him a bit better, my boss. So I can like tell him that, you know, I don't work at nights or I will do it in the morning . . . I always tell my boss, like, to deliver work and sometimes, like, if there's lots and lots of work and the passage is filled up, I'll say to him, 'Don't give me all this much, just give me as much as sits over here.' Because too much work and then, it's so difficult to go out of the house. And in the house, like, even if you have a fire or something, it's going to be difficult to get out and in, if you fill the house up too much with work. So I always say to him, 'Collect it on time.' So he always comes about three times a day to collect it, morning, afternoon and evening.
>
> (Meena; homeworker)

Rather than trying to iron out swings in work load, another approach is to become adept at working intensively for bouts of time, with the objective of securing the reward of holiday or 'down-time' later on. This 'famine and feast' pattern of working – reminiscent of pre-industrial temporalities (Joyce 1987; Thompson 1967; Reid 1976) – can result in periods when work activity takes priority over all else, engulfing domestic times and spaces. When demand slackens the work splurge is ended and domestic regimes reassert themselves:

> If there's a rush order on . . . I feel as if I'm pressurised and I have to sit there, no matter how long it takes and get it all done. And I tend to neglect the house. But then I have a mad clean up on a Thursday night, before I know my husband's coming home on a Friday.
>
> (Elizabeth; homeworker)

> The work has to be back in on the Wednesday, so I can put a bill in to get some money. Normally on Monday and Tuesday, I do more work than I will on a Thursday and Friday, 'cause that's sort of like the end of the week. I've got to get it done by then.
>
> (Tracy; homeworker)

In extreme cases of work pressure, the whole household can be drawn into the support of the home-located producer, with children and other household members taking up auxiliary work roles. This has been described as 'Family Inc.'; that is, not a family business but a family or household organised around supporting home-located production (Beach 1989). Something along these lines appeared to occur in the households of some of our respondents at moments of extreme pressure.

Invisibility

Research suggests that home-located production is often perceived by friends, relatives and other household members as not 'real' work, precisely because its times and spaces are located in the home. It may be presumed that the home-located producer is readily available for a social call or a chat. Within the firm, too, home-located wage labourers may be marginalised by colleagues or supervisors. Female homeworkers may be particularly vulnerable in these respects (Costello 1988; Haddon and Lewis 1994; Huws *et al.* 1990; Miraftab 1996; Weiss 1996). Such stigmatising or marginalising of the home-located producer's identity is by no means inevitable and a number of our respondents specifically reported that they had not experienced this kind of treatment. However, others were less sanguine. It might be expected that men would be more alarmed by being regarded as 'not really working', thereby threatening conventional masculine identities. However, both male and female respondents commented in this vein:

> They think it's pin money . . . pin money, as they call it . . . It's not pin money, it just gives me a bit of spending money for sort of Christmas time or the kids' birthdays or whatever, just a bit extra.
>
> (Tracy; homeworker)

> I think sometimes you aren't taken so seriously especially if you're a woman. I still think there could be a bit of – 'Oh, she works from home, I bet she doesn't work all the time, it's only part-time.'
>
> (Isobel; home-located employer)

> People like the wife who thinks: 'You're here all day – why haven't you hung the washing out? Why haven't you done the washing up?' There is a prejudice against homeworkers because you don't go out and struggle to earn a living . . . there's that kind of little bit like a macho thing . . . a lot of businesses think that if you're working at home you're a 'mickey-mouse', 'micro', 'don't take it seriously' type of thing.
>
> (Stephen; home-located petty commodity producer)

Various techniques may be adopted by home-located producers in order to maintain credibility and status, both in their households and wider communities. One is to distinguish between 'insiders', who can be trusted to understand and whose opinions are valued, and others who require more careful impression management:

The professional, who understands what homeworking is about, knows. You don't get it there, because they realise what you're giving them, how you're doing it and . . . that you have to keep up certain standards. When you get into a sort of social group and you say – 'Oh, I work from home' – you are then classed as a sort of second-class citizen, you're not quite 'us'.

(Bella; home-located petty commodity producer)

Another technique is deliberately to avoid revealing that the work is done at home, especially to key business and employment contacts:

There's something we've found actually with getting supplies of fabrics from people. We try to disguise the fact that we work from home. We disguise that by leaving part of the address off orders and things so that they don't realise it's a house that they're being delivered to. Because a lot of companies if you want samples from them, then want to order from them, can be quite difficult.

(Henrietta; home-located petty commodity producer)

Actually what I do say, and it's not totally untrue, is that I have offices attached to my home. What I'm really doing or trying to is to give the impression that it's a separate building but it's on the same site as home . . . When I'm sat here and I'm 'phoning people up, they aren't aware what I look like, where I'm sitting to make the 'phone call . . . I wouldn't want a client to see where I live because that would give them a false impression. I meet them in probably a local hotel or I go to their offices . . . People who I know quite well, clients I've worked with for a while, know that I'm based at home. But that doesn't bother them at all because they know that I'll deliver what they want. So they haven't got a problem. But you do have to be careful with the positioning.

(Isobel; home-located employer)

Various technological devices may aid the process of concealing the true location of the work:

The one thing you want if you're a small business is somebody to answer the 'phone for you. Answerphones are not very good because people won't use them or they hang up. If you've got a virtual team – and there are more and more examples of this now – if you work together, say six people form a collective, they have one number for all six people. You dial that number and it hunts for the first line that is available. You answer with a common name or there are other ways that you can answer. This is the way Call Centres work . . . So it looks like you're actually dealing with a lot of people all in one office. The outside client doesn't know they're all working at home. If you present as a big company, you are quite capable of delivering the same level of service but it overcomes that credibility gap.

(Stephen; home-located petty commodity producer)

Another way of countering negative stereotypes is to create an alternative value system that reinvests home-located production with credibility. For one of our respondents this involved evoking a reading of the historical past:

> If you go back into the history of this village and look at the knitting industry in the seventeenth and eighteenth centuries – you will find that 80 to 90 per cent of households at that time had knitting machines – frame knitters. The history of the frame knitters in [this county] shows that during that time the backbone of the economy was the people working at home. All we've seen now is the knitting machines being replaced by computers.
>
> (Stephen; home-located petty commodity producer)

Conclusion

The above do not exhaust the technologies of the self entailed in home-located production. For example, Ahrentzen (1992: 130) has drawn attention to the management of personal security by women working alone in the home. However, rather than elaborating these further, we wish to turn in the next chapter to teasing out some of the more general themes underlying the processes discussed here. By way of conclusion to this chapter, there are a number of general features of technologies of the self that our discussion has highlighted.

- Technologies of the self are performances. They are aspects of self-management and self-presentation. There is a knowing and reflexive adoption of these modes of behaviour.
- Technologies of the self commonly deal with dilemmas, uncertainties, ambiguities and contradictions. They are most elaborate and self-conscious at points in the social fabric where performances are fragile, vulnerable, stretched or are breaking up. Consequently, they are often not characterised by neat and untroubled behaviours. The solution to one dilemma may generate other problems.
- Technologies of the self incorporate relationships of both knowledge and power. The knowledge entailed in management of the self simultaneously establishes relationships of power with others. They constrain and limit in the same moment as they enable and empower.
- Technologies of the self call for a high degree of self-discipline and self-organisation. Like the respondents of other studies – such as Huws *et al.* (1996: 67) – our interviewees often found this self-discipline difficult to achieve in practice and they not uncommonly chided themselves for not doing better. Since this was one of the issues our respondents commented on most freely, we shall end this chapter with their words:

The requirement is to be self-motivated and . . . it's the horror story sometimes. It's so difficult to explain to anybody who doesn't have the opportunity to work from home. A lot of people say, it's a good idea. The way I feel at the moment, with the pressures that I have with the family, I wish I could go to the factory every day . . . I've really got to work a lot harder and discipline myself to accommodate the family and the business.

(Geoff; high discretion home-located wage labourer)

You have to be very self-disciplined. I've talked to people, I've worked with a lot of people who work from home, and some of them are better than others. It's very tempting when it's nice to think, 'I'll just nip out and do a bit of gardening.' Or someone could pay you a visit. Or get on the 'phone to someone. And it's amazing how difficult it is to switch off from all that.

(Isobel; home-located employer)

You have to be disciplined, 'cause you have to do it . . . I mean, sometimes, I think: 'Oh, I can't be bothered to do this.' If it's a nice day, you want to stay out in the garden, you want to be out there in the garden. So, you know, if I do take time off in the day, I sometimes have to do a bit of it in the evening, but I've got to do the work . . . if you're not feeling too clever, then it's still got to be done, can't get time off, can't have a week off . . . I have to be disciplined, you can always find something else that you'd rather be doing.

(Shirley; homeworker)

As time gets on I am finding it harder and harder to make myself do the work – that's the problem.

(Barbara; home-located petty commodity producer)

Chapter 9

Combining home and work

> It is *precisely* the location of the work which raises one of the most signifi-
> cant aspects of the social relationships involved: working at home involves
> a *second* set of production relationships, those between members of the
> household in the domestic labour process of producing use values. People's
> location in the social relations of both production processes are different
> and interactive, but when the two are merged in a single location, the web
> becomes ever more complex and the possibilities more numerous.
>
> (Walker 1987: 7; original emphasis)

Introduction

Underlying the specific characteristics of particular technologies of the self, discussed in the previous chapter, can be discerned more general strategies for
combining home and work deployed by home-located producers. These involve
principles that shape the ordering of time and space within the home. In this chapter we will analyse these principles and their relationship to different types of
households and household understandings.

Home-located production problematises the temporal and spatial organisation
of household relationships. Bulos and Chaker (1995) argue that it represents a
potential disruption to the home on physical, interactional and personal levels. An
issue for research is how home-located producers deal with this disruption and, at
the same time, seek to maintain an enduring sense of integrity and personal identity. In reaching decisions about how to accommodate paid employment in the
home, home-located producers and other household members may be forced to
articulate and operationalise principles and beliefs about domestic time and space
that are not commonly expressed in an explicit and direct form. It is the deep
rooted beliefs and values about home, family and private life that they draw upon
in this process that are the subject of this chapter.

It must be emphasised at the outset that the arguments presented here are speculative hypotheses rather than the outcome of our own or others' empirical
research. Although they are derived from the findings of studies of household relations and gender divisions, they represent an agenda for future investigation

rather than a summation of completed work. Indeed, the themes we explore are ones which have so far rarely been the focus of attention. It should also be noted that this chapter is largely devoted to a discussion of home-located production in general rather than homeworking in particular. This is because we wish to comment upon the broadest level of analysis identified at the outset of the book in Chapter 2: that is, the conjunction of social relations of production and reproduction. We are interested in the collision of two worlds of meaning and organisation within one locale. It is perfectly possible to consider the issues raised in this chapter solely in relation to homeworking, as we have defined it. This task, however, will not be tackled here.

The chapter begins by identifying a number of temporal and spatial strategies for combining home and work. These concern the extent to which boundaries of time and space between the home and the outside world, and boundaries of time and space within the home itself, are maintained. The chapter then moves on to consider the main social forces that determine the different decisions that home-located producers make with respect to these household boundaries. It is suggested that labour markets, labour processes, gender relations, ethnicity and household understanding all play a part. However, this chapter focuses on household understandings. This is partly because household understandings have been under-researched but mainly because, as argued in Chapter 2, the household context is central to the definition of home-located production. Next we outline four ideal types of household understanding, derived from research in contemporary Britain. It is suggested that these household understandings offer a variety of opportunities and constraints to those of their male and female members who seek to engage in home-located production. These are explored in turn. It is further argued that, in managing home-located production, each household understanding generates a characteristic pattern of spatial and temporal divisions. These highlight particular combinations of technologies of the self among home-located producers.

Strategies for combining home and work

Relatively little is known about the grounds on which home-located producers organise time and space in combining home and work. There is a dearth of research – especially with respect to men who work at home and with respect to different types of households (though see, for example, Ahrentzen 1990; Haddon and Silverstone 1993; Fothergill and Rose 1998).

Nevertheless, it is commonly suggested that there are two contrasting strategies adopted by home-located producers. These ideal types – defining the extreme ends of a continuum of responses – refer to the ways in which home-located producers define and use space and time in the home (cf. Haddon and Silverstone 1993; Haddon and Lewis 1994; Bulos and Chaker 1993, 1995; Ahrentzen 1990; Christensen 1985; Beach 1989; Huws *et al.* 1996: 41–46; Michelson and Lindén 1997; Miraftab 1996: 70; Shamir 1992). One approach, it is argued, is to establish a clear separation between domesticity and employment. This strategy seeks to replicate the conventional divisions of home and work within the household. The other strategy represents a fusion of the two activities, thereby generating a synthesis that reshapes and redefines the home. These options are summed up by one of the respondents interviewed in a Swedish study:

> There are two models, one is to integrate the job with the dwelling and then I think the furniture must be subordinated to the home. The other one is, like some people do, to establish a real office at home. It's like opening the door to the working-room and then at once one is at work, in a completely different environment. Those are the alternatives.
>
> (Michelson and Lindén 1997: 16)

It is our contention that this conceptualisation offers a helpful beginning but does not fully capture the complexities of the situation or the range of options open to home-located producers. In our discussion of technologies of the self, in Chapter 7, we identified two different types of boundaries that home-located producers confront and negotiate. We distinguished between, on the one hand, the management of boundaries *between* the household and the outside world and, on the other, the organisation of boundaries among activities conducted *within* the household. In this chapter, we will argue that the spatial and temporal strategies of home-located producers entail decisions that may maintain or erode both these sets of boundaries.

The strength of spatial and temporal boundaries *between* the household and the outside world shapes the sense of privacy, inclusion and belonging experienced by household members. It also may determine their sense of threat, danger and anxiety. Households that maintain clear and unambiguous divisions with the outside world typically construct material and symbolic walls and thresholds around the home. There are clear markers delineating household time and space from those of the public sphere. Ports of entry and exit are explicitly identified, guarded by ritual and charged with emotion. External influences may be regarded as polluting, threatening, alien or exotic. In contrast, where divisions between inside and outside the home are weak or ill-defined it is relatively easy to come and go without comment or supervision. Membership of the household is fluid and changing. External interventions are not seen as intrinsically threatening or unwelcome.

The organisation of boundaries *within* the home among different activities reflects the extent to which rigid internal divisions characterise household life. Where such boundaries are strong there is a place for everything and everything is in its place. Different parts of the house may be regarded as the domain of particular sub-groups, such as the old or young, male or female, married or single, guests or family. Each room has its own clearly designated function, and the mixing of activities – such as eating in the bedroom or sleeping in the lounge – is regarded as abhorrent. In contrast, in households where internal separations of these kinds are not sustained, times and spaces commonly have multiple and flexible uses. Members move freely around the space of the home, there are few locks on the doors and few *a priori* grounds for objecting to the presence of others. Similarly, timetables are contingent and provisional, rarely invested with sacred significance or symbolic power.

Home-located producers belonging to households constructed around these different patterns of division and inclusion are faced with contrasting problems and opportunities when seeking to combine home and work. The constraints and choices inherent in their domestic relationships shape the underlying strategies that determine their deployment of technologies of the self. With respect to boundaries between the household and the outside world, we shall distinguish between home-located producers who pursue strategies of *openness* and *closure*. With respect to internal divisions among household activities and relationships, we shall distinguish home-located producers who adopt strategies of *segregation* and *integration*. In case there is any doubt, it should be emphasised that these concepts are ideal types and that they represent the ends of continua rather than discrete entities (see Table 9.1).

Openness refers to a strategy for managing the boundary between the household and the outside world that allows for an easy and ready interaction between, on the one hand, members of the household (including the home-located producer) and, on the other, suppliers, clients and other business associates. There is no prohibition, for example, on members of the family answering the telephone to clients. The unexpected arrival of suppliers is not routinely perceived as an assault on the integrity of home life. In general, home-located producers feel relatively comfortable with employment relations spilling over into the times and places of the home. Their household relationships permit them to cope with such eventualities relatively easily. None of the respondents we interviewed in our qualitative study, discussed in the previous chapter, appeared to have fully adopted this strategy for managing the interface between the worlds of domesticity and employment, although, as we have seen, a number sought to combat the experience of isolation by tentatively opening their homes to outside contacts.

Closure comprises a strategy for managing the boundary between the household and the outside world that draws a clear and unambiguous line between the private life of the home and the demands of employment. Among our respondents in the qualitative interviews, for example, we saw that Sarah and Barbara refused to allow the demands of clients to infringe on key aspects of their family commitments. Furthermore, Lorna, Henrietta, Stephen and Isobel adopted various other aspects of this strategy; for example, preventing business associates interacting with, or even knowing about, members of their households. Closure entails the construction of thresholds – literal and symbolic – which suppliers, employers and clients are not permitted to cross. The home is sealed off from outside influences, interventions and interactions. Home-located producers may well experience moral and material pressures from other members of their households to sustain this division.

Table 9.1 **Management of temporal and spatial boundaries within and around the home**

Terms used	Explanation
Open	*Weak external* boundaries between the home and the outside world
Closed	*Strong external* boundaries between the home and the outside world
Segregation	*Strong internal* boundaries within the home between the times and places of paid work and domestic life
Integration	*Weak internal* boundaries within the home between the times and places of paid work and domestic life

Segregation entails establishing strict boundaries within the household between the times and spaces allocated to, on the one hand, paid work and, on the other, domestic life. This was, for instance, characteristic of the way Charles organised his life, though not his wife who was also in work at home. Segregation typically entails the specification of clearly defined and exclusive hours of work – the simulation of 'industrial time' and specially designated working spaces; the mimicking of factory or office – within the life of the home. Such arrangements are likely to occur in households where the domestic sphere is itself divided into functionally differentiated localities and temporalities. Where home is internally differentiated, home-located production is compartmentalised in its own spatial and temporal cocoon. Such an arrangement might indicate that the home-located producer commands power and authority within the household, laying claim to precious and scarce domestic resources. On the other hand, it might be indicative of a relative lack of power, such that the home-located producer is relegated to, and hemmed within, marginal spaces and times in the household.

Integration entails intermingling and eliding the times and spaces of paid work and the home. Work and domestic labour are threaded in, through and between one another, resulting in the fusion or multiple use of time and space for different functions. This, for example, was a feature of the timetables described in Chapter 8 by Chantelle, Maureen, Henrietta, Sarah, Isobel and, to some extent, Stephen. Integration means that domestic and work regimes may be conducted within sight and sound of one another. It would encompass situations such as a homeworker who works on the dining room table while keeping an eye on children playing elsewhere in the room (cf. Elizabeth); or a petty commodity producer who routinely breaks into her working time for short periods in order to carry out domestic tasks such as putting clothes in the washing machine or a meal into the oven (cf. Henrietta). Such an approach to the organisation of home-located production may entail continuous negotiation of access to time and space in the home. It implies a tolerance of ambiguity and the reconciliation of divergent needs. However, it may also be the product of a failure by other household members to recognise the work loads entailed in home-located production and/or domestic labour.

Openness and closure, segregation and integration are referred to in this chapter as *strategies* for managing the relationship between home and work. It is perhaps as well to note that our use of the term 'strategy' here does not necessarily imply deliberate planning and premeditated intent. Rather, it is intended to capture an emergent pattern which can be discerned within the outcomes of a series of specific technologies of the self. Whether such patterns are the product of conscious planning, or emerge in a cumulative and unreflexive way, may be regarded as an empirical question to be established in particular instances (M. Anderson *et al.* 1994).

Strategies based around openness and integration are likely to involve ongoing processes of negotiation between household members. Spatial and temporal divisions within the home and between the home and the wider world are a movable feast, open to reinvention and reconfiguration depending upon circumstances. This implies discussion, debate and the explicit expression of meaning entailed in the use of elaborated linguistic codes (Bernstein 1975). Households that institutionalise strategies of closure and segregation are characterised by much more immutable spatial and temporal boundaries. They are more likely to celebrate ritualised, symbolic and mythical modes of communication (Cohen 1985), incorporating the implicit or intuitive meanings typical of restricted linguistic codes (Bernstein 1975). The everyday life of such households is focused upon policing and defending entrenched boundaries rather than negotiating and renegotiating their movement.

Sources of variation in strategies

Thus far in this chapter we have identified a number of ideal typical ways in which the social relations of households containing home-located producers may differ in character. These variations we have conceptualised in terms of the relative strength of two sets of spatial and temporal boundaries; that is, those within households and those between households and the wider society. In this section we shall begin to consider, in general terms, the social forces which give rise to these variations.

Home-located producers have generated a wide variety of different responses to the challenges of making a living at home. Indeed, it sometimes seems, when reading descriptive or case-study research reports, that just about every possible variation on the organisation of time and space has been adopted at some time or other. The sources of variation in these patterns cannot be reduced to a single 'factor', such as gender, ethnicity or the labour process. Rather, there are a multiplicity of forces at work. Principle among these are the following:

- the labour market, which determines how much income is available to the home-located worker;
- the nature of the activities and tasks entailed in the labour process, which shape the temporal and spatial requirements of the job;
- beliefs, values and practices entailed in 'doing' gender, ethnicity, class and age;
- the social relations of the household, including the numbers of co-residents, stage in the life cycle and the character of collective values, beliefs and lifestyles.

All of these are routinely involved in determining the temporal and spatial structures of home-located production. Within the confines of this book we cannot seek to capture all this complex diversity but rather we aim to develop some general principles which may enable us to classify, and distinguish between, different types of lifeworlds created by home-located producers. We shall proceed by briefly considering the significance of each of the four sets of social relationships identified above.

Income differentials generated in the labour market impose stark limitations on strategies available in managing the spatial and temporal boundaries of home-located production. Previous research suggests that few homeworkers, as we define them, have separate spaces in their homes, such as dedicated rooms, where they are able to conduct their work (Hakim 1987b; Bulos and Chaker 1993, 1995; Allen 1983). This lack of separation may contribute to the impression, on the part of other household members, that their work is not 'real' or demanding. Huws *et al.* (1996), however, found that three-quarters of their sample of 'tele-workers' did have a separate place to work (as noted in Chapter 1, the concept of 'teleworker' is not one that can be readily mapped onto our classificatory scheme). Such findings may well reflect differences in income levels which, in turn, determine the availability of spacious and congenial accommodation. In most European countries, for example, the availability of a separate room is often a function of earnings (Huws *et al.* 1996: 43). Economic circumstances may dictate, therefore, that it is not possible to carry out home-located production in the preferred manner. For example, in a small terraced house it is difficult to separate home-working from other household activities, however much all parties might prefer it. Some degree of integration may become the only option (see, for example, the remarks of Elizabeth and Meena in Chapter 8). In this situation, homeworking may be conducted under circumstances that cause friction among household members.

It is also apparent that the nature of the labour process has much to do with whether integration or segregation are feasible or desirable. Forms of employment that require high levels of concentration, confidentiality, use of valuable raw materials or use of dangerous machinery are all obvious candidates for segregation from the rest of the life of the household. For example, in our qualitative interviews one respondent – Elizabeth – was able to carry out her homeworking job in the living room on a tray in the company of her children because the task – inspecting and repairing cooker filaments – facilitated this approach. In contrast, Barbara, who was also very heavily committed to supporting her husband and family, nevertheless had to work upstairs in a small spare room. This was because there was no other way she could make the long curtains, involving expensive fabrics, that were an important aspect of her business.

The times and spaces of home are, of course, gendered. Home means different things to men and women and this has implications for the experience and use of the home as a workplace (Allen and Wolkowitz 1987; Ahrentzen 1992; Boris and Daniels 1989; Boris 1996). For women home is often a place of unpaid work, especially with respect to nurturing, caring and emotional labour. The gendered nature of household regimes may, under certain circumstances, enable women to perceive paid employment at home as affording them more power and control than employment in the workplace. Similarly, in some ethnic minority communities, religious requirements and cultural practices may shape the availability of space and time for home-located employment.

Haddon and Silverstone (1993), Haddon and Lewis (1994) and Salmi (1997a), in their research, found integration to be a strategy more commonly associated with women than men. The articulation of different tasks, temporalities and spaces characteristic of integration mirrors more general findings about the gendered nature of temporal and spatial divisions within the household. Thus, for example, the temporal experience of women in the home tends to be more cyclical, fragmented and multiple than that of men. Women's household time commonly involves switching between a variety of activities and commitments that involve a repetitive round of tasks. The household temporalities of men more frequently maintain a linear, singular and focused pattern, reminiscent of industrial time (Gershuny *et al.* 1994; Sullivan 1997; Hantrais 1993; see also Fothergill and Rose 1998). We should, however, avoid an essentialist analysis and seek instead to understand time and space in terms of the relationships of the household (Glucksmann 1995, 1998).

Integration is, perhaps, most likely to be attempted by women with young children, who seek to combine home-located production with responsibilities for childcare and other domestic tasks (Salmi 1996, 1997a, 1997b). It may also be an approach which is more suited to certain types of work activity that can be easily put down and picked up again. However, Michelson and Lindén (1997) found in their study of 22 Swedish 'teleworkers' that gender was less important in determining whether an integration or segregation strategy was followed than employment status (self-employed/employee), hours of work (full time/part time) and length of time spent in the home.

In addition to the above, the expectations, practices and values entailed in 'household understandings' – defined and discussed in Chapter 1 – may well play a major role in determining strategies for combining home and work. They entail spatial and temporal regimes which are typically established in advance of the introduction of home-located production. We do not wish to suggest that household understandings are the *sole* influence on the strategies adopted by home-located producers in combining home and work. Indeed, in this section we have noted a wide range of other forces at work. It is our contention, however, that household understandings do play a significant part and that their influence has not received sufficient attention. The relationship between, on the one hand, the specific characteristics of different types of household understandings and, on the other, the temporal and spatial regimes of home-located production remains relatively unexplored.

We regard this omission as particularly serious. As we made plain in Chapter 2, it is essential that the study of home-located production focuses on the interaction between two sets of social relationships – those of production and reproduction – within one spatial location. The importance of this conjunction has often been asserted within the literature but less frequently have its implications been followed through in theoretical analysis and empirical research. It is our contention that the distinctive features of home-located production arise from the way in which relations of production become embedded within differing household contexts. This is what justifies regarding home-located production as a suitable subject for sociological investigation and as a clearly delineated field of enquiry. Home-located production comprises a distinctive social configuration, characterised by the spatial and temporal juxtaposition of relations of household and economy.

In the remainder of this chapter, therefore, we shall develop a model of the links between types of household understandings and strategies for combining home and work. Our proposals are based on analysis of our qualitative case-study interviews and reflection upon existing research literature concerning the domestic division of labour and control over household finances. We claim no more for our model than that it suggests a number of hypotheses for further research.

Four types of household understanding

We wish to distinguish four ideal types of 'household understanding'. Each of these, we shall argue, represents a distinctive collection of opportunities and constraints that face household members who seek to become home-located producers. Consequently, each household understanding tends to prioritise or highlight a particular combination of technologies of the self.

Our ideal types draw upon the basic conceptual dimensions that are outlined in Chapter 2. These concern the extent to which the domestic division of labour and the management of household resources are characterised by egalitarian or non-egalitarian and joint or segregated social relations. However, our four household understandings do not represent a comprehensive theoretical summation of all possibilities. Rather they are derived from an analysis of research studies of the actually existing household arrangements in Britain. They are the four most commonly encountered household understandings to be found in the empirical research.

The first type of household understanding is based on the premise that one party will adopt sole and total responsibility for the functioning of the household and the maintenance of social relations of social reproduction. Thus, the burdens of domestic labour and financial management are shouldered by one individual. We shall refer to this as the *sole responsibility* model. Other members consume the outputs of household labour without contributing to their production in word or deed. Examples would include those 'traditional' working class households based on an extreme version of the 'female homemaker, male breadwinner' model, in which men appeared almost as visitors in the home. Although, in practice, the solely responsible household member is highly likely to be a woman, in principle this model would also include role reversal situations in which a man became a solely responsible house-husband and a female partner or partners took responsibility for breadwinning.

In these circumstances, the distribution of domestic labour is extremely unequal, negotiation between household members is minimal, and segregation of functions is total. The party vested with sole responsibility may have a very difficult, invisible and thankless task. On the other hand, she may also reign as 'queen of the family' within the household domain, exercising a high degree of autonomy and control in the construction of time and space within the home.

The second household understanding we wish to highlight is one in which one member of the household exercises a predominant degree of power and authority over the distribution of resources and the allocation of domestic tasks. We designate this as the *hierarchical responsibility* model. Such a situation would be one in which a wife is expected to carry full responsibility for day-to-day management of household expenditures while her male partner retains control over the amount of housekeeping allowance, choice of major purchases and the extent of his personal spending money. Similarly, with respect to domestic labour, the female party may have responsibility for carrying out menial tasks while the male partner exercises supervisory, surveillance and managerial functions. This might be combined with – and to some extent legitimated or mitigated by – occasional male assistance with light domestic tasks or personal gifts to the female partner. Here negotiation often tends to become concerned with detailed terms rather than the underlying principles of the arrangement. Another example might be a situation in which an older woman is the lead party and a number of younger women – such as daughters or daughters-in-law – are junior members of the household (e.g., some Asian families in Britain and elsewhere).

A third type of household understanding is one in which adult members of the household have equal but separate responsibilities. We call these *divided responsibility* households. For example, a husband and wife may distribute among themselves responsibility for various household chores and aspects of money management, allocating distinct spheres of operation to each on the basis of principles perceived by both to be equitable. Gender stereotypes may guide the division of labour but the burdens are seen to be equally shared. Each does what is required of them, reporting back to the other at appropriate moments. Here, then, separation is combined with equality. Negotiation is confined to the initial – and possibly subsequent – allocation of responsibilities. The execution of tasks is achieved by the autonomous actions of each individual.

A fourth household understanding is characterised by joint and equal responsibility for domestic tasks and financial management. We describe these as *shared responsibility* households. For example, partners may collaborate in and share as many domestic tasks as possible – making joint shopping trips, gardening together, tackling redecorating as a joint task, and so on. Similarly, they typically work out together how to meet their financial obligations and how to spend their money. Actual execution of decisions – such as paying the gas bill – might be done by either, by agreement and as convenient. However, unlike hierarchical responsibility understandings, decision-making at all levels is shared. Here negotiation, debate and discussion are built into the everyday functioning of all aspects of the household unit, since it is constantly necessary to elicit and to consider the feelings and beliefs of the other. From menus to mortgages, decisions are joint and talked through.

Home-located production and household understandings

In this section, we will consider the implications of the four household understandings, outlined above, for the strategies adopted by home-located producers in managing time and space within the home (see Table 9.2).

Sole responsibility households

Members of sole responsibility households in charge of the domestic regime – typically older women – have a good deal of latitude in deciding how they will fit home-located production into the times and spaces of the home. At the same time, however, they carry a considerable burden of responsibility for organising and conducting domestic work, in addition to managing the demands of home-located production. They have few opportunities to delegate tasks. Moreover, failure to complete domestic labour to the expected standard may bring shame on themselves and the household as a whole. Nevertheless, provided that housekeeping does not fall below the culturally expected norms, they may adopt a wide range of different solutions to the problem of combining home and work.

The combination of multiple household duties with freedom to construct domestic routines will tend to favour strategies of integration, combined with frequent and rapid switching between domestic and paid labour. Domestic demands will continue to exert their sway but they may be manoeuvred in and around the times and spaces of paid employment. Problems generated by the invasion of work into the home and the intrusion of home into work may be considerable, in the sense that there may not be enough hours in the day to encompass everything. However, home-located producers running such households do have the scope to adjust and reorder the home/work interface. The sheer volume of their tasks is formidable but they have some degree of domestic autonomy.

Home-located producers running sole responsibility households may also exercise discretion over the extent to which they insist upon strong boundaries between the household and the outside world. They may, if they choose, opt for an open strategy. This might extend, for example, to bringing in the members of other households – such as kin or neighbours – to assist with production deadlines or domestic outputs. Network connections and kinship ties may be crucial in determining the availability of such ancillary support, both practical and emotional. In the absence of network support, home-located producers may suffer

Table 9.2 **Household understandings, gender divisions and the management
of temporal and spatial boundaries in home-located production***

Household understandings	Male members	Female members
Sole responsibility	Segregated	Integrated
	Closed	Open
Hierarchical responsibility	Segregated	Segregated
	Closed/open	Closed
Divided responsibility	Segregated	Segregated
	Closed	Closed
Shared responsibility	Integrated	Integrated
	Closed	Closed

Note
* This table simplifies some of the possible combinations of gender divisions and household
understanding. For the purposes of presentation it assumes that: those in charge of sole
responsibility households are female; subordinate members of hierarchical responsibility households
are female; and superordinate members of hierarchical responsibility households are male.

from isolation and exhaustion since their work load – both paid and unpaid – may
leave them with little time or strength for anything else.

The management of credibility with other household members and with suppliers of work rests upon being able to cope with variable and unpredictable
employment demands whilst maintaining standards in the home. This may be
achieved in high income homes by buying in aspects of housework and childcare.
In some cases, however, completion of domestic tasks in person may be regarded
as highly desirable or even mandatory. Another tactic for improving credibility
with employers and business associates may be the cultivation of informal personal
ties, possibly facilitated by strategies of openness. This may enable the home-
located producer to negotiate with the supplier of work and/or with clients, even
though the scope for negotiation with other household members is low.

When women bear the burdens in sole responsibility households, male members are often treated as privileged guests – but not ones in a position to define the
shape and character of household life. Alternatively, they may be regarded as a nui-
sance under the feet of the real rulers of the home. Male home-located producers
in such a position are likely to constitute an intrusive element in the home. As a
result, male home-located producers who are members of 'sole responsibility'
households may be excluded from the main arenas where domestic life are played
out. Moreover, their best chance of commanding credibility within the household
may depend on ensuring that their home-located production mimics the temporal and spatial rhythms of workplace employment, where men as sole
breadwinners exercise supreme authority. The combination of these circumstances
means that home-located production by male members of sole responsibility
households is likely to be conducted in times and spaces separate from the heart
of the home (e.g., shed, garage or outhouse) and during regular working hours;
in short, segregation.

Switching by male home-located producers in such households is likely to be based around the reproduction of male full-time working patterns. Intrusion of home-located production into the spatial and temporal orders of the home is unlikely to be tolerated by powerful female members of the household and, hence, demarcation lines are likely to be clearly drawn. As a corollary, however, there is unlikely to be much need for male home-located workers to defend their work routines against domestic interruptions, since home-located production is banished from the main times and places of household life. None the less, it follows that isolation is likely to be a problem faced by male home-located producers in this household understanding, since popping in and out of the family scene is unlikely to be popular with female members.

Variability of work loads may be managed by male home-located producers by increasing or diminishing working hours, but only provided that this does not lead to encroachments on the domestic order. Similarly the dominant women of the household may well place limitations on the extent and location of visits to male home-located producers by business associates. It is likely, therefore, that male home-located producers will pursue strategies of closure with respect to boundaries with the outside world.

Hierarchical responsibility households

Subordinate (usually female) members of hierarchical responsibility households have little scope in determining the pattern of domestic labour. Whilst they are charged with most of the practical execution of housework they have little control over the management of the home, which rests with superordinate male or female members. Opportunities for them to renegotiate or reconstruct the spatial and temporal order are not likely to be extensive. Where subordinate female members take up home-located production, therefore, they are likely to be required to continue to give their domestic responsibilities their full attention and priority. This implies that home-located production will be consigned to separate times and spaces that do not disturb existing domestic routines – in short, segregation.

It also follows that the domestic work loads of subordinate household members engaged in home-located production are likely to remain unchanged in character and extent. Even if income from home-located production is sufficient to purchase hired help to relieve the burdens of housework and childcare, gender divisions and stereotypes are likely to result in household disapproval of this tactic. Arguably, therefore, subordinate members of hierarchical responsibility households face the most difficult circumstances when they seek to take up home-located production.

Home-located producers who perform subordinate duties in hierarchical responsibility households may, therefore, be under great pressure. They are likely to find themselves giving up leisure times and spaces in order to meet their production targets. Intrusion of home-located production into housework will be heavily frowned upon but invasion of domestic responsibilities into working times and places will be routine. Isolation is likely to be extensive. Variable work loads may create extreme pressure – and home-located producers in this situation may well discover that there is little credibility to be gained from successfully managing this difficult balancing act. It is unlikely that senior members of the household will tolerate encroachments by the business associates of junior members engaged in home-located production, forcing them to pursue strategies of closure.

Where home-located producers are among the superordinate (male or female) members of hierarchical responsibility households, they will enjoy far more scope to arrange the temporal and spatial divisions of the home in ways which facilitate their economic activities. Indeed, of all the groups we discuss in this chapter, superordinate members of hierarchical responsibility households have the greatest degree of latitude, autonomy and control in combining home and work, precisely because of their distinctive *household* position. Although they may have important managerial or supervisory responsibilities in the household, it is unlikely that they will be called upon to carry out ongoing physical domestic labour. In these circumstances, superordinate members may not only claim precious resources of household space and time but may also not wish to be interrupted while conducting paid work. Segregation strategies are likely to be the result.

Those in this position – particularly perhaps males – are most at danger of becoming workaholics. They are not subject to the imposed timetables of the workplace but also are not likely to be interrupted by other household members. They are able to use their authority in the household to repel invasions and, on the same basis, may well be able to get away with intrusions into the routines and resources of other household members. They can take on surges in work loads knowing that domestic hindrances can be overcome or ignored. Their control over the household context of home-located production may, therefore, lead them into situations where they can devote themselves to their careers. This may have a variety of results – including increased earnings, upward social mobility, crushing work loads and increased distance from family ties.

Superordinate members of hierarchical responsibility households are relatively free to bring business associates, suppliers or other visitors into the home without fear of effective resistance. This means that strategies of openness are an option. However, as we have seen in the previous chapter, their credibility with business associates and clients may depend upon creating a business which as much as possible simulates traditional (male) employment patterns or even one which disguises its location. For these reasons, superordinate members of hierarchical responsibility households may opt for strategies of closure. The significant point is that their position in the social relations of the household offers them a *choice* between openness and closure.

Divided responsibility households

Male and female members of divided responsibility households are separate but equal. Discrete tasks and responsibilities are allocated to particular household members. The focus is on collective convenience and individual agreement rather than traditional expressions of gender identity or ingrained ideas about the 'proper' way to run a home. Hence, the emotional charge surrounding particular domestic arrangements or household practices is relatively low. The details of household life are regarded pragmatically – as a practical matter rather than a moral imperative. However, a high value is placed on the processes of negotiation and agreement as well as on the delivery of the bargain struck. The household understanding is based, then, on mutual acceptability, consideration and personal empathy but not on shared activities.

The implications of this type of household understanding are similar for both male and female home-located producers. There is, therefore, likely to be relatively little gender inequality in opportunities for home-located production in divided responsibility households, unlike sole responsibility and hierarchical responsibility households.

Divided responsibility households are likely to recognise clearly defined internal divisions and boundaries of time and space. These may be legitimately open to renegotiation and reorganisation should circumstances change but the parties are expected to stay within them under normal circumstances. The introduction of home-located production is acceptable to other members provided that the commitments of each partner are agreed and the needs of each are respected. Strategies of segregation seem a likely outcome in these circumstances. The home-located producer is likely to establish and stay within negotiated boundaries of time and space, allowing the other members of the household to get on with their lives undisturbed. Partners might be called upon to cover in an emergency but they are not expected or required to step outside their own working regimes and domestic involvement on a regular basis.

The home-located producer's credibility among household members thus lies in staying within boundaries. Provided this is achieved, home-located producers may exercise considerable autonomy in managing how they deliver on both domestic and employment fronts. They can exercise autonomy and control in completion of both employment and domestic tasks. Skill at switching – being disciplined and organised – will be crucial in keeping the boundaries distinct. Isolation may be attenuated by discussions with partners, who may well have a genuine interest in the home-located producer's career and progress. However, offers of help from others to deal with surges in work levels may be limited. As a result, variability in work loads may represent a chronic threat to the way of life that all household members regard as appropriate.

To maintain legitimacy within the household it is important for the home-located producer to minimise disruptions to the regimes of other members by suppliers, clients and other business visitors. Hence, home-located producers are likely to hold such visitors at bay, resulting in strategies of closure to the outside world. However, where it is possible to make arrangements for business to be conducted without impinging on household agendas (e.g., by constructing a separate entrance to self-contained office space or by putting in dedicated business telephone lines), then the home-located producer is unlikely to encounter opposition in *principle* to strategies of openness.

Shared responsibility households

Shared responsibility household understandings are constructed around processes of negotiation and communication. The details of the agreements reached are less important to the parties than the principles of consensus, equality and mutual understanding. Togetherness is the watchword. Inclusion within household relations rests on personal acceptability, based around readings of attributes such as intention, motivation, moral worth, love and affection. Perceived failure in respect of these qualities of character – rather than in the execution of prescribed rules concerning formal definitions of roles and status – is likely to generate powerful sanctions based on processes of emotional exclusion from the household circle. These features shape the strategies adopted by both male and female members of shared responsibility households in attempting to combine home and work. As with divided responsibility households, there are relatively few gender differences in the opportunities and constraints faced by those within shared responsibility households who wish to embark on home-located production.

It is likely to be the case that *internal* boundaries within the home are few and relatively permeable. We would expect members of the household to share space and time and to carry out activities together. Temporal and spatial boundaries within the home, therefore, are not immutable but can be changed in the light of shared decisions. However, the very process of negotiation, joint decision-making and sharing may strengthen *external* boundaries between home and the outside world.

The introduction of home-located production into the household represents an encroachment of the outside world into the domestic sphere. This may be possible to achieve but will need to be based on discussion and negotiation. Thus home-located producers do not have a high degree of individual autonomy in deciding how to reconcile home and work, but they may, in the course of collective negotiations with other household members, ultimately be able to establish a high degree of control over domestic and employment routines.

Once such routines have been put in place, partners or other household members may feel the need, or even obligation, to offer support to the home-located producer. In these circumstances, temporal and spatial integration of home-located production and domestic routines is a feasible, and even likely, strategy. Home-located production may become an integral part of the life of the *whole* household. Variability of work loads may be tackled by drawing upon the support and understanding of other household members.

It may be hypothesised that this household understanding is the one most compatible with the 'Family Inc.' approach, discussed by Beach (1989) (the concept of 'Family Inc.' here refers not to a family business but to the rallying of cooperative support by all family members in completing home-located production tasks). Credibility will be maintained within the household provided that all members accept the legitimacy of the home-located producer's employment career. This collective expression of support may provide emotional resources and status confirmation that enables the home-located producer to weather criticism, misunderstanding or lack of visibility in the outside world. Equally, however, if home-located producers breach promises given to other household members concerning family and domestic commitments, as a result of their involvement in home-located production, this may well be regarded as a serious misdemeanour, warranting withdrawal of support. There may be strong household barriers, therefore, to becoming a self-absorbed workaholic.

Issues surrounding defending work routines from domestic disruptions and managing the intrusion of work into home life are likely to be dealt with through the household negotiation process. Although the potentiality for disagreements should not be underestimated, the commitment to working out a mutually acceptable arrangement is at the heart of this household understanding. Indeed, such problems might be perceived as an opportunity for sharing and joint responsibility. Keeping the burdens of home-located production to oneself might even be regarded as contravening the spirit of household life. Isolation is unlikely to be a major problem in this household, therefore.

However, the strong boundaries between home and the outside world may mean that the introduction of business visitors or suppliers of work to the home may well be regarded as unacceptable. The household members will happily work together in a joint effort to support the home-located producer in completing his or her tasks but will not allow the labour market to breach the symbolic walls surrounding their private world of the family nest. Hence strategies of closure are very likely to be favoured by home-located producers in shared responsibility households. It is to be expected that this is a non-negotiable arrangement that all household members will intuitively feel to be right and proper. This will call for technologies of the self that enable home-located producers to appear eager and enthusiastic to their supplier of works while at the same time holding them at arm's length from the domestic setting.

Conclusion

This chapter has presented a theoretical model of the strategies adopted by home-located producers in combining the contrasting demands of household and employment relations. These strategies involve ways of managing spatial and temporal boundaries, both within the home and between the home and the outside world. In generating coping strategies, home-located producers draw on entrenched sets of beliefs and assumptions concerning home, household and family that we have called household understandings. Typically household understandings are expressed implicitly and intuitively rather than explicitly and reflexively.

Household understandings specify a series of attitudes and feelings which are embedded in the ways in which household boundaries are drawn in time and space. Such boundaries may be relatively strong and immutable or weak and permeable. They set the framework within which home-located producers function when introducing paid employment into the home. There are a number of sources of variation in the strategies that home-located producers may pursue in combining home and work. For example, their options are constrained by their incomes and by the character of the work processes they do. However, household understandings represent a powerful source of influence that has yet to be extensively researched or theorised.

We identify four ideal types of household understanding, each of which is characterised by distinctive patterns with respect to the domestic division of labour and the management of household finances. It is argued that male and female home-located producers in each type are faced with a range of contrasting choices and constraints. We specify a series of hypotheses about the nature and form of the options open to them. Of particular importance, it is suggested, are two factors. First the balance of power between household members – i.e., whether household relations are egalitarian or hierarchical. Second, the extent to which domestic tasks and activities are regarded by household members as joint enterprises – i.e., whether the household is based around shared or divided responsibilities.

It should be emphasised that this chapter offers hypotheses and theoretical speculations – albeit ones derived from reflection upon our qualitative interviews and the research literature that documents existing patterns of household relations. The analysis presented above seeks to distinguish between different types of households and household relations, rather than assuming that all home-located producers are subject to similar domestic pressures. It argues that the degree of autonomy and restraint encountered by home-located producers varies between different types of households. Thus, it is our contention that not only do different types of home-located production entail contrasting social relations but also that different household contexts shape the possibilities for personal autonomy and self-regulation.

Chapter 10

Conclusion
Mapping the broader perspective

Introduction

This book has focused on an aspect of work and employment that has been the subject of much popular speculation and fascination. It has explored the implications of earning a living at home or, in the words of the title, of being 'in work, at home'. More and more people are spending at least some part of their working lives in this way. Those who follow this path may do so under different circumstances and in many contexts. They pursue a wide variety of careers and jobs. Some work part-time, others full-time. Some combine working at home with workplace jobs – either simultaneously or at different periods in their careers. Some regard working at home as an adjunct to their main job, while others see it as their principal commitment. Some do repetitive tasks and are badly paid, while others pursue professional and entrepreneurial careers that generate handsome rewards.

We have highlighted one element of this very mixed bag, conventionally described as 'homeworking'; that is, routine manufacturing and service occupations done in the home. This type of employment has a long history. It sometimes receives rather less attention than it deserves in the midst of the publicity that surrounds the idea of the 'telecottage' and the promise that information technology will turn all our living rooms into remote offices. In order to develop an understanding of homeworking we have found it essential to locate this kind of employment in the context of all the different types of work that can be done at home. This book is not only about homeworking, therefore, but also a much broader field which we have called 'home-located production'. Our aim has been to identify the features and characteristics that are unique to homeworking and those which it has in common with home-located production more generally.

Previous research on people who work at home has tended to concentrate on a limited range of themes. Key among these has been the documentation of their terms and conditions, and the estimation of their overall numbers (e.g., Huws 1984, 1994; Hakim 1985, 1987a, 1987b; Felstead and Jewson 1996). These themes are certainly not neglected here. However, this book has cast its net rather wider to include many additional issues that have so far received scant coverage.

It offers a systematic conceptual analysis that distinguishes between a series of different groups engaged in home-located production. It assembles key findings from a wide range of data sources and research studies drawn from many different countries. The methodological and theoretical foundations of these are brought under scrutiny and their contribution to our understanding evaluated. This enables us to provide a 'state of the art' assessment of the quantitative data available world-wide on those who earn a living at home.

The book also contains a number of innovative arguments and hypotheses about the significance of the spatial location of home-located production. A major aspect of this analysis concerns the implications for patterns of managerial control of introducing employment relations into the social life of the households. This provides a framework within which to investigate the distinctive emotional and psychological dispositions of those who work at home. Here, original qualitative materials are presented, derived from the authors' research interviews. The differing strategies devised by home-located producers in combining the competing demands of household and employment relations are considered in the context of the overall character of their domestic lives. All of these are themes currently under-researched and under-theorised in existing literature.

An underlying motif of this book, hinted at on several occasions, is the view that the study of home-located production raises a range of general issues that extend well beyond the specific features of the lives of those who are 'in work, at home'. Home-located production is at the interface of a series of broad social processes and institutional spheres that characterise capitalist societies. These include, *inter alia*, divisions between the public and the private, production and consumption, the global and the local, work and leisure, and the formal and informal economies. In recent years the articulation of these divisions has been characterised by processes such as time–space compression, transformations in relations of intimacy and challenges to established sources of ontological security. Home-located production thus exemplifies or incorporates many general aspects of what has been designated as 'late' or 'high' modernity (e.g., Giddens 1990, 1992).

This final chapter will, very briefly, attempt to locate the central arguments and findings of the book in the context of some of these broader issues. A full account would, undoubtedly, require another book, while a truncated version might easily generate misunderstandings. We have, therefore, tackled this task by identifying a series of points for discussion and further development rather than spelling out detailed conclusions or assertions. This chapter does not, then, represent a full exposition of the issues nor is it even a comprehensive agenda for further research. Instead it aims to map out some of the ways in which the issues raised in this book connect with broader themes in contemporary debates in the social sciences.

Defining the field

A rock on which many previous studies of home-located production have foundered is that of conceptualisation and definition. Regrettably, there remain

many examples of the confused application of terminology. There is no standardised way of distinguishing and referring to different groups of home-located
producers. As long as this situation prevails efforts to move towards a better
understanding of home-located production, and homeworking in particular, are
likely to be frustrated. We are well aware of the difficulties of rigorously identifying and consistently applying even a limited set of distinctions. Indeed, the
eagle-eyed reader may well spot the occasional lack of consistency in our earlier
work! Nevertheless, we have found it essential to develop further our own terminology in order to provide a framework for this book. We believe that the
inconvenience of introducing a set of new terms is outweighed by the potential
benefits to be had from enhanced methodological rigour and systematic comparative analysis.

The starting point of our conceptual analysis was to define the field of enquiry
as the *totality* of social relationships characteristic of those who work at home.
These include both the social relations of production and the social relations of the
household. The conjunction of these two sets of practices, beliefs and constraints
within one spatial location – the home – is what makes this form of employment
distinctive and of particular interest. By distinguishing between a range of contrasting social relations of production, we are able to identify a series of different
categories or types of people who work at home. These include, *inter alia,* groups
we denote as: 'home-located producers'; 'home-located employers'; 'home-
located workers'; 'home-located petty commodity producers'; 'home-located
wage labourers'; and 'homeworkers'. Among these, the terms which have
appeared most frequently in the pages of this book are 'home-located producers'
(i.e., all those engaged in any commodity production at home) and 'homeworkers' (i.e., low discretion home-located wage labourers). We went on to introduce
a number of concepts and distinctions that are central to our analysis of the
household relations of home-located producers. Principal among these is the
notion of 'household understandings'. These, we argue, refer to the ingrained and
taken-for-granted practices, values and beliefs that guide and order domestic life
and relationships between household members (cf. Bourdieu's concept of 'habitus' 1990a, 1990b). At the end of the book we went on to identify a series of
different forms of household understandings, with contrasting implications for
gender and other divisions in the home.

It follows that our conceptualisation of the field highlights the diversity, com-
plexity and multi-faceted character of home-located production in general and of
homeworking in particular. We do not wish to be unnecessarily complex or over-
elaborate. However, it is our contention that the defining feature of this kind of
work – i.e., the conjunction of two sets of practices, beliefs and constraints within
one location – *necessarily* generates a multiplicity of forms of home-located production. Thus, the same social relations of production may, in principle, be found
in a range of different types of household understandings. Equally similar households may incorporate a variety of different relations of production. It follows that
home-located production is decentred and fractured. Failure to recognise the

categorical differences in the social relationships of home-located producers is to neglect a key aspect of their lived experience and overlook a vital feature of the overall structure of this segment of the labour market.

Generating transparent terminology, disentangling contradictory arguments and mapping contrasting perspectives are among the most important contributions that social scientists make to both public and professional audiences. We have seen that a deceptively simple term like 'homeworking' has been used by different authors to refer to contrasting types of economic activities and social relationships. As a result, protagonists in the debate are often talking at cross-purposes. This raises the urgent need for clarification of terms and hence the avoidance of unnecessary confusion and disagreement. Such a plea applies across the social sciences and pushes high up the agenda the need for conceptual and theoretical clarification.

Generating data

One of the penalties of devising rigorous concepts is that the process of generating samples for research becomes increasingly difficult. Moreover, it is well known that homeworkers in particular and home-located producers in general are often reluctant to participate in research studies. There are many reasons for this which, to some extent, vary between different categories of home-located producers. In searching for subjects, therefore, researchers must ensure that their techniques of sample generation both target the required groups and secure their cooperation. Certain methods are more appropriate for particular kinds of research questions and types of home-located production than others. The diverse and fractured nature of home-located production, noted above, itself implies the need for a range of different techniques of investigation.

National estimates of home-located production are more readily available from official data sources such as population censuses and labour force surveys. Other ways of identifying subjects – such as doorstep surveys, direct appeals and chasing known points of contact – offer alternative perspectives and insights. For example, they are useful in providing information on working conditions, the management of time and space in the household, the strategies used to combine home and work, and so on. One of our aims has been to spell out the advantages and disadvantages of each search technique, including possible sources of bias. A wide ranging series of examples are cited from around the world. An understanding of homeworking in its entirety requires several techniques of searching for subjects as well as comparison between the results thereby generated. Such an all-encompassing approach calls for a keen awareness of differences within and between the category of subjects captured by the available research techniques. This, in turn, requires the rigorous application of theoretical and conceptual frameworks.

Technical difficulties in data gathering must also be taken into account. Estimating the number of people working at home, for example, is a task fraught with technical as well as conceptual difficulties. This book shows that counts vary markedly within as well as between countries. Differences between estimates often derive from technical decisions about measurement instruments as well as a failure rigorously to follow through conceptual distinctions. These decisions can serve to narrow or widen the focus and hence diminish or raise the final count. It is largely for this reason that one can find contrasting and contradictory estimates within a single country.

Our empirical research, and our account of the work of others, highlights another way in which data collection methods comprise a mediating influence on research results. Gathering data entails making social relationships with respondents – albeit particular kinds of social relationships guided by distinctive principles and practices. It inevitably follows that the quality and quantity of information gathered is a function of the dynamics of social interaction within the research relationship. Of crucial importance in this context is the social identity of researchers, in particular their gender, age, class, ethnicity and 'racialisation' (O'Connell Davidson and Layder 1994). Our experience, discussed in this book, has demonstrated these points to the full. We have found it essential to take particular care in constructing and training research teams. In the case of researching homeworkers, it is also vital to consider whether respondents will perceive interviewers as representatives of punitive state authorities, such as those administering welfare benefits and tax liabilities. In short, in evaluating and interpreting data about those 'in work, at home' it is essential to remember that to do research is to make social relationships.

We have strongly argued against the view that there is one best research technique to be used in the investigation of home-located production. We also reject the notion that particular research techniques are, in themselves, inherently radical or conservative. Each technique reveals its own truths, the totality of results creating a composite picture comprising many dimensions and perspectives. A multi-faceted form of employment calls for a multiplicity of research techniques. Moreover, results from any particular research method may be put to a variety of different political uses (O'Connell Davidson and Layder 1994: xiii).

Even when a variety of techniques are adopted, however, there is a danger of generating results which present an oversimplified picture. For example, many surveys – whether based upon direct appeals via the media, chasing known contacts or doorstepping in local areas – have failed to reveal the full diversity of the social characteristics of those involved. Indeed, many of the techniques adopted by social scientists in searching for subjects make it very likely that the stereotypical images of homeworkers are reproduced rather than challenged. This is because they are carried out via mechanisms, networks or in areas that researchers themselves assume to be fruitful. As a result, 'untypical' homeworkers and 'untypical' localities are often excluded from view. Official data sets and government surveys also suffer from a variety of weaknesses. We argued that they probably under-record and under-count certain types of homeworkers – such as members of ethnic minorities. A balanced view about the social characteristics of those who work at home, therefore, suggests that homeworking in particular – and home-located production in general – is characterised by greater diversity than is often acknowledged.

Two stereotypes have gained prominence in popular and academic discourses. One portrays a rosy picture of people, often men, in high level non-manual occupations, possessing good qualifications and working at home out of choice. The other is of mothers of small children, often from ethnic minority communities, toiling over sewing machines in cramped conditions. In reality, there is more diversity than either of these images allows. It is, for example, wide of the mark to suggest that home-located production is a mainly female activity. In Britain there is probably a roughly equal balance in numbers of men and women working at home and similar evidence can be found in other countries. Moreover, official data sets do not suggest that, at the national level, members of ethnic minorities dominate the homeworking labour force – although there may be localised pockets where they are more numerous. There is certainly reason to believe that women with children and members of some ethnic minority communities are heavily represented among some categories of home-located producers. Homeworkers, for example, include some of the most deprived groups in the labour market. Nevertheless, our own and other research (Phizacklea and Wolkowitz 1995) suggests that even among homeworkers there are significant variations in levels of pay and opportunities for work. Earlier chapters have provided evidence of sharp contrasts not only between white and non-white homeworkers but also between different ethnic minorities. In addition, there are comparable differences between male and female homeworkers leading to significant differences in their reasons for and experience of homeworking.

Overall our conclusion with respect to gathering data is that detecting individuals who fall within the remit of particular research questions should be a preoccupation – even an obsession – of those who carry out empirical work. However, the presentation of findings in this field is not always accompanied by a detailed account of the data collection methods used. This makes comparisons difficult and must be frowned upon by the critical reader (a point well made by Phizacklea and Wolkowitz 1995: 44). The nature of data collection techniques constantly needs to be borne in mind, especially when the target group feels vulnerable and is fearful of being seen. In these circumstances, novel and innovative strategies may have to be adopted. This heightens the importance of keeping a track of the source of research results.

Restructuring labour markets

Home-located production straddles the division of home and work which is widely regarded as typical of the development of capitalist industrialisation. The separation of home and work has often been regarded as an early consequence of large-scale capitalist development. However, both historical and contemporary research testifies not just to the long-standing survival of home-located production but its current world-wide growth (e.g., Boris 1994; Boris and Daniels 1989;

Phizacklea and Wolkowitz 1995; Felstead and Jewson 1996; Mitter 1986a). It is an important manifestation of the enhanced flexibility and contingency of employment in contemporary societies. Notwithstanding the importance of traditional homeworking in manufacturing and routine services, a relatively small proportion of home-located producers fall into this category. A higher percentage are 'white collar' workers of various kinds. Indeed, a significant proportion of professionals, managers, freelancers, small entrepreneurs and clerical staff work at home for most or part of the time (Felstead and Jewson 1995; Felstead 1996; Hakim 1998). The figures indicate that large numbers of home-located producers in general, and homeworkers in particular, are to be found in the US, Australia, Canada and Europe. Furthermore, the evidence suggests that their numbers have risen in recent decades. People earning a living at home appear to have doubled in the US over the period 1991–1997, while in Britain and Canada similar rates of increase have also been recorded. 'Futurologists', and commercial organisations such as British Telecom, have produced a range of current estimates and future predictions of the numbers involved. Some estimates go so far as to suggest that every other worker in Britain could work at home in the future (cited by Hodson 1993). While there is dispute about these figures, few analysts have doubted that working at home is set to grow. Policy-makers have been quick to acknowledge the implications this might have for jobs, transport, housing design and the environment (e.g., Parliamentary Office of Science and Technology 1995; European Commission 1994; Huws 1996b; Gillespie *et al.* 1995).

The world-wide growth of home-located production has been accompanied by much broader processes of employment restructuring. These include the growth of part-time jobs, temporary employment contracts and self-employment. A common feature of these jobs is that they diverge in some way from the pattern which was regarded in mid-twentieth-century advanced capitalist economies as the 'norm'. Such 'standard' jobs and careers are defined as full-time, permanent, open-ended, secure and workplace-located. Those which do not match this template are collectively referred to as 'non-standard' forms of employment (see Felstead and Jewson 1999). The future – according to some (e.g., Handy 1995) – belongs to 'portfolio people' who offer their skills to many different clients, move between different employers and, frequently, work at home at some point in their lives.

Home-located production is sometimes neglected in this context. However, it also has to be recognised that 'non-standard' forms are a disparate collection of employment relations and cannot be reduced to a single pattern or set of characteristics. Even more than home-located production, 'non-standard' forms are diverse, fragmented and non-comparable. Indeed, the category itself is a negative one which is in increasing danger of breaking down under the weight and variety of employment types that it is required to embrace. Different authors focus on different attributes of this *mélange* in an effort to highlight generic or defining features. This has resulted in the growth of a variety of different terms, each putting the accent on a different issue (Felstead and Jewson 1999). In summary, the fractured forms of home-located production are located in a wider labour market that itself is increasingly differentiated and fragmented.

The issue of the changing spatial location of employment does raise the question of whether spatial location, in itself, constitutes conclusive evidence of deviation from 'standard' terms and conditions of employment. In other words, are all of those who are 'in work, at home' by definition to be regarded as part of the 'non-standard' workforce? Can home-located production be an integral part of a traditional career path? Consider, for example, two academics who routinely work at home for part of the week, one with established tenure and the other on a short-term contract. Are both to be regarded as 'non-standard' workers or is there an important distinction to be made between their circumstances? Ultimately, a resolution of these issues necessitates closer examination of terms and definitions. However, this prompts us to ask whether the growth of home-located production should simply be regarded as one example of the rise of 'non-standard' forms of employment or whether there is a more complex relationship between these two phenomena.

Protecting and organising labour

Homeworkers often receive extremely low rates of pay, are exposed to health and safety hazards and receive meagre fringe benefits. Those who endure the worst terms and conditions tend to be drawn from among groups with specific social characteristics – for example, ethnic minorities and women. Moreover, home-located producers generally appear to be relatively worse off compared to their workplace-located peers. Despite their disadvantaged material conditions, however, the relative isolation of those who work at home has made it difficult to mobilise or organise. There have been few successful attempts to incorporate them within conventional labour organisations. To make matters worse, their employment status in national law is rarely clear-cut, reflected in the often contradictory and ambiguous decisions of courts and tribunals. Few countries have specific laws to protect homeworkers – and many of those which do, fail to define them by statute as employees. The result is that homeworkers are often denied rights commonly accorded to employees because, correctly or incorrectly, they are defined as self-employed or believe themselves to be self-employed.

The growth of 'non-standard' forms of employment and the rise of global commodity chains both present formidable new challenges for the organisation and protection of home-located producers. These trends offer employers opportunities to utilise and switch between a variety of 'non-standard' forms of employment. The fluid position in which workers find themselves makes it difficult for labour organisations to maintain regular contact with their members. Short-term engagements, limited hours of work and remoteness from the workplace all make organisation difficult. Coupled with this has been the increasingly global nature of production. Globalisation has been associated with the world-wide growth in subcontracting chains and the spatial division of elements of the production process. With the advent of an increasingly integrated economy, business linkages are becoming more global in nature (see Lui and Chiu 1999), so that products manufactured in Calcutta are eventually finding their way into department stores in Manhattan and Paris. Immediate employers of labour often have little room for manoeuvre since they supply large multinational organisations which place severe downward pressure on profit margins, turnaround times and delivery dates. Transnational corporations and high street retailers standing at the apex of these chains can remain relatively invisible, denying formal responsibility for the terms and conditions of those who produce the goods and services they sell. While there is much anecdotal evidence, formally tracing subcontracting chains is inherently difficult and has been successfully pursued by a limited number of researchers (e.g., Mitter 1986a; Hendry 1994; Tate 1996a).

Notwithstanding these difficulties, when novel and innovative strategies for organising homeworkers have been pursued they have, on occasion, made an impact. Examples include 'naming and shaming' campaigns in Britain, Canada and India, as well as dedicated recruitment drives by pressure groups in Australia, the Netherlands, Canada and India. As a result, the labour movement is developing new forms of resistance, such as harnessing consumer power and strengthening its community-based links, thereby influencing the product market and providing an alternative means of contact with its client group. Effective forms of resistance and assertion of collective demands necessarily reflect the diversity of types of home-located production and household contexts that we have identified in our analysis. A single or unified campaign is unlikely to reflect the multiple situations of those 'in work, at home'.

It is apparent that home-located production has a number of implications for equal opportunities, which are likely to become of increasing significance. In part these arise because of the general trend of so-called 'non-standard' forms of employment (see pp. 166–168), many of which pose challenges to equal opportunities policies as they are conventionally conceived. Equal opportunities legislation and programmes are typically based around comparing the careers of people with open-ended jobs, fixed contracts of employment and legally regulated employment rights (Jewson and Mason 1986; Jewson et al. 1995). However, often 'non-standard' forms of employment erode or eliminate these, making comparisons problematic (Jewson and Mason 1992, 1994). In addition, there are specific difficulties faced by home-located workers who wish to make comparisons with others in the same position. Managerial strategies of control, variations in work loads and the personal circumstances of households all generate differences. Problems of comparison are further compounded by the relative invisibility and isolation of home-located workers.

We have seen that there are considerable variations in the gender composition of different types of home-located producers. Women are particularly represented at the low discretion – and low paid – end of the spectrum. We might hypothesise that the poorer the terms and conditions of any particular job, the more likely are female employees to be recruited to home-located production. Furthermore, whilst all home-located producers potentially face problems in having their employment activities taken seriously, women at home are particularly likely to become invisible workers whose paid employment is wholly or partly obscured by their wider responsibilities for domestic labour. The conjunction of these processes suggests, therefore, that the continuing growth of home-located production may have serious implications with respect to equal opportunities for women in the labour market.

Another equal opportunities issue concerns the personal attributes that are widely perceived to be advantageous by employers and home-located workers alike. They are aspects of personality, character and individual disposition such as self-discipline. These are culturally specific qualities, typically conveyed and recognised in recruitment situations in terms of subjective and intuitive readings of personal conduct, linguistic codes, body language, social skills and other value-laden performances. In short, what Jenkins calls 'acceptability criteria' may well play a major role in selection for home-located production (Jenkins 1986). This is not to deny that such attributes are occupationally relevant but rather to suggest that detecting their presence is open to a good deal of capriciousness, prejudice and the vagaries of 'gut reaction'. There may well be implications here for the gender, class and ethnicity of those recruited, as well as their age and disability status.

For those recruited as home-located labour, the strategies of their employers with respect to the design of the labour process may be crucial in determining whether their future opportunities are equal to those of other members of the firm or other workers in the industry. Thus, for example, firms that deliberately shunt the least important and most routine jobs to their home-located staff may well prejudice the latter's promotion prospects. If they also recruit more women to these posts than men, arguably their actions constitute indirect sexual discrimination and could be open to challenge.

Controlling the work

Homeworking and home-located production are not only of interest because of their increasing incidence and association with social disadvantage. One of the characteristics of this type of production that makes it of particular theoretical and analytical importance is the social and geographical distance between producers and supervisors/managers. The distance between home-located wage labourers and management has been said to enable the former to enjoy a high degree of autonomy, although this has been hotly contested (Toffler 1980; Allen and Wolkowitz 1987; Phizacklea and Wolkowitz 1995). It does mean, however, that employers are driven to devise distinctive managerial strategies and techniques that are currently not fully researched (see Hendry 1994; Allen and Wolkowitz 1987; Shamir 1992). These, in turn, generate forms of resistance that seek either to contest or subvert relations of control.

The control and supervision of work is often conceptualised in terms of external measures used to 'police' an individual's productivity. This policing function is usually carried out by a supervisor, manager or colleagues who allocate work, monitor progress and impose deadlines. Probably the single most important method of controlling homeworkers is 'payment by results' – the piece rate. Workers are typically only paid for work completed accurately or to a specified quality standard. This device is increasingly used by companies and organisations involved in remote but routine data entry tasks, where keystroke monitoring governs payment. However, American and European research indicates not only a widespread management fear of 'losing control' but a reluctance to experiment with supervisory methods different from those which currently prevail in most organisations (Olson 1989; Huws et al. 1990; Shamir 1992).

We have argued that homeworkers in particular, and home-located producers in general, are subject to a range of coercive managerial controls exerted by employers and their agents. In addition, those who work at home face a range of pressures by virtue of their membership of a household – pressures that are highly gendered. However, we have also argued that, whilst we do not underestimate the constraints on them, home-located producers of all kinds typically engage in resistance and struggle against the limitations inherent in their circumstances. This, we have suggested, leads them to develop forms of self-discipline and self-regulation that are in contrast to those of their workplace-located peers. This is because home-located producers are routinely required to regulate aspects of their working lives that in the workplace are typically subsumed under management or are embedded in the moral and social fabric of the office or factory. These include decisions about where and when to work, the monitoring and policing of work schedules, and management of the interface between household and employment relationships. As a result, we argued, home-located producers develop a distinctive psychological disposition or attitude that incorporates processes of self-discipline that have much in common with Foucault's concept of 'technologies of the self' (Foucault 1988, 1990; Martin et al. 1988). These constitute a distinctive mode of governance. Regulation, control and supervision are not achieved simply by externally coercive measures – extensive though these may be – but also by training the emotions and thought processes of the self.

Foucault's notion of technologies of the self enabled him to introduce to his work the idea that individuals, to a degree, take an active part in making themselves into subjects (Dreyfus and Rabinow 1982). This concept is in contrast to the themes of his earlier work which represent the individual as a product of knowledge, discourses and power. The objective of this book is not to comment on Foucault or engage in an exegesis of his work. We are solely interested in adopting and developing ideas, wherever they are to be found, which are useful in generating a systematic and consistent understanding of home-located production. Thus, for example, Foucault and Giddens have very different notions of identity and individuality but we have drawn on both in developing our analysis. It is, however, important to note that Foucault's concept of technologies of the self does not imply that subjects are autonomous beings free from social constraints and able to invent themselves as they please; rather, technologies of the self arise within struggles and resistance generated in social relationships which are themselves constituted in and by dominant discourses.

This general perspective is the one which we adopt in analysing the situation of home-located producers. We suggest that, in order to make sense of their circumstances and to cope with a multitude of pressures from many different sources, they are driven to generate a series of technologies of the self. These enable home-located producers to mobilise for themselves their own energies, motivations, negotiating skills and sense of self-esteem. This represents a form of empowerment – but it is an empowerment that also traps them within the assumptions and practices of discourses surrounding home and work. It locks them into particular circuits of power at the same time as it enables them to pursue the struggle for self-actualisation within those relationships.

Ironically, the mentality characteristic of home-located producers is one which has much in common with an entrepreneurial personality type increasingly sought and encouraged by modern management strategies. However, as far as the workplace is concerned, innovations in approaches to management have been accompanied by heightened surveillance, new panoptical devices and an increased emphasis on participation in corporate culture. Home-located producers, in contrast, are at the edge – or indeed may be beyond the scope – of conventional surveillance techniques and corporate consciousness raising. Hence, the very attributes of home-located producers which make it possible for them to function effectively – and which employers value in office and factory-located employees – problematise their relationships with management.

Reconciling two worlds

The spatial location of home-located production not only problematises relationships with employers but also potentially threatens to disturb relationships with other household members. Home-located producers have to find a way of accommodating their work routines within the context of their domestic lives – of reconciling two worlds within one. Prominent among the challenges they face is that of ordering and maintaining the times and places of work and the home. Our interviews document a range of technologies of the self that are adopted by home-located producers in managing temporal and spatial divisions *within* their households and *between* their households and the outside world. These, we argue, include the social skills and techniques entailed in such matters as: drawing spatial and temporal boundaries; switching between the times and places of work and family; preventing unwanted intermingling of domestic and work life; coping with isolation; responding to unpredictable variations in work loads; combating encroachments by employers and others into the home; and maintaining a credible employment identity. This part of our analysis is derived from our qualitative interviews and is supported by extensive quotations from our respondents. They describe in their own words the lived experience of home-located production in its various forms – emphasising the need for self-discipline and self-motivation.

The politics of the household – constructed around class, racialised and gendered identities – are the terrain on which such strategies are devised. At present, there is a paucity of evidence about the interactions between working at home and household relations, although there is a burgeoning interest (e.g., Armstrong 1999; Salmi and Lammi-Taskula 1998). Most studies have been based on small samples and have rarely examined the impact of different *types* of household on working practices (e.g., Haddon and Silverstone 1993; Fothergill and Rose 1998). It seems likely, however, that home-located producers have contrasting experiences and adopt divergent solutions to the problems of combining home and work. For example, some seek to integrate work into the home while others attempt to maintain a sharp division (see Ahrentzen 1990, 1992).

Our discussion of technologies of the self devised by home-located producers has resonances with broader debates in the social sciences about the transformation of relations of intimacy in contemporary societies. A number of authors have argued that men and women in advanced capitalist societies are not merely offered the opportunity to invent and create identities for themselves but are indeed obliged to do so and to monitor their own choices (Rose 1990). Giddens (1992) argues that 'pure relationships' – based on intrinsic personal satisfaction and emotional trust – increasingly characterise intimate ties between friends, lovers and family. Such relationships are highly reflexive, freely chosen and based on mutual revelation. They eschew handed-down values, traditional notions of duty and unquestioning acceptance of limitations. In a similar vein, Wellman's research (Wellman 1979; Wellman and Berkowitz 1988) has documented the rise of geographically dispersed, flexible and choice-based personal networks, which he calls 'personal communities'. Both Giddens and Wellman see the grip of local communities and ascribed roles as weakened, the geographical and social scope of relationships as widened, and the presentation of personality as an ongoing performance that has to be 'polished' and 'worked at'. The self becomes a reflexive project woven around the maintenance of a biographical narrative. Such a world may be more egalitarian, democratic and sophisticated than those of the past, but may also be more vulnerable to anomie, doubt and uncertainty.

These arguments have attracted criticism. It has been suggested that they neglect the ways in which constraints of gender, ethnicity, class and age mediate the extent and nature of reflexivity. This, in turn, leads Giddens to underestimate the multiple, contradictory and fragmented character of individual subjectivity and the collective constraints on patterns of group consciousness (Layder 1997). Recognition of this diversity is clearly crucial to our analysis of home-located work. Nevertheless, both empirical research and theoretical analysis suggest a general movement in the direction of reflexively based, personally chosen intimate relations. This, then, is the context in which home-located production has to be understood. Whatever the detailed beliefs and practices of household understandings, all are increasingly based on the assumption that the reflexive construction of an individual self is the ultimate legitimate goal in life. Such an outlook shapes the character of family communications, struggles and compromises (Finch and Mason 1993).

The personal goals of all household members have, therefore, to be accommodated in the reconciliation of home-located production with domestic regimes. The tensions and fragility inherent in such negotiations and calculations can be seen running throughout the quotations from our interview respondents. Moreover, rarely can solutions to these problems be drawn from established routines or precedents. In the case of home-located production this is in part because the household arrangements devised by others in a similar position generally have a low visibility. More generally, however, the transformation of intimacy described by Giddens and others suggests that there can be no routinised solutions to these dilemmas. Each individual and each household is required to work out their own distinctive arrangements. These are the circumstances in which technologies of the self are invented – as a tool-kit with which to fashion identities.

Sustaining ontological security

One of the implications of transformations in relations of intimacy is that home has become an increasingly important site in late modern capitalist societies. It is one of the key locations in which the reflexive project of the self is sustained and developed. Home – as a specialised site of residence, consumption, leisure and family life – is a recent phenomenon, generated by the high levels of structural differentiation typical of modern societies. Prior to the industrialisation of production, the greater part of the labour process was located in places of residence (Quinney 1986). In modernity home becomes the classic expression of 'habitus' and everyday lifeworlds (Bourdieu 1977; Deprés 1991). Home becomes more than just a place of shelter. It incorporates past and present, images and memories, fantasies and desires.

Given the uncertainty and perceived riskiness of modern life, a sense of ontological security has become of crucial importance to personal identity but also has become inherently problematic (Giddens 1992). Ontological security, argues Giddens, entails trust and confidence in the regularity and predictability of paths – individual and collective – through time and space. It facilitates a sense of composure, inner-connectedness and ease with oneself. Saunders (1990) has argued that home is one of the main venues in which people are afforded a chance to obtain a sense of ontological security in modern societies. Home offers the possibility of control over the environment, freedom from surveillance, relaxation, escape from threat, safety, stability and self-expression (see also Dupuis and Thorns 1998).

However, it also has to be said that home can be a place of profound insecurity. Home can be a place of hidden abusive relationships. It can be a place of disappointment when the myths and reality of home life do not match. Home is a site where gender inequalities with respect to unpaid labour and control over personal resources are routinely reproduced. Moreover, in a capitalist society home is a commodity – to be bought and sold in exchange for money, subject to the twists and turns of market forces (Gittins 1993; Hampton 1993; Morgan 1985; Pacione 1997).

This, then, is the site of home-located production. It is an ambivalent and ambiguous context. The introduction of home-located production may disturb or upset relationships of profound emotional significance for all members of the household – relationships based on face-to-face, emotionally charged gift-giving rather than contractual exchanges. The presence of deep pre-existing anxieties or tensions within the household may make undertaking home-located production much more difficult or emotionally wearing than would otherwise be the case. Equally, however, the warmth of personal ties of trust and a sense of ontological security may make it possible for home-located producers to generate work routines that are highly productive and rewarding. It is imperative, therefore, to avoid the simplistic extremes of both those who see home as a haven in a heartless world and those who see it as nothing but a source of exploitation and misery. It may be either, both, or something in between. Ambiguity, ambivalence and diversity characterise the context of home-located production.

In the later chapters in this book we took up these themes and developed a speculative conceptual model of the ways in which home-located producers seek to combine home and work. We argued that members of households organise their domestic lives around sets of taken-for-granted values, beliefs and practices, which we call household understandings. They include ingrained notions about the proper way to organise the domestic division of labour and manage household finances. These intuitive and implicit forms of consciousness are embedded within the spatial and temporal boundaries of the home. Home-located producers develop their working habits and practices within this framework of assumptions and expectations. Household understandings set the parameters within which they negotiate with other household members for time, space and resources. We identified four ideal types of household understandings and suggested that each represents a distinctive pattern of opportunity and constraint. Moreover, we suggested, each impinges on the lives of male and female home-located producers in different ways. An analysis of household understandings thus enables us to situate contrasting patterns of gender divisions within the everyday lives of households. We emphasise that our theoretical analysis is intended to be no more than a source of hypotheses to guide further empirical research. However, it is our conclusion that the degree and form of autonomy and control experienced by home-located producers in part reflects differences between the household contexts in which they operate.

If the analysis of transformations in intimate relations presented by authors such as Giddens (1992) is accepted, it follows that home-located workers today face a somewhat different challenge to those of, say, a century ago in combining their work and domestic regimes. They have far fewer fixed points of reference or guides from which to draw when reconciling household understandings with the spatial and temporal regimes of their employment. They have the potential to create a new type of environment and new forms of social relationships. However, they may also encounter a heightened sense of risk and uncertainty, a chronic feature of those who live in late modern societies (Beck 1992; Bauman 1991). This sense of insecurity may be intensified by increases in the fluidity and diversity of household and family relationships during the second half of the twentieth century. Divorce, family breakdown, remarriage, cohabitation, lone parent families, 'reconstituted' families, births out of wedlock – all have grown rapidly. As a result, many home-located producers find themselves negotiating difficult issues surrounding their employment in the context of household relationships that are themselves fraught with novelty, distress and unpredictability.

Arguably, threats to ontological security in contemporary societies are not confined to developments in family and household relations but also extend to changes in the labour market. Sennett (1998) has recently argued that 'non-standard' forms of employment in general – which he specifically suggests includes home-located production – have an inherently corrosive effect on personal identities. He suggests that the temporary, disjointed, discontinuous, and fluid character of these kinds of employment undermine personal biographical narratives, create a sense of inner emotional drift and problematise relationships of long-term commitment to family life. While Sennett's arguments are extremely interesting, the tenor of our analysis here tends to run counter to them. Our investigations suggest that, to a greater or lesser extent, home-located producers develop technologies of the self that constitute the intellectual and emotional tools with which to construct new worlds of meaning and routine. These exercises in self-invention and self-policing may, in some respects, be fragile and vulnerable but nevertheless they suggest a capacity for reinventing identities in changing circumstances. Our analysis, therefore, leads us towards more optimistic conclusions than those of Sennett. Despite all the problems, home-located producers may yet succeed in developing new spatial and temporal regimes that embrace their lives as a whole. Moreover, there may well be more than one viable solution to their dilemmas, reflected in diverse types of household relationships.

At present, the division between home and work is so ingrained within the popular cultural consciousness that there is a tendency among some home-located producers to seek to reproduce this division, in one form or another, within their households. A conceptual leap is required to envisage a unified, holistic locale that fuses what are, in fact, the quite recently created divisions of time and space surrounding home and work. Thus, we can see in the lives of some household producers, including some of those we interviewed, what Foucault and others have called 'heterotopias': that is, really existing sites that are organised on principles that contest or invert the values of the wider social order in which they are located (Foucault 1986; Soja 1995; Hetherington 1997). Often, heterotopias juxtapose in one space apparently incompatible, incommensurate or foreign ideals and themes. It is their apparently contradictory character which gives them the power to attract and to involve others. It may be as well to remember that such bastions of contemporary modernity as the factory, school, asylum, prison, holiday resort and pleasure arcade began life as heterotopias (Hetherington 1997; Shields 1991).

Putting home-located work in its place

We have made spatial location the defining feature of home-located production. The one characteristic that the diverse forms of home-located production share is that they all take place in a domestic context. It follows that a spatial analysis of relations of production and reproduction is central to an understanding of those who are 'in work, at home'. Of particular interest are the contrasting effects of modernity on conceptions of space and place in contemporary societies – and their implications for the experiences of home-located producers.

Space is an abstract concept. It refers to the distance between objects, as measured in formal units and by standardised instruments. Place, in contrast, conjures up the particularities of a specific locality, experienced comparatively and expressed in relative terms. Modernity has compressed space – as measured by the amount of time taken to travel or communicate across distances – to an unprecedented degree and at an ever-accelerating rate (Giddens 1991, 1992; Harvey 1989). As a result, more and more aspects of social relations have been progressively disembedded from particular places. On the other hand, modernity is associated with a reinvention of place. Threats to ontological security have led to the reinvention of local identities within emotionally charged, visible places – reflected, for example, in the revival of ethnic, regional and communal identities (cf. Westwood and Williams 1997).

Home-located production is poised on the cusp of these developments in space and place. The growth of home-located production has been stimulated by technological innovations in communications and transport, the spatial separation of economic functions and the globalisation of economic activities (Massey 1984; Sassen 1991, 1994). All these have loosened the claims of traditional communities and established localised identities. They make it possible for the workforce to be dispersed to geographically isolated sites. In one perspective, therefore, home-located producers are analogous to tiny, scattered islands in a vast ocean of advanced capitalist space (cf. Sennett 1998: 55, 59). In principle, the home-located worker could be anywhere, even a different time zone on the other side of the planet.

Home-located production appears, then, to be a paradigm case of the compression of time–space and the disembedding of economic relations from place. However, it is also the case that the home invests economic activity with a very specific sense of place and time. The home has become a site where the narratives of individual biographies are played out. The times and spaces of home are where individuals construct, experience and invent their lifeworlds (Saunders 1990; Dupuis and Thorns 1996, 1998; Allan and Crow 1991). The home is one of the key sites in the late modern world where individual and personalised identities are constructed by members within a bounded geographical locality as an assertion and expression of their unique selves. Home is, thus, crucial to the reinvention of place (Saunders 1989, 1990; Crow and Allan 1990, 1994). As a result, home-located production is to be found within one of the key *places* in the western world.

Home-located production thus reflects contradictory processes with respect to space and place in late modernity. It is, simultaneously, an expression of enormous advances in time–space compression and of the reinvention of localised individualised practices embedded in particular places.

Endings and beginnings

The reader may discern in this last chapter a certain tension in our desire to summarise the arguments presented in this book and our eagerness to open up new themes for analysis and enquiry. We are all too well aware that many of our closing thoughts have offered no more than a preliminary sketch of ideas that will require much further development elsewhere. In conclusion, therefore, we would like in our final paragraph to bring the focus back to those issues which earlier chapters have enabled us to discuss in greater depth.

This book has sought to address what we perceive to be a number of serious deficiencies in the current state of knowledge about people 'in work, at home'. Research findings are scattered, fragmentary and not readily available to scholars within one volume. Academic, popular and policy-oriented writing in the field is plagued by serious conceptual confusions and misunderstandings that undermine the value of much of the work that has been done and make comparison very difficult. Few studies seek to encompass the totality of social relations – both relations of production and of the household – that, in our estimation, comprise the field of enquiry. Little work has been done to relate the psychological disposition of homeworkers to differences in their household contexts. We hope that this volume makes a contribution to ending some of the confusions in all these areas and stimulates the beginning of new lines of research.

Appendix

The following is a full list of the respondents to the qualitative interviews, referred to by pseudonyms. All were engaged in home-located production for at least some of their working time. Not all respondents are quoted in the text.

Home-located employers

Diane
: Diane is a part owner of a small family firm producing soft furnishings for local retail outlets. She is involved in manufacture, her husband concentrates on planning and fitting. They employ two homeworkers and a range of other assistants. Both are in their late fifties and are white. They live in a small market town in Britain and have two grown-up children.

Isobel
: Isobel is a freelance communications adviser, conference organiser and trainer. She runs her own business employing administrative and other staff on short-term or part-time basis as required. Isobel is in her mid-thirties. She is white, married, with one child, living in a very exclusive village in the English shires.

Lorraine
: Lorraine runs a nursing agency supplying staff to private and public sector hospitals. She employs a range of professional and administrative staff. Lorraine is in her mid-forties. She is white, has two grown-up children and lives in a large house in a market town in Britain.

Home-located petty commodity producers

Barbara
: Barbara makes a range of high quality curtains and soft furnishings and sells direct to private clients. She is in her early forties, is white, married, has two teenage children and lives on a farm in rural Britain.

Bella
: Bella is a freelance management consultant. She is in her mid-fifties, is white and is married with one child. She lives with her husband, daughter and granddaughter in a large house in a small industrial town in Britain.

Bill
: Bill is a self-employed business and management consultant. He is in his late forties and is white, married, has two children and lives in a middle-class modern estate in a small town in Britain.

Charles	Charles is a self-employed surveyor. He is in his early forties, is white, married to Sarah (also interviewed), has one child and lives in an affluent commuter village on the outskirts of a major provincial British city.
Daniel	Daniel is a freelance exhibition designer and also manages a joint business with Henrietta (also interviewed). He is in his mid-fifties, is white and is married to Henrietta. They live in an affluent rural commuter village in the English shires.
Harry	Harry is a self-employed freelance surveyor. He is in his mid-forties, white, married with five children and lives in a very large and well appointed cottage in rural England.
Henrietta	Henrietta is a designer of fabric novelties sold as mail order kits direct to end-users. She is in her mid-fifties and white. Henrietta is married to Daniel (also interviewed). They live in an affluent rural commuter village in the English shires.
Lorna	Lorna is a freelance design consultant. She is in her mid-forties and is white. Lorna and her partner have one child and live in a well-to-do rural commuter village in the English shires.
Maureen	Maureen is a childminder looking after five children in her own home. She is in her late forties and white. She is a divorcee and has two children in their twenties and two in their teens.
Niall	Niall is a self-employed architect and designer. Half of his time is devoted to private practice and half to commissions from a range of residential projects across London. Single, Irish, and in his early thirties, he lives in the East End of London.
Sarah	Sarah is a self-employed dressmaker specialising in *haute couture* and high quality bridal gowns. She is in her early forties, white and married to Charles (also interviewed). They have a child and live in an affluent commuter village on the outskirts of a major provincial British city.
Stephen	Stephen is a freelance information technology consultant and trainer. He is in his late forties, white and is married with one child. Stephen and his family live on a new estate in a middle-class commuter village outside of a major provincial British city.

High discretion home-located wage labourers
| Geoff | Geoff sells industrial packaging and labelling for a well known local company. He is in his early fifties, white, and married. He has two children in their early twenties. |

Low discretion home-located wage labourers (homeworkers)
| Abdul | Abdul is a textile machinist and lockstitcher working in the front room of an inner city terraced house in a major provincial British city. He is in his early thirties, is Muslim and lives a strict Islamic lifestyle. He is married with two young children. |

Chantelle	Chantelle is a bookkeeper currently working for her husband's building business. She is in her early thirties and has two children under school age. She lives in Central London and is of African-Caribbean origin.
Elizabeth	Elizabeth inspects and repairs cooker filaments. She is in her late twenties, is white and is married with three children. She lives in a suburban area of a major provincial British city.
Meena	Meena lockstitches and overlocks garments such as leisure wear and fashion items. She is in her early thirties and of Asian origin, born in the UK. Meena is married with two children. She lives in a two-bedroom suburban house on an outer estate of a major provincial British city.
Shirley	Shirley undertakes routine bookkeeping for one long-standing client. In her mid-forties, she is white, married, has one son and lives in a suburban area of a major provincial British city.
Tracy	Tracy is a machinist primarily working on the finishing of children's ankle socks. She is in her mid-thirties, white and married with four children. She lives in an outer suburb of a major provincial British city.
Vikash	Vikash is a lockstitcher and machinist finishing a range of garments, including those sold in high street stores. In his mid-thirties, of Indian origin, he is married with one child. Vikash lives in a small terraced house in an inner city neighbourhood in a provincial British town and works in an outhouse in his backyard. He has limited English and was interviewed in Gujerati.

References

Abrera-Mangahas, A. (1993) 'New national survey findings: profile of homeworkers in the Philippines', in Lazo, L. (ed.) *From the Shadows to the Fore: Practical Actions for the Social Protection of Homeworkers in the Philippines*, Bangkok: International Labour Organisation.

ACAS (1978a) *Button Manufacturing Wages Council*, Report No. 11, London: Advisory, Conciliation and Arbitration Service.

ACAS (1978b) *Toy Manufacturing Wages Council*, Report No. 13, London: Advisory, Conciliation and Arbitration Service.

Adkin, E. (1994) 'Contractual considerations of employing homeworkers: a case study', *Employment Law and Practice*, vol. 2, no. 2, 38–40.

Ahrentzen, S. (1987) 'Blurring boundaries: socio-spatial consequences of working at home', *Center for Architecture and Urban Planning Research, University of Wisconsin-Milwaukee, Report R87–4.*

Ahrentzen, S. (1990) 'Managing conflict by managing boundaries: how professional home-workers cope with multiple roles at home', *Environment and Behavior*, vol. 22, no. 6, November, 723–752.

Ahrentzen, S. (1992) 'Home as a workplace in the lives of women', in Altman, I. and Lowe, S. M. (eds) *Place Attachment*, New York: Plenum Press.

Akyeampong, E. B. (1997) 'Work arrangements: 1995 overview', *Perspectives on Labour and Income*, Spring, Catalogue No. 75–001–XPE, 48–52.

Akyeampong, E. B. and Siroonian, J. (1993) 'Work arrangements of Canadians – an overview', *Perspectives on Labour and Income*, Autumn, Catalogue No. 75–001E, 8–10.

Allan, G. and Crow, G. (1991) 'Privatization, home-centredness and leisure', *Leisure Studies*, vol. 10, 1–13.

Allen, S. (1983) 'Production and reproduction: the lives of women homeworkers', *Sociological Review*, vol. 31, no. 4, 649–655.

Allen, S. and Wolkowitz, C. (1987) *Homeworking: Myths and Realities*, London: Macmillan.

Anderson, G., Brosnan, P. and Walsh, P. (1994) 'Homeworking in New Zealand: results from a workplace survey', *International Journal of Employment Studies*, vol. 2, no. 2, October, 229–247.

Anderson, M., Bechhofer, F. and Gershuny, J. (eds) (1994) *The Social and Political Economy of the Household*, Oxford: Oxford University Press.

Armstrong, N. (1997) 'Negotiating the boundaries between "home" and "work": a case-study of teleworking in New Zealand', paper presented at the Gender and Teleworking Conference, National Resource Centre for Women (NUTEK), Stockholm, Sweden, 14 March.

Armstrong, N. (1999) 'Flexible work in the virtual workplace: discourses and implications of teleworking', in Felstead, A. and Jewson, N. (eds) *Global Trends in Flexible Labour*, London: Macmillan.

Bagihole, B. (1986) *Invisible Workers: Women's Experience of Outworking in Nottinghamshire*, Nottingham: Benefits Research Unit, University of Nottingham.

Bailyn, L. (1988) 'Freeing work from the constraints of location and time', *New Technology, Work and Employment*, vol. 3, no. 2, 143–152.

Bauman, Z. (1991) *Modernity and Ambivalence*, Oxford: Polity Press.

Beach, B. (1989) *Integrating Work and Family Life: The Home-Working Family*, Albany, New York: State University of New York Press.

Beck, U. (1992) *Risk Society*, London: Sage.

Benería, L. and Roldán, M. (1987) *The Crossroads of Class and Gender: Industrial Homework, Subcontracting, and Household Dynamics in Mexico City*, Chicago: University of Chicago Press.

Benjamin, O. and Sullivan, O. (1996) 'The importance of difference: conceptualising increased flexibility in gender relations in the home', *Sociological Review*, vol. 44, no. 2, 225–251.

Berch, B. (1985) 'The resurrection of outwork', *Monthly Review*, 37: 37–46.

Berg, M. (1987) 'Women's work, mechanisation and the early phases of industrialisation in England', in Joyce, P. (ed.) *The Historical Meanings of Work*, Cambridge: Cambridge University Press.

Berik, G. (1987) *Women Carpet Weavers in Rural Turkey: Patterns of Employment, Earnings and Status*, Geneva: ILO.

Berk, S. F. (1985) *The Gender Factory*, New York: Plenum.

Bernstein, B. (1975) *Class, Codes and Control*, 3 volumes, London: Routledge and Kegan Paul.

Bhatt, E. (1987) 'The invisibility of home-based work: the case of piece rate workers in India', in Menefee Singh, A. and Kelles-Viitanen, A. (eds) *Invisible Hands: Women in Home-Based Production*, New Delhi: Sage.

Birmingham City Council (1993) *Profile of Homeworking Issues in Birmingham*, Birmingham: Birmingham City Council.

Bisset, L. and Huws, U. (1984) *Sweated Labour: Homeworking in Britain Today*, London: Low Pay Unit.

Blackburn, R. M. (1998) 'A new system of classes: but what are they and do we need them?', *Work, Employment and Society*, vol. 12, no. 4, 735–742.

Boris, E. (1994) *Home to Work: Motherhood and the Politics of Industrial Homework in the United States*, Cambridge: Cambridge University Press.

Boris, E. (1996) 'Sexual divisions, gender constructions', in Boris, E. and Prügl, E. (eds) *Homeworkers in Global Perspective: Invisible No More*, London: Routledge.

Boris, E. and Daniels, C. R. (eds) (1989) *Homework: Historical and Contemporary Perspectives on Paid Labour at Home*, Urbana: University of Illinois Press.

Boris, E. and Prügl, E. (eds) (1996) *Homeworkers in Global Perspective: Invisible No More*, London: Routledge.

Bourdieu, P. (1977) *Outline of a Theory of Practice*, Cambridge: Cambridge University Press.

Bourdieu, P. (1990a) *In Other Words*, Cambridge: Polity.

Bourdieu, P. (1990b) *The Logic of Practice*, Cambridge: Polity.

Brosnan, P. and Thornthwaite, L. (1997) '"The TV work is not so bad": the experiences of a group of homeworkers', Centre for Research on Employment and Work, Griffith University, unpublished mimeo.

Brown, M. (1974) *Sweated Labour: A Study of Homework*, London: Low Pay Unit.

Bulos, M. and Chaker, W. (1993) 'Homebased workers: studies in the adaptation of space', in Bulos, M. and Teymur, N. (eds) *Housing: Design, Research, Education*, Aldershot: Avebury.

Bulos, M. and Chaker, W. (1995) 'Sustaining a sense of home and personal identity', in Benjamin, D. N., Stea, D. and Saile, D. (eds) *The Home: Words, Interpretations, Meanings, and Environments*, Aldershot: Avebury.

Burchell, G. (1993) 'Liberal government and techniques of the self', *Economy & Society*, vol. 22, no. 3, 266–282.

Burdett, J. (1980) 'The clothing industry in the Cypriot community', Haringey Employment Project, mimeo.

Bureau of Labor Statistics (1998) 'Work at home in 1997', http://stats.bls.gov/newsrels.htm

Bythell, D. (1978) *The Sweated Trades: Outwork in Nineteenth-Century Britain*, London: Batsford Academic.

Callus, R., Morehead, A., Cully, M. and Buchanan, J. (1991) *Industrial Relations at Work: The Australian Workplace Industrial Relations Survey*, Canberra: AGPS Press.

Cameron, B. and Mak, T. (1991) *Working Conditions of Chinese-speaking Homeworkers in the Toronto Garment Workers' Union*, Ontario: International Ladies' Garment Workers' Union, Ontario District Council.

Carney, L. and Brent, N. (1997) *The Hidden Workers of Sheffield: The Health and Safety Needs of Homeworkers*, Sheffield: Sheffield Occupational Health Project.

Casey, C. (1995) *Work, Self and Society*, London and New York: Routledge.

Census of Population Office (1994) *Singapore Census of Population 1990: Transport and Geographic Distribution*, Singapore: SNP Publishers.

Chiu, S. W. K. and Lui, T.-L. (1996) 'Hong Kong: unorganised industrialism', in Clark, G. and Kim, W. B. (eds) *Asian Newly Industrialised Economies and the Global Economy*, Baltimore, Maryland: Johns Hopkins University Press.

Christensen, K. (1985) *Impacts of Computer-mediated Home-based Work on Women and their Families*, New York: Center for Human Environments.

Christensen, K. (1988) *Women and Home-Based Work: The Unspoken Contract*, New York: Henry Holt.

Christensen, K. (1989) 'Home-based clerical work: no simple truth, no single reality', in Boris, E. and Daniels, C. (eds) *Homework: Historical and Contemporary Perspectives on Paid Labor at Home*, Urbana and Chicago: University of Illinois Press.

Christian Aid (1997) *A Sporting Chance: Tackling Child Labour in India's Sports Goods Industry*, London: Christian Aid.

CIR (1973) *Pin, Hook and Eye and Snap Fastener Wages Council*, Report No. 49, HMSO: London.

Cockburn, C. (1983) *Brothers: Male Dominance and Technological Change*, London: Pluto Press.

Cohen, A. (1985) *The Symbolic Construction of Community*, London: Tavistock.

Coltrane, S. (1989) 'Household labour and the routine production of gender', *Social Problems*, 36: 473–490.

Costello, C. B. (1988) 'Clerical home-based work: a case study of work and family', in Christensen, K. E. (ed.) *The New Era of Home-Based Work: Directions and Policies*, Boulder, Colorado: Westview Press.

Council of Europe (1989) *The Protection of Persons Working at Home*, Strasbourg: Council of Europe.

Cragg, A. and Dawson, T. (1981) 'Qualitative research among homeworkers', *Department of Employment Research Paper*, No. 21.

Crine, S. (1979) *The Hidden Army*, London: Low Pay Unit.

Crow, G. and Allan, G. (1990) 'Constructing the domestic sphere: the emergence of the modern home in post-war Britain', in Corr, H. and Jamieson, L. (eds) *Politics of Everyday Life: Continuity and Change in Work and the Family*, London: Macmillan.

Crow, G. and Allan, G. (1994) *Community Life: An Introduction to Local Social Relations*, London: Harvester Wheatsheaf.

Cummings, K. (1986) *Outworkers and Subcontractors: Non-Standard Employment and Industrial Democracy*, Canberra: AGPS Press.

Dagg, A. (1996) 'Organizing homeworkers into unions', in Boris, E. and Prügl, E. (eds) *Homeworkers in Global Perspective: Invisible No More*, London: Routledge.

Dagg, A. and Fudge, J. (1993) 'Sewing gains: homeworkers in the garment trade', in Lowe, G. S. and Krahn, H. J. (eds) *Work in Canada: Readings in the Sociology of Work and Industry*, Ontario: Nelson Canada.

Dawson, W. and Turner, J. (1989) *When She Goes to Work, She Stays at Home: Women, New Technology and Home-Based Work*, Canberra: AGPS Press.

Deming, W. (1994) 'Work at home: data from the CPS', *Monthly Labor Review*, vol. 117, no. 2, February, 14–20.

Deprés, C. (1991) 'The meaning of home: literature review and main directions for future research and theoretical development', *Journal of Architectural and Planning Research*, vol. 8, no. 2, 96–115.

Dholakia, R. H. (1989) 'On estimating home workers in India', in Patel, B. B. (ed.) *Problems of Home-Based Workers in India*, Ahmedabad: Gandhi Labour Institute.

Direction des Statistiques Sociales (1991) *Enquête main-d'oeuvre 1989*, ONS: Algiers.

Donzelot, J. (1991) 'Pleasure in work', in Burchell, G., Gordon, C. and Miller, P. (eds) *The Foucault Effect: Studies in Governmentality*, London: Harvester Wheatsheaf.

Douglas, M. (1973) *Natural Symbols: Explorations in Cosmology*, London: Barrie and Jenkins.

Dreyfus, H. L. and Rabinow, P. (1982) *Michel Foucault: Beyond Structuralism and Hermeneutics*, Chicago: University of Chicago Press.

Du Gay, P. (1996a) *Consumption and Identity at Work*, London: Sage.

Du Gay, P. (1996b) 'Organising identity: entrepreneurial governance and public management', in Hall, S. and Du Gay, P. (eds) *Questions of Cultural Identity*, London: Sage.

Dundee Inner City Neighbourhood Action Centre (1984) *Working at Home: A Feasibility Study into the Extent, the Problems and the Future Requirements of Homeworkers in Dundee*, Dundee: Dundee Inner City Neighbourhood Action Centre.

Dupuis, A. and Thorns, D. L. (1996) 'The meaning of home', *Housing Studies*, vol. 11, no. 4, 485–501.

Dupuis, A. and Thorns, D. L. (1998) 'Home, home ownership and the search for ontological security', *Sociological Review*, vol. 46, no. 1, 24–47.

Ellem, B. (1991) 'Outwork and unionism in the Australian clothing industry', in Bray, M. and Taylor, V. (eds) *The Other Side of Flexibility*, Sydney: ACIRRT, University of Sydney.

Elwin, T. (1994) *Outworking: A Code of Practice*, Nottingham: Nottingham County Council.

Employment Gazette (1992) 'LFS Help-Line', *Employment Gazette*, vol. 100, no. 12, 615–620.

European Commission (1994) *High Level Group on the Information Society, Europe and the*

Global Information Society, Luxembourg: Office for Official Publications of the European Communities.

Eurostat (1992) *Labour Force Survey: Methods and Definitions, 1992 Series*, Luxembourg: Office for Official Publications of the European Communities.

Eurostat (1993) *Labour Force Survey Results 1992*, Luxembourg: Office for Official Publications of the European Communities.

Eurostat (1994) *Labour Force Survey Results 1993*, Luxembourg: Office for Official Publications of the European Communities.

Eurostat (1995) *Labour Force Survey Results 1994*, Luxembourg: Office for Official Publications of the European Communities.

Eurostat (1996) *Labour Force Survey Results 1995*, Luxembourg: Office for Official Publications of the European Communities.

Eurostat (1997) *Labour Force Survey Results 1996*, Luxembourg: Office for Official Publications of the European Communities.

Faricellia Dangler, J. (1989) 'Electronic subassemblers in Central New York: nontraditional homeworkers in a nontraditional homework industry', in Boris, E. and Daniels, C. R. (eds) *Homework: Historical and Contemporary Perspectives on Paid Labor at Home*, Urbana and Chicago: University of Illinois Press.

Felstead, A. (1988) 'Technological change, industrial relations and the small firm: a study of small printing firms', unpublished Ph.D. thesis, University of London.

Felstead, A. (1993) *The Corporate Paradox: Power and Control in the Business Franchise*, London: Routledge.

Felstead, A. (1996) 'Homeworking in Britain: the national picture in the mid-1990s', *Industrial Relations Journal*, vol. 27, no. 3, September, 225–238.

Felstead, A. and Jewson, N. (1995) 'Working at home: estimates from the 1991 Census', *Employment Gazette*, vol. 103, no. 3, March, 95–99.

Felstead, A. and Jewson, N. (1996) *Homeworkers in Britain*, London: HMSO.

Felstead, A. and Jewson, N. (1997) 'Researching a problematic concept: homeworkers in Britain', *Work, Employment and Society*, vol. 11, no. 2, June, 327–346.

Felstead, A. and Jewson, N. (eds) (1999) *Global Trends in Flexible Labour*, London: Macmillan.

Fernández-Kelly, M. P. and García, A. M. (1988) 'Hispanic women and homework: women in the informal economy of Miami and Los Angeles', in Christensen, K. E. (ed.) *The New Era of Home-Based Work: Directions and Policies*, Boulder, Colorado: Westview Press.

Financial Times (1996) 'Ragtrade probes work practices', 3 October, p. 14 (Jenny Luesby and William Lewis).

Finch, J. and Mason, J. (1993) *Negotiating Family Responsibilities*, London: Tavistock/Routledge.

Flecker, J. and Hofbauer, J. (1998) 'Capitalising on subjectivity: the "new model worker" and the importance of being useful', in Thompson, P. and Warhurst, C. (eds) *The Future Workplace*, London: Macmillan.

Foster, K., Jackson, B., Thomas, M., Hunter, P. and Bennett, N. (1995) *General Household Survey 1993*, London: HMSO.

Fothergill, A. and Rose, M. (1998) 'Teleworking: gender roles and the influence of gender on the space in the home', paper presented at the Gender, Work and Organization Conference, Manchester Metropolitan University and University of Manchester Institute of Science and Technology, 9–10 January.

Foucault, M. (1977) *Discipline and Punish: The Birth of the Prison*, London: Allen Lane.

Foucault, M. (1979) *The History of Sexuality, Vol. 1: An Introduction*, London: Allen Lane.

Foucault, M. (1986) 'Of other spaces', *Diacritics*, vol. 16, no. 1, 22–27.

Foucault, M. (1987) *The History of Sexuality, Vol. 2: The Use of Pleasure*, London: Penguin Books.

Foucault, M. (1988) 'Technologies of the self', in Martin, L., Gutman, H. and Hutton, P. (eds) *Technologies of the Self*, London: Tavistock.

Foucault, M. (1990) *The History of Sexuality, Vol. 3: The Care of the Self*, London: Penguin Books.

Fox, A. (1974) *Beyond Contract*, London: Faber and Faber.

Gershuny, J., Godwin, M. and Jones, S. (1994) 'The domestic labour revolution: a process of lagged adaptation', in Anderson, M., Bechhofer, F. and Gershuny, J. (eds) *The Social and Political Economy of the Household*, Oxford: Oxford University Press.

Gerson, J. (1993) 'Clerical homeworkers: are they organizable?', in Cobble, S. (ed.) *Women and Unions: Forging a Partnership*, Ithaca, New York: Industrial and Labor Relations Press.

Gerson, J. M. and Kraut, R. E. (1988) 'Clerical work at home or in the office: the difference it makes', in Christensen, K. E. (ed.) *The New Era of Home-Based Work: Directions and Policies*, Boulder, Colorado: Westview Press.

Ghavamshahidi, Z. (1996) '"Bidi Khanum": carpet weavers and gender ideology in Iran', in Boris, E. and Prügl, E. (eds) *Homeworkers in Global Perspective: Invisible No More*, London: Routledge.

Giddens, A. (1990) *Consequences of Modernity*, Cambridge: Polity Press.

Giddens, A. (1991) *Modernity and Self Identity: Self and Society in the Late Modern Age*, Cambridge: Polity Press.

Giddens, A. (1992) *Transformation of Intimacy*, Cambridge: Cambridge University Press.

Gillespie, A., Richardson, R. and Cornford, J. (1995) *Review of Telework in Britain: Implications for Public Policy*, CURDS, University of Newcastle.

Gittins, D. (1993) *The Family in Question: Changing Households and Familiar Ideologies*, London: Macmillan.

Glucksmann, M. (1995) 'Why "work"? Gender and the "total organization of labour"', *Gender, Work and Organization*, vol. 2, no. 2, 63–75.

Glucksmann, M. (1998) '"What a difference a day makes": a theoretical and historical exploration of temporality and gender', *Sociology*, vol. 32, no. 2, 239–258.

Gordon, C. (1987) 'The soul of the citizen: Max Weber and Michel Foucault on rationality and governmentality', in Lash, S. and Whimster, S. (eds) *Max Weber, Rationality and Modernity*, London: Allen and Unwin.

Granger, B., Stanworth, J. and Stanworth, C. (1996) 'Self-employment career dynamics: the case of "unemployment push" in UK book publishing', *Work, Employment and Society*, vol. 9, no. 3, September, 499–516.

Gregson, N. and Lowe, M. (1993) 'Renegotiating the domestic division of labour? A study of dual career households in North East and South East England', *Sociological Review*, vol. 41, no. 3, 475–505.

Gutek, B. (1983) 'Women's work in the office of the future', in Zimmerman, J. (ed.) *The Technological Woman: Interfacing with Tomorrow*, New York: Praeger.

Haddon, L. (1992) *Clerical Teleworking – How it Affects Family Life*, Martlesham: British Telecom.

Haddon, L. and Lewis, A. (1994) 'The experience of teleworking: an annotated review', *The International Journal of Human Resource Management*, vol. 5, no. 1, 195–223.

Haddon, L. and Silverstone, R. (1993) 'Teleworking in the 1990s: a view from the home', *SPRU CICT Report Series*, No. 10.

Hakim, C. (1980) 'Homeworking: some new evidence', *Employment Gazette*, vol. 88, no. 10, October, 1105–1110.

Hakim, C. (1985) 'Employers' use of outwork: a study using the 1980 Workplace Industrial Relations Survey and the 1981 National Survey of Homeworking', *Department of Employment Research Paper*, No. 44.

Hakim, C. (1987a) 'Home-based work in Britain: a report on the 1981 National Homeworking Survey and the DE research programme on homework', *Department of Employment Research Paper*, No. 60.

Hakim, C. (1987b) 'Homeworking in Britain: key findings from the national survey of home-based workers', *Employment Gazette*, vol. 95, no. 2, February, 92–104.

Hakim, C. (1991) 'Grateful slaves and self-made women: fact and fantasy in women's work orientations', *European Sociological Review*, vol. 7, no. 2, September, 101–121.

Hakim, C. (1998) *Social Change and Innovation in the Labour Market: Evidence from the Census SARs on Occupational Segregation and Labour Mobility, Part-Time Work and Student Jobs, Homework and Self-Employment*, Oxford: Oxford University Press.

Hakim, C. and Dennis, R. (1982) 'Homeworking in Wages Council industries: a study based on Wages Inspectorate records of pay and earnings', *Department of Employment Research Paper*, No. 37.

Hamblin, H. (1995) 'Employees' perceptions on one dimension of labour flexibility: working at a distance', *Work, Employment and Society*, vol. 9, no. 3, 473–498.

Hampton, R. L. (1993) *Family Violence*, London: Sage.

Handy, C. (1995) *The Future of Work*, London: W. H. Smith Contemporary Papers 8.

Hantrais, L. (1993) 'The gender of time in professional occupations', *Time and Society*, vol. 2, no. 2, 139–157.

Harris, R. (1997) *Homeworking in Glasgow: Key Issues Arising from a Preliminary Investigation*, Glasgow: Scottish Low Pay Unit.

Harvey, D. (1989) *The Condition of Post Modernity*, New York: Basil Blackwell.

Heck, R. K. Z. (1993) 'A profile of home-based workers', *Human Ecology Forum*, vol. 15, 15–18.

Hendry, K. (1994) 'Invisible threads: from homeworkers to the high street: investigating the links in the sub-contracting chain', unpublished Masters thesis, University of Warwick.

Hetherington, K. (1997) *The Badlands of Modernity: Heterotopia and Social Ordering*, London: Routledge.

Hirshey, G. (1985) 'How women feel about working at home', *Family Circle*, 5 November, 70–74.

Hodson, N. (1993) *The Economics of Teleworking*, British Telecommunications.

HomeNet (various) *HomeNet: The Newsletter of the International Network for Homebased Workers*, Leeds: HomeNet.

Hope, E., Kennedy, M. and de Winter, A. (1976) 'Homeworkers in North London', in Barker, D. L. and Allen, S. (eds) *Dependence and Exploitation in Work and Marriage*, London: Longman.

Hopkins, M. (1992) 'Empowerment or escape? Technical training for homeworkers in Britain', in Mitter, S. (ed.) *Computer-Aided Manufacturing and Women's Employment: The Clothing Industry in Four EC Countries*, Berlin: Springer-Verlag.

Horvath, F. W. (1986) 'Working at home: new findings from the Current Population Survey', *Monthly Labor Review*, vol. 109, November, 31–35.

Hsiung, P.-C. (1996) *Living Rooms as Factories: Class, Gender, and the Satellite Factory System in Taiwan*, Philadelphia: Temple University Press.

Huws, U. (1984) *The New Homeworkers: New Technology and the Changing Location of White-Collar Work*, London: Low Pay Unit.

Huws, U. (1993) 'Teleworking in Britain', *Employment Department Research Series*, No. 18.

Huws, U. (1994) *Home Truths: Key Results from a National Survey of Homeworkers*, Leeds: National Group on Homeworking.

Huws, U. (1996a) *No Sweat! Why Britain's One Million Homeworkers Need a New Deal*, London: Trades Union Congress.

Huws, U. (1996b) *Teleworking: An Overview of the Research*, DoT/DoE/DTI/DfEE report, London.

Huws, U., Korte, W. B. and Robinson, S. (1990) *Telework: Towards the Elusive Office*, Chichester: John Wiley.

Huws, U., Podro, S., Gunnarsson, E., Weijers, T., Arvanitaki, K. and Trova, V. (1996) 'Teleworking and gender', *Institute for Employment Studies Report*, No. 317.

Illawara Migrant Resource Centre (1984) *Outwork: A Guide for Community and Welfare Workers*, Wollongong: Illawara Migrant Resource Centre.

ILO (1989) *Home Work: Conditions of Work Digest*, Geneva: International Labour Office.

ILO (1994) *Homework Report V (1)*, Geneva: International Labour Office.

ILO (1995) *Invisible Workers in Viet Nam: An Exploratory Survey of Home-Based Workers in Selected Areas*, Geneva: International Labour Office.

ILO (1996) *Home Work Report IV (2B)*, Geneva: International Labour Office.

Industrial Relations Law Bulletin (1995) 'Employment status 2: specific categories', December, 2–6.

Irwin, M. H. (1902) *The Problems of Homework*, Glasgow: Scottish Co-operative Wholesale Society.

Jaques, E. (1956) *Measurement of Responsibility*, London: Tavistock.

Jaques, E. (1967) *Equitable Payment*, revised edition, Harmondsworth: Penguin.

Jenkins, R. (1986) *Racism and Recruitment*, Cambridge: Cambridge University Press.

Jewson, N. and Mason, D. (1986) 'The theory and practice of equal opportunities policies: liberal and radical approaches', *Sociological Review*, vol. 34, no. 2, 307–334.

Jewson, N. and Mason, D. (1992) '"Race", equal opportunities and employment practice: reflections on the 1980s, prospects for the 1990s', *New Community*, vol. 19, no. 1, 99–112.

Jewson, N. and Mason, D. (1994) '"Race", employment and equal opportunities: towards a political economy and an agenda for the 1990s', *Sociological Review*, vol. 42, no. 4, 591–617.

Jewson, N., Mason, D., Drewett, A. and Rossiter, W. (1995) *Formal Equal Opportunities Policies & Employment Best Practice*, Department for Education & Employment Research Series, No. 69, November.

Jhabvala, R. (1994) 'Self-Employed Women's Association: organising women by struggle and development', in Rowbottom, S. and Mitter, S. (eds) *Dignity and Daily Bread: New Forms of Economic Organising Among Women in the Third World and the First*, London: Routledge.

Joeman, L. (1994) 'Homeworking in Britain: findings from the Spring 1992 Labour Force Survey', Employment Department mimeo.

Joyce, P. (1987) *The Historical Meanings of Work*, Cambridge: Cambridge University Press.

Judkins, P., West, D. and Drew, J. (1985) *Networking and Organisations: The Rank Xerox Experiment*, Aldershot: Gower.

Kamio, K. (1995) 'The Kyoto Homeworkers' Friendship Associations – Japan', in Huws, U. (ed.) *Action Programmes for the Protection of Homeworkers: Ten Case Studies from Around the World*, Geneva: International Labour Organisation.

Korns, A. (1993) 'Where are the homeworkers in the labour force survey? Indonesian statistics for manufacturing by homebased workers', in Lazo, L. (ed.) *From the Shadows to the Fore: Practical Actions for the Social Protection of Homeworkers in Indonesia*, Bangkok: ILO.

Kraut, R. E. (1988) 'Homework: what is it and who does it?', in Christensen, K. E. (ed.) *The New Era of Home-Based Work: Directions and Policies*, Boulder, Colorado: Westview Press.

Kraut, R. E. and Grambsch, P. (1987) 'Home-based white collar employment: lessons from the 1980 Census', *Social Forces*, vol. 66, no. 2, December, 410–426.

Kumar, K. (1995) *From Post-Industrial to Post-Modern Society: New Theories of the Contemporary World*, Oxford: Blackwell.

Kyoto Labour Standards Bureau (1994) *The Present Situation of Homeworking in Kyoto Prefecture*, Kyoto: Kyoto Labour Standards Bureau.

Labour Market Trends (1996) 'Labour Force Survey: Help-Line', *Labour Market Trends*, June.

Labour Research (1993) 'Homeworkers help themselves', *Labour Research*, vol. 82, no. 5, May, 17–18.

Lafferty, G., Hall, R., Harley, B. and Whitehouse, G. (1997) 'Homeworking in Australia: an assessment of current trends', *Australian Bulletin of Labour*, vol. 23, no. 2, June, 143–156.

Lauric, H. and Taylor, M. P. (1995) 'Homeworkers in Britain: using the BHPS wave one data', *ESRC Research Centre on Micro-social Change Working Paper*, No. 95–3.

Layder, D. (1997) *Modern Social Theory: Key Debates and New Directions*, London: UCL Press.

Lazo, L. (ed.) (1992a) *Homeworkers of Southeast Asia: The Struggle for Social Protection in Indonesia*, Bangkok: International Labour Organisation.

Lazo, L. (ed.) (1992b) *Homeworkers of Southeast Asia: The Struggle for Social Protection in the Philippines*, Bangkok: International Labour Organisation.

Lazo, L. (ed.) (1992c) *Homeworkers of Southeast Asia: The Struggle for Social Protection in Thailand*, Bangkok: International Labour Organisation.

Lazo, L. (ed.) (1993a) *From the Shadows to the Fore: Practical Actions for the Social Protection of Homeworkers in Indonesia*, Bangkok: International Labour Organisation.

Lazo, L. (ed.) (1993b) *From the Shadows to the Fore: Practical Actions for the Social Protection of Homeworkers in the Philippines*, Bangkok: International Labour Organisation.

Lazo, L. (ed.) (1993c) *From the Shadows to the Fore: Practical Actions for the Social Protection of Homeworkers in Thailand*, Bangkok: International Labour Organisation.

Leidner, R. (1988) 'Home work: a study in the interaction of work and family organization', *Research in the Sociology of Work*, vol. 4, 69–94.

Littlefield, D. (1996) 'Danger at work in the supply chain', *People Management*, 4 April, 22–27.

Loveridge, A. and Schoeffel, P. (1991) 'Who works at home? A New Zealand profile', *Working Papers on Information Technology and Society No. 2*, DSIR Social Science, Christchurch.

Loveridge, A., Graham, P. and Schoeffel, P. (1996) 'The impact of tele-work on working at home in New Zealand', *New Zealand Sociology*, vol. 11, no. 1, May, 1–37.

Low Pay Unit (1995) *The New Review*, May/June.

Lui, T.-L. (1994) *Waged Work at Home: The Social Organization of Industrial Outwork in Hong Kong*, Aldershot: Avebury.

Lui, T.-L. and Chiu, T. (1999) 'Global restructuring and non-standard work in Newly Industrialised Economies: the organisation of flexible production in Hong Kong and Taiwan', in Felstead, A. and Jewson, N. (eds) *Global Trends in Flexible Labour*, London: Macmillan.

McLennan, W. (1989) *Persons Employed at Home, Australia, April 1989*, Catalogue No. 6275.0, Canberra: Australian Bureau of Statistics.

McLennan, W. (1996) *Persons Employed at Home, Australia, September 1995*, Catalogue No. 6275.0, Canberra: Australian Bureau of Statistics.

Madden, R. (1992) *Persons Employed at Home, Australia, March 1992*, Catalogue No. 6275.0, Canberra: Australian Bureau of Statistics.

Marglin, S. (1974) 'What do bosses do? The origins and functions of hierarchy in capitalist production', *Review of Radical Political Economy*, vol. 6, no. 2, 60–112.

Marsh, C. (1993) 'The sample of anonymised records', in Dale, A. and Marsh, C. (eds) *The 1991 User's Guide*, London: HMSO.

Marshall, A. (1992) *Circumventing Labour Protection: Non-Standard Employment in Argentina and Peru*, Geneva: International Institute for Labour Studies.

Martin, L., Gutman, H. and Hutton, P. (eds) (1988) *Technologies of the Self*, London: Tavistock.

Massey, D. (1984) *Spatial Divisions of Labour: Social Structures and the Geography of Production*, London: Macmillan.

Mayhew, C. and Quinlan, M. (1998) *Outsourcing and Occupational Health and Safety: A Comparative Study of Factory-based and Outworkers in the Australian TCF Industry*, Sydney: Industrial Relations Research Centre, University of New South Wales.

Meulders, D., Plasman, O. and Plasman, R. (1994) *Atypical Employment in the EC*, Aldershot: Dartmouth Publishing.

Michelson, W. and Lindén, K. P. (1997) 'Home and telework in Sweden', a paper presented at the Gender and Teleworking Conference, National Resource Centre for Women (NUTEK), Stockholm, Sweden, 14 March.

Ministry of Labour (1995) *Annual Survey on Homeworking*, Tokyo: Ministry of Labour.

Miraftab, F. (1996) 'Space, gender, and work: home-based workers in Mexico', in Boris, E. and Prügl, E. (eds) *Homeworkers in Global Perspective: Invisible No More*, London: Routledge.

Mitter, S. (1986a) *Common Fate, Common Bond: Women in the Global Economy*, London: Pluto Press.

Mitter, S. (1986b) 'Industrial restructuring and manufacturing homework: immigrant women in the UK clothing industry', *Capital and Class*, no. 27, Winter, 37–80.

Mitter, S. (1994) 'Women organising in casual work: a global view', in Rowbottom, S. and Mitter, S. (eds) *Dignity and Daily Bread: New Forms of Organising Among Poor Women in the Third World and the First*, London: Routledge.

Mitter, S., Phizacklea, A. M., Totterdill, P. and Wolkowitz, C. (1993) *Tower Hamlets Homeworkers' Co-operative Project: Feasibility Report*, Tower Hamlets: Tower Hamlets Homeworkers' Co-operative.

Morgan, D. H. J. (1985) *The Family, Politics and Social Theory*, London: Routledge and Kegan Paul.

Morokvasic, M. (1987) 'Immigrants in the Parisian garment industry', *Work, Employment and Society*, vol. 1, no. 4, December, 441–462.

Morris, L. (1987) 'Constraints on gender: the family wage, social security and the labour market: reflections on research in Hartlepool', *Work, Employment and Society*, vol. 1, no. 1, March, 85–106.

Morris, L. (1990) *The Workings of the Household: A US–UK Comparison*, London: Polity Press.

Morris, L. (1993) 'Household finance management and the labour market: a case study in Hartlepool', *Sociological Review*, vol. 41, no. 3, August, 506–536.

Mulholland, K. (1996) 'Entrepreneurialism, masculinities and the self-made man', in Collinson, D. and Hearn, J. (eds) *Men as Managers, Managers as Men: Critical Perspectives on Men, Masculinities and Managements*, London: Sage.

Nadwodny, R. (1996) 'Canadians working at home', *Canadian Social Trends*, Spring, 16–20.

Noon, M. and Blyton, P. (1997) *The Realities of Work*, London: Macmillan.

O'Connell Davidson, J. and Layder, D. (1994) *Methods, Sex and Madness*, London: Routledge.

O'Donnell, C. (1987) *Self-Employed or Employee? A Survey of Women in New South Wales Doing Paid Work at Home*, New South Wales: Department of Industrial Relations and Employment.

O'Reilly, K. and Rose, D. (1998) 'Changing employment relations: plus ça change, plus c'est la même chose?', *Work, Employment and Society*, vol. 12, no. 4, 713–734.

Olson, M. H. (1989) 'Organizational barriers to professional telework', in Boris, E. and Daniels, C. R. (eds) *Homework: Historical and Contemporary Perspectives on Paid Labor at Home*, Urbana and Chicago: University of Illinois Press.

Olson, M. H. and Primps, S. B. (1984) 'Working at home with computers: work and non-work issues', *Journal of Social Issues*, vol. 40, no. 3, 97–112.

Oxfam (1996) *Oxfam UK/I Briefing Paper on the Proposed New ILO Convention on Home-Working*, Oxford: Oxfam.

Pacione, M. (1997) *Britain's Cities: Geographies of Division*, London: Routledge.

Pahl, J. (1983) 'The allocation of money and the structuring of inequality within marriage', *Sociological Review*, vol. 31, no. 2, May, 237–262.

Pahl, J. (1989) *Money and Marriage*, London: Macmillan.

Parliamentary Office of Science and Technology (1995) *Working at a Distance: UK Teleworking and its Implications*, London: POST.

Pennington, S. and Westover, B. (1989) *A Hidden Workforce: Homeworkers in England, 1850–1985*, London: Macmillan.

Phizacklea, A. (1990) *Unpacking the Fashion Industry: Gender, Racism, and Class in Production*, London: Routledge.

Phizacklea, A. and Wolkowitz, C. (1995) *Homeworking Women: Gender, Ethnicity and Class at Work*, London: Sage.

Prandy, K. (1998) 'Deconstructing classes: critical comments on the revised social classification', *Work, Employment and Society*, vol. 12, no. 4, 743–754.

President of the Board of Trade (1998) *The National Minimum Wage: First Report of the Low Pay Commission*, Cm 3976, London: The Stationery Office.

Presser, H. B. and Bamberger, E. (1993) 'American women who work at home for pay: distinctions and determinants', *Social Science Quarterly*, vol. 74, no. 4, December, 815–837.

Probert, B. and Wacjman, J. (1988a) 'New technology outwork', in Willis, E. (ed.) *Technology and the Labour Process: Australian Case Studies*, Sydney: Allen and Unwin.

Probert, B. and Wacjman, J. (1988b) 'Technological change and the future of work', *Journal of Industrial Relations*, vol. 30, no. 2, September, 432–448.

Pugh, H. S. (1984) 'Estimating the extent of homeworking', *Social Statistics Research Unit Working Paper*, No. 15.

Pugh, H. S. (1990) 'Making the best of a bad job: homeworking in the secretarial and clerical industry', unpublished Ph.D. thesis, City University, London.

Quinney, A. (1986) *House and Home: A History of the Small English House*, London: BBC.

Rainnie, A. (1984) 'Combined and uneven development in the clothing industry: the efforts of competition on accumulation', *Capital and Class*, no. 22, Spring, 142–156.

Rangel de Paiva Abreu, A. and Sorj, B. (1996) '"Good housewives": seamstresses in the Brazilian garment industry', in Boris, E. and Prügl, E. (eds) *Homeworkers in Global Perspective: Invisible No More*, London: Routledge.

Reid, D. A. (1976) 'The decline of Saint Monday: 1766–1876', *Past and Present*, no. 71, 76–101.

Richards, W. (1994) 'The flexible labour market: the case of homeworking', *Irish Business and Administration Research*, vol. 15, 165–177.

Richards, W. (1996) 'The homeworker – exploited and underpaid?', *Evening Press*, 19 November.

Rose, D. (1998) 'Once more unto the breach: in defence of class analysis yet again', *Work, Employment and Society*, vol. 12, no. 4, 755–767.

Rose, K. (1992) *Where Women Are Leaders: The SEWA Movement in India*, London and New Jersey: Zed Books.

Rose, N. (1990) *Governing the Soul: The Shaping of the Private Self*, London: Routledge.

Rowbotham, S. (1993) *Homeworkers Worldwide*, London: Merlin Press.

Roxby, B. C. (1984) *The Forgotten Workers: A Study of the Legal Problems Faced by Homeworkers*, Leicester: Leicester Outwork Campaign.

Rubery, J. and Wilkinson, F. (1981) 'Outwork and segmented labour markets', in Wilkinson, F. (ed.) *The Dynamics of Labour Market Segmentation*, London: Academic Press.

Rubery, J., Humphries, J. and Horrell, S. (1992) 'Women's employment in textiles and clothing', in Lindley, R. (ed.) *Women's Employment: Britain and the Single European Market*, Manchester: Equal Opportunities Commission.

Salmi, M. (1996) 'Finland is another world: the gendered time of homework', in Boris, E. and Prügl, E. (eds) *Homeworkers in Global Perspective: Invisible No More*, New York: Routledge.

Salmi, M. (1997a) 'Home-based work, gender and everyday life', paper presented at the Gender and Teleworking Conference, National Resource Centre for Women (NUTEK), Stockholm, Sweden, 14 March.

Salmi, M. (1997b) 'Autonomy and time in home-based work', in Heiskanen, T. and Rantalaiho, L. (eds) *Gendered Practices in Working Life*, London: Macmillan.

Salmi, M. and Lammi-Taskula, J. (1998) 'Work, family and gendered practices', paper presented at the Gender, Work and Organization Conference, Manchester Metropolitan University and University of Manchester Institute of Science and Technology, 9–10 January.

Sassen, S. (1991) *The Global City: New York, London, Tokyo*, Princeton: Princeton University Press.

Sassen, S. (1994) *Cities in a World Economy*, London: Pine Forge Press.

Saunders, P. (1989) 'The meaning of home in contemporary English culture', *Housing Studies*, vol. 4, no. 3, 177–192.

Saunders, P. (1990) *A Nation of Home Owners*, London: Unwin Hyman.

Sayer, A. and Walker, R. (1992) *The New Social Economy: Reworking the Division of Labour*, Oxford: Blackwell.

Schoeffel, P., Loveridge, A. and Davidson, C. (1991) 'Telework in New Zealand: the present situation and future prospects', *Working Papers in Information Technology and Society*, No. 1.

Self Employed Women's Union (SEWU) (1995) *Homework Research Project*, Durban, South Africa: SEWU.

Sennett, R. (1998) *The Corrosion of Character: The Personal Consequences of Work in the New Capitalism*, New York and London: W. W. Norton and Company.

Sewell, G. and Wilkinson, B. (1992) 'Empowerment or emasculation? Shopfloor surveillance in a total quality organisation', in Blyton, P. and Turnbull, P. (eds) *Reassessing Human Resource Management*, London: Sage.

Shah, S. (1975) *Immigrants and Employment in the Clothing Industry: The Rag Trade in London's East End*, London: Runnymede Trust.

Shamir, B. (1992) 'Home: the perfect workplace?', in Zeldeck, S. (ed.) *Work, Families and Organizations*, San Francisco: Jossey-Bass.

Shields, R. (1991) *Places on the Margin: Alternative Geographies of Modernity*, London: Routledge.

Silver, H. (1989) 'The demand for homework: evidence from the US Census', in Boris, E. and Daniels, C. (eds) *Homework: Historical and Contemporary Perspectives on Paid Labor at Home*, Urbana and Chicago: University of Illinois Press.

Silverstone, R., Hirsch, E. and Morley, D. (1994) 'Information and communication technologies and the moral economy of the household', in Silverstone, R. and Hirsch, E. (eds) *Consuming Technologies*, London: Routledge.

Siroonian, J. (1993) *Work Arrangements*, Catalogue No. 71–605, Ottawa: Statistics Canada.

Smith, G. A. (1902) 'Preface', in Irwin, M. H., *The Problem of Home Work*, Glasgow: Scottish Co-operative Wholesale Society Ltd.

Smith, S. L. and Anderson, J. (1992) 'Over the threshold? Private and public choices in new information homeworking', in Gilbert, N., Burrows, R. and Pollert, A. (eds) *Fordism and Flexibility: Divisions and Change*, Basingstoke: Macmillan.

Soja, E. W. (1995) 'Heterotopologies: a remembrance of other spaces in the citadel-LA', in Watson, S. and Gibson, K. (eds) *Postmodern Cities and Spaces*, Oxford: Blackwell.

Standen, P. (1997) 'Home, work and management in the Information Age', Mimeo, Department of Management, Edith Cowan University.

Stanworth, C. (1996) *Working at Home: A Study of Homeworking and Teleworking*, London: Institute of Employment Rights.

Stanworth, C. (1998) 'Telework and the information age', *New Technology, Work and Employment*, vol. 13, no. 1, 51–62.

Statistics Bureau (1995) *Annual Report on the Labour Force Survey*, Tokyo: Statistics Bureau, Management and Coordination Agency.

Statistics Canada (1998) *The Daily*, 17 March, Cat. No. 11–001E.

Stinson, J. F. (1986) 'Moonlighting by women jumped to record highs', *Monthly Labor Review*, vol. 109, 22–25.

Sullivan, O. (1997) 'Time waits for no (wo)man: an investigation of the gendered experience of domestic time', *Sociology*, vol. 31, no. 2, 221–239.

Sunday Times (1996) 'End of the line', 24 November, p. 13 (anon).

Suzuki, Y. (1993) 'Home-based work in Japan', unpublished paper commissioned by the International Labour Organisation.

Tate, J. (1993) 'Unions and homeworkers: organizing homeworkers in the informal sector in Australia, the Netherlands and Canada', *Equality for Women in Employment: An Interdepartmental Project, Working Paper No. 7*, International Labour Office, Geneva.

Tate, J. (1994a) 'Canada', in Martens, M. H. and Mitter, S. (eds) *Women in Trade Unions: Organizing the Unorganized*, Geneva: International Labour Office.

Tate, J. (1994b) 'Homework in West Yorkshire', in Rowbottom, S. and Mitter, S. (eds) *Dignity and Daily Bread: New Forms of Economic Organising Among Women in the Third World and the First*, London, Routledge.

Tate, J. (1994c) 'Organizing homeworkers in the informal sector', in Martens, M. H. and Mitter, S. (eds) *Women in Trade Unions: Organizing the Unorganized*, Geneva: International Labour Office.

Tate, J. (1996a) 'Every pair tells a story', Report on a Survey of Homeworking and Subcontracting Chains in Six Countries of the European Union, unpublished mimeo, March.

Tate, J. (1996b) 'Making links: the growth of homeworker networks', in Boris, E. and Prügl, E. (eds) *Homeworkers in Global Perspective: Invisible No More*, London: Routledge.

Textile, Clothing and Footwear Union of Australia (1995) *The Hidden Cost of Fashion*, Sydney: Textile, Clothing and Footwear Union of Australia.

The Times (1983) 'Home from home in the office', 31 October, p. 9 (Penny Perrick).

Thompson, E. P. (1967) 'Time, work-discipline and industrial capitalism', *Past and Present*, no. 38, 56–97.

Thompson, P. and Warhurst, C. (eds) (1998) *Workplaces of the Future*, London: Macmillan.

Toffler, A. (1980) *The Third Wave*, London: Collins.

US Department of Commerce (1998a) 'Increases in at-home workers reverses earlier trend', *Census Brief*, CENBR/98–2, March.

US Department of Commerce (1998b) 'Working at home: 1990', CPH-L-195, US Bureau of the Census, http://www.census.gov/main//www.subjects.html#w

Varesi, P. A. and Villa, P. (1986) *Homeworking in Italy, France and the United Kingdom*, Brussels: Commission of the European Communities – Employment, Social Affairs and Education.

Vogler, C. (1989) 'Labour market change and patterns of financial allocation within households', *ESRC Social Change and Economic Life Initiative Working Paper No 12*, Oxford: Nuffield College.

Vogler, C. (1994) 'Money in the household', in Anderson, M., Bechhofer, F. and Gershuny, J. (eds) *The Social and Political Economy of the Household*, Oxford: Oxford University Press.

Vogler, C. and Pahl, J. (1993) 'Social and economic change and the organisation of money within marriage', *Work, Employment and Society*, vol. 7, no. 1, March, 71–93.

Vogler, C. and Pahl, J. (1994) 'Money, power and inequality within marriage', *Sociological Review*, vol. 42, no. 2, May, 263–288.

Walker, J. (1987) 'Home-based working in Australia: issues and evidence', *Research School of Social Sciences Working Paper No. 1*, Urban Research Unit, Canberra: Australian National University.

Warde, A. and Hetherington, K. (1993) 'A changing domestic division of labour? Issues of measurement and interpretation', *Work, Employment and Society*, vol. 7, no. 1, 23–45.

Weiss, A. M. (1996) 'Within the walls: home-based work in Lahore', in Boris, E. and Prügl, E. (eds) *Homeworkers in Global Perspective: Invisible No More*, London: Routledge.

Wellman, B. (1979) 'The community question: the intimate networks of East Yorkers', *American Sociological Review*, vol.84, 1201–1231.

Wellman, B. and Berkowitz, S. D. (eds) (1988) *Social Structures: A Network Approach*, Cambridge: Cambridge University Press.

West, C. and Zimmerman, D. H. (1987) 'Doing gender', *Gender and Society*, no. 1, 125–151.

West Yorkshire Homeworking Group (1990) *A Penny a Bag: Campaigning on Homework*, Batley: Yorkshire and Humberside Low Pay Unit.

West Yorkshire Homeworking Unit (1992) *Outwork in Leeds: A Report by the West Yorkshire Homeworking Unit*, Batley: West Yorkshire Homeworking Unit.

Westwood, S. and Williams, J. (eds) (1997) *Imagining Cities: Scripts, Signs, Memory*, London: Routledge.

Whipp, R. (1987) '"A time to every purpose": an essay on time and work', in Joyce, P. (ed.) *The Historical Meanings of Work*, Cambridge: Cambridge University Press.

Wirutomo, P. (1993) 'Homeworkers of Indonesia: who are they, where are they?', in Lazo, L. (ed.) *From the Shadows to the Fore: Practical Actions for the Social Protection of Homeworkers in Indonesia*, Bangkok: International Labour Organisation.

Wolkowitz, C. (1996) 'Close to home: men's and women's homeworking in an inner city North London neighbourhood', paper presented to the 14th Annual International Labour Process Conference, University of Aston, 27–29 March.

Wong, Y. C. (1983) 'Outworkers', *Department of Economics, University of Hong Kong, Discussion Paper No. 25*.

Wood, S. (ed.) (1989) *The Transformation of Work? Skill, Flexibility and the Labour Process*, London: Unwin Hyman.

Yorkshire and Humberside Low Pay Unit (1991) *A Survey of Homeworking in Calderdale*, Batley: Yorkshire and Humberside Low Pay Unit.

Young, M. and Willmott, P. (1973) *The Symmetrical Family*, New York: Pantheon.

Index